Ivo van Hove

Ivo van Hove

From Shakespeare to David Bowie

Edited by Susan Bennett and Sonia Massai

methuen | drama

LONDON • NEW YORK • OXFORD • NEW DELHI • SYDNEY

METHUEN DRAMA
Bloomsbury Publishing Plc
50 Bedford Square, London, WC1B 3DP, UK

BLOOMSBURY, METHUEN DRAMA and the Methuen Drama logo are trademarks of
Bloomsbury Publishing Plc

First published in Great Britain 2018

Cover design: Adriano Brioso
Cover images: (front) *Kings of War*, Amsterdam, 2015; (back) *Lazarus*, New York, 2015. (© Jan Versweyveld)

A catalogue record for this book is available from the British Library.

Library of Congress Cataloging-in-Publication Data
Names: Bennett, Susan, 1955– editor. | Massai, Sonia editor.
Title: Ivo Van Hove : from Shakespeare to David Bowie / edited by Susan
Bennett and Sonia Massai.
Description: London ; New York : Metheun Drama, 2018. | Series: Performance books |
Includes bibliographical references and index.
Identifiers: LCCN 2017061326 (print) | LCCN 2018000059 (ebook) |
ISBN 9781350031555 (epub) | ISBN 9781350031524 (epdf) | ISBN 9781350031531
(hb : alk. paper) | ISBN 9781350031548 (pb : alk. paper)
Subjects: LCSH: Hove, Ivo van, 1958–Criticism and interpretation.
Classification: LCC PN2708.H68 (ebook) | LCC PN2708.H68 I94 2018 (print) |
DDC 792.02/33092—dc23
LC record available at https://lccn.loc.gov/2017061326

ISBN: HB: 978-1-3500-3153-1
         PB: 978-1-3500-3154-8
         ePDF: 978-1-3500-3152-4
         eBook: 978-1-3500-3155-5

Series: Performance Books

Typeset by RefineCatch Limited, Bungay, Suffolk
Printed and bound in India

To find out more about our authors and books visit www.bloomsbury.com
and sign up for our newsletters.

Contents

Illustrations

Plates

1   *Hedda Gabler* (2016), photograph by Philip Carter, reproduced by permission of Philip Carter and the National Theatre, London.

2   *Kings of War* (2015), photograph by Jan Versweyveld, reproduced by permission of Toneelgroep Amsterdam.

3   *Othello* (2012), photograph by Jan Versweyveld, reproduced by permission of Toneelgroep Amsterdam.

4   *The Taming of the Shrew* (2012), photograph by Jan Versweyveld, reproduced by permission of Toneelgroep Amsterdam.

5   *Hedda Gabler* (2016), photograph by Jan Versweyveld, reproduced by permission of Toneelgroep Amsterdam.

6   *A View from the Bridge* (2014), photograph by Jan Versweyveld, reproduced by permission of Toneelgroep Amsterdam.

7   *The Crucible* (2016), photograph by Jan Versweyveld, reproduced by permission of Toneelgroep Amsterdam.

8   *The Little Foxes* (2010), photograph by Jan Versweyveld, reproduced by permission of Toneelgroep Amsterdam.

9   *Götterdämmerung* (2008), photograph by Jan Versweyveld, reproduced by permission of Toneelgroep Amsterdam.

10   *Idomeneo* (2010), photograph by Jan Versweyveld, reproduced by permission of Toneelgroep Amsterdam.

11   *Macbeth* (2012), photograph by Jan Versweyveld, reproduced by permission of Toneelgroep Amsterdam.

Notes on Contributors

Susan C. W. Abbotson is Professor of English at Rhode Island College, where she mostly teaches drama. She is the author of *A Critical Companion to Arthur Miller* (2007) and *Student Companion to Arthur Miller* (2000), as well as numerous articles on Arthur Miller. She also authored *Thematic Guide to Modern Drama* (2003), *Masterpieces of Twentieth Century American Drama* (2005) and *Modern American Drama: Playwriting in the 1950s* (Methuen Drama, 2018). She has published articles on Sam Shepard, Tom Stoppard, Mae West, Tennessee Williams, Thornton Wilder, August Wilson, Eugene O'Neill and Paula Vogel in a variety of books and journals.

Kate Bassett is Literary Associate at Chichester Festival Theatre, as well as a freelance script consultant and dramaturg for theatre and film companies. As an arts journalist and long-standing theatre critic, she wrote for *The Times, Daily Telegraph, Independent on Sunday, New Statesman, TLS* and other publications. Her book *In Two Minds: A Biography of Jonathan Miller* (2013) was shortlisted for the Theatre Book Prize, the Sheridan Morley Prize for Theatre Biography and the HW Fisher Best First Biography Prize; it is now available in paperback. She previously was Associate Professor of Creative Writing at the University of Reading (2014–2016), served on many theatre, comedy and literary awards panels, and hosts platform talks at the National Theatre, British Library, Barbican Centre and elsewhere.

Susan Bennett is Professor of English at the University of Calgary, Canada. She is widely published in a variety of topics across theatre and performance studies, with particular interest in contemporary productions of Shakespeare's plays. Her books include *Theatre & Museums* (2013), *Shakespeare Beyond English* (co-edited with Christie Carson, 2013), *Performing Environments* (co-edited with Mary Polito, 2014) and *Theatre Audiences* (2nd edition, 1997). With Kim Solga, she is series editor of 'Theory for Theatre Studies', to be published by Methuen Drama with the first titles appearing in 2018.

Marcin Bogucki is a PhD candidate in Theatre and Performance at the Institute of Polish Culture, University of Warsaw, with a background in cultural studies, art history and musicology. His research focuses on the cultural history and modern staging of opera; he is the author of the first book in Polish about Peter Sellars' operatic work, *Teatr operowy Petera Sellarsa* (2012). In 2015, he was a visiting scholar at the Jacobs School of Music, Indiana University, Bloomington. Marcin is also a member of the Polish Society for Theatre Research and has served as secretary since 2016.

Laurens De Vos is Assistant Professor in Theatre Studies at the University of Amsterdam. He obtained his PhD in 2006 from the University of Ghent. De Vos is co-author of *Shakespeare: Auteur voor alle seizoenen* (2016), a book that explores the ways Dutch and Flemish theatre makers (including Ivo van Hove) have dealt with Shakespeare's work over the last fifty years. He also published *Cruelty and Desire in the Modern Theatre: Antonin Artaud, Sarah Kane, and Samuel Beckett* (2011) and is the co-editor of *Sarah Kane in Context* (2010). His current research focuses on the role of the gaze in the theatre.

Denis Flannery is Associate Professor of American and English Literature at the University of Leeds. His published works include his first monograph, *Henry James: A Certain Illusion* (2000) and *On Sibling Love, Queer Attachment and American Writing* (2007). His most recent book is the collection *Alan Hollinghurst: Writing Under the Influence* (co-edited with Michèle Mendelssohn, 2016). His current projects include *The Chamber and the World: Reading, Theatre, Toneelgroep Amsterdam* and the completion of a collaborative memoir begun with his father, Denis Kevin Flannery (1919–2009).

François Jongen is a lawyer, journalist, professor at the Université Catholique de Louvain and visiting associate professor at the University of Neuchâtel. Under the pen name Nicolas Blanmont, he writes about music (classical and rock) for *La Libre Belgique*, is a radio producer at the Radio Télévision Belge de la Communauté Française (RTBF) and opera critic for *Opera* and *Opéra Magazine*. He has published three novels and several books about media law and music.

Mark Lawson is a UK-based journalist, broadcaster and author. He is a reviewer and reporter on culture for *The Guardian*, a regular contributor to *New Statesman* and *Radio Times*, as well as a theatre critic for *The Tablet*. His work as a writer-presenter on radio and TV includes *The Late Review* and *Newsnight Review* (BBC Two), *Mark Lawson Talks To. . .* (BBC Four) and *Front Row* (BBC Radio 4). His novels include *Enough is Enough* (Picador,

2005), *The Deaths* (Picador, 2013) and *The Allegations* (Picador, 2016). He has written numerous radio dramas for BBC Radio 4, including *The Third Soldier Holds His Thighs* (2005), *Expand This* (2009), *Suspicion for Ten Voices* (2013) and *Holy Father* (2016). He is a fellow of the Royal Society of Literature and an honorary fellow of the Royal Institute of British Architecture, University College London and University of Northampton.

Sonia Massai is Professor of Shakespeare Studies in the English Department at King's College London. She has published widely on the history of the transmission of Shakespeare on the stage and on the page. Her publications include *Shakespeare and the Rise of the Editor* (2007), the edited collections *Shakespeare and Textual Studies* (co-edited with Margaret Jane Kidnie, 2015) and *World-Wide Shakespeares: Local Appropriations in Film and Performance* (2005), as well as critical editions of *The Paratexts in English Printed Drama to 1642* (2014) and John Ford's *'Tis Pity She's a Whore* (Arden Early Modern Drama, 2011).

Frédéric Maurin is Associate Professor in the Department of Theatre Studies at Université Sorbonne Nouvelle – Paris 3. His research focuses on contemporary performance, international crossovers and the interplay between the arts. He has written extensively on European and North American directors such as Robert Wilson, Peter Sellars, Ivo van Hove and Thomas Ostermeier, as well as on issues such as technology and theatre, festivals and large-scale works. On Ivo van Hove, Dr Maurin has given papers and lectures at academic conferences; research seminars and theatres; published a number of articles in such journals as *Alternatives théâtrales*, *Théâtre/Public*, *L'avant-scène théâtre* and *Prospero European Review*; compiled a book-length interview (2014) and edited a seminal collection of essays entitled *Ivo van Hove, la fureur de créer* (2016).

José Máximo Leza is Senior Lecturer and Department Head in the Departamento de Didáctica de la Expresión Musical, Plástica y Corporal at the Universidad de Salamanca, Spain. His research focuses on theatre music and opera, with special emphasis on eighteenth-century Spain, including Spanish *zarzuela* and reception of Italian opera. He has published a wide array of articles dealing with musical dramaturgy of opera. He has collaborated on texts for the Teatro de la Zarzuela and the Teatro Real in Madrid, as well as edited stage works of the Spanish composer José de Nebra. He is co-author (with L. K. Stein) of the chapter dedicated to Spanish and Latin American opera in the *Cambridge Companion to Eighteenth-Century Opera* (2009). He has recently edited the volume *La música en el siglo XVIII* within the work *Historia de la música en España e Hispanoamérica*.

Joseph V. Melillo is Executive Producer for Brooklyn Academy of Music (BAM), responsible for overseeing artistic direction and programming for Howard Gilman Opera House, Harvey Theatre, BAM Fisher and Rose Cinemas. He previously served as producing director for BAM and founding director of the Next Wave Festival. Melillo has fostered the work of emerging and established artists, forging international partnerships such as *DanceMotion USAsm*, an international cultural engagement program of the US Department of State. Awards include the Chevalier and Officier de L'ordre des Arts et des Lettres (France) and an OBE (Great Britain). He is a member of the National Order of Québec and has served on the US Nominating Committee for the Praemium Imperiale, a global arts prize awarded by the Japan Art Association. Melillo has served on the faculty of Brooklyn College and as a lecturer at colleges, universities and arts agencies in the US and abroad. He is the recipient of the 2018 Bessies Presenter Award for Outstanding Curating.

Rachael Nicholas is a PhD student in the Department of Drama, Theatre and Performance at the University of Roehampton. Her doctoral research investigates the reception of Shakespeare through live theatre broadcasts in cinemas, online and in schools. She has a chapter forthcoming in *Shakespeare and the 'Live' Theatre Broadcast Experience* (Arden Shakespeare) and is working on a chapter about recent theatre broadcasts of *King Lear*. She is Co-Chair of the New Researchers' Network, a sub-committee of The Society for Theatre Research.

Joshua E. Polster is Associate Professor of Theatre at Emerson College. He was President of the Arthur Miller Society and currently serves on their Board of Directors. His publications include *Stages of Engagement: U.S. Theatre and Performance 1898–1949* (2015), *The Routledge Anthology of U.S. Theatre 1898–1949* (2016), *Reinterpreting the Plays of Arthur Miller* (2010), a critical edition of Miller's *A Memory of Two Mondays* (Methuen Drama, 2011) and numerous articles on Arthur Miller and US theatre. Dr Polster has presented work at numerous national and international conferences.

Toni Racklin joined the Barbican Centre in 1996 as Producer, launching the year-round programme of distinctive international dance, drama and music theatre. In 2010, she became Head of Theatre at the Barbican. During her tenure, Toni has line-produced and internationally toured four major in-house productions: Deborah Warner's *Julius Caesar*; Peter Brook's *11* and *12*; Ivo van Hove's *Antigone*, featuring Juliette Binoche, and his *Obsession*, featuring Jude Law. She has also curated large-scale seasons of international work in tribute to Beckett, Ibsen and Shakespeare. She forged a relationship with Ivo van Hove and his company, Toneelgroep Amsterdam, in 2009 with the staging of *Roman Tragedies* at the Barbican. In 2017, she invited Toneelgroep Amsterdam to lead a residency across the year with the return of *Roman Tragedies*, the creation of *Obsession* based on the film by Luchino Visconti and a double-bill of *After the Rehearsal/Persona* based on films by Ingmar Bergman.

Halina Reijn is a renowned actress and author. She has won multiple awards, including the Dutch Film Award for Best Actress, the Theo Mann-Bouwmeester Ring and the Dutch theatre awards Theo D'Or, Colombina and Courbois Pearl. Halina was trained at the Maastricht Academy of Dramatic Arts and debuted on stage in 1997 as Ophelia in *Hamlet*. She has continued to act in such productions as *Shopping & Fucking, Mourning Becomes Electra, Hedda Gabler, La Voix Humaine, The Fountainhead* and opposite Jude Law in *Obsession*. She starred in the Oscar-nominated film *Zus & Zo*, Paul Verhoeven's critically acclaimed *Black Book* and opposite Tom Cruise in *Valkyrie*. Her novels include *Prinsesje Nooitgenoeg* (Prometheus, 2005), *Doen alsof ik iemand anders ben* (Prometheus, 2009), *Antiglamour* (co-written with Carice van Houten, Nijgh & Van Ditmar, 2013) and *Loos* (Nijgh & Van Ditmar, 2016). Currently, she works with Ivo van Hove at Toneelgroep Amsterdam.

George Rodosthenous is Associate Professor of Theatre Directing in the School of Performance and Cultural Industries at the University of Leeds. His research interests are the body in performance, refining improvisational techniques and compositional practices for performance, devising pieces with live musical soundscapes as interdisciplinary process, the director as coach, updating Greek Tragedy and the British Musical. He has edited the books *Theatre as Voyeurism: The Pleasures of Watching* (2015), *Contemporary Adaptations of Greek Tragedy: Auteurship and Directorial Visions* (Methuen Drama, 2017), *The Disney Musical on Stage and Screen: Critical Approaches from Snow White to Frozen* (Methuen Drama, 2017) and *Twenty-First Century Musicals: From Stage to Screen* (2017).

Julie Sanders is Professor of English Literature and Drama and Deputy Vice-Chancellor at Newcastle University in the UK. She is the author of *Adaptation and Appropriation* (2006), which recently went into a revised and updated second edition (2015). She has published widely on Shakespeare and adaptation, including articles in *Shakespeare Survey* and *The Shakespeare International Yearbook*. She is also recognized for her work on early modern literary geographies, including *The Cultural Geography of Early*

Modern Drama, 1620–1650 (2011), which won the British Academy's Rose Mary Crawshay Prize.

Emile Schra studied Theatre and Dutch Literature at Utrecht University (MA, 1985) and Anthropology at the University of Amsterdam. He worked as a dramaturg at the HKU University of the Arts Utrecht, as well as for theatre groups and individuals. In 1998, he became Artistic Director of PassePartout Summer School, aiming at an international exchange amongst theatre professionals. That same year, he started a book series on intercultural developments in the performing arts. Combining his interest in practice and theory, Schra wrote articles and books on subjects ranging from Peter Brook to Asian theatre traditions. Since 2002, he is Professor of World Drama for Emerson College at the European Centre in the Netherlands and teaches creative storytelling and creativity at Hogeschool Utrecht. He is currently working on a book on Ivo van Hove, focusing on the development of his work and ideas since the start of his career in 1981.

P. A. Skantze is a director, writer and teacher working in London and Italy. She is also co-founder of the international performance group Four Second Decay, whose performances range from chamber opera, *Humpty Agonistes: After the Smash* (London, 2015), to promenades through hell, *Orfeo and Eurydice: How to Save Someone You Cannot See* (Greece, 2016). Her books *Stillness in Motion in the Seventeenth-Century Theatre* (2003) and *Itinerant Spectator/Itinerant Spectacle* (2013) think through early modern theatre and spectatorship as practice in twenty-first-century Europe. Her essays include lyric theory written in quixotic pentameter, work on sound and Shakespeare and on race and reception. Current projects include a 2018 production of her musical *Stacks*, in which New York City is saved from flattening into a single dimension by the New York Public Library.

Johanna Wall studied dramaturgy and Japanology at the Bayerische Theaterakademie August Everding and the Ludwig-Maximilians University in Munich, Germany. As a dramaturg, she collaborated in the fields of opera, drama, performance and dance with performance artists Alexeij Sagerer (proT, Munich), Darren O'Donnell (Mammalian Diving Reflex, Toronto), Chris Thorpe (Third Angel, Sheffield) and Marcel Leemann (Physical Dance Theatre, Bern). She also performed in theatres and opera houses all over Germany (Hamburg, Tübingen, Munich, Oldenburg, Heidelberg) with directors Thom Lutz, Anna Bergmann, Niklaus Helbling, Jan Christoph Gockel, Nina Gühlstorff,

Albrecht Hirche and many more. Since 2012, she has worked as a dramaturg at the Komische Oper Berlin where she has collaborated with directors Kirill Serebrennikov, Herbert Fritsch, Viesturs Kairish, Lydia Steier, Tobias Kratzer and Barrie Kosky, as well as conductors Henrik Nánási, Antonello Manacorda, Konrad Junghänel and Christian Curnyn. Future projects include productions with France-based Laura Scozzi and Canadian opera director Robert Carsen.

Ruth Wilson is a two-time Olivier Award winner, Golden Globe winner and Tony Award nominated actress. Best known for her television work in *The Affair* and *Luther*, as well as her performances on the London stage, Wilson has quickly become one of Britain's most lauded young actresses. Wilson studied history at the University of Nottingham. She later graduated from the London Academy of Music and Dramatic Art, appearing in the BBC mini series *Jane Eyre* and on the London stage in 2007 in the National Theatre Presentation of *Philistines*. She continued to act in such works as Donmar Warehouse productions of *A Streetcar Named Desire* and *Anna Christie*, as well as the films *Saving Mr. Banks, The Lone Ranger* and Joe Wright's film adaptation of *Anna Karenina*. In 2017, she returned to the National Theatre to star in the title role of *Hedda Gabler* directed by Tony Award-winning director Ivo van Hove.

Maja Zade grew up in Germany and Sweden. She studied English Literature at London University and at Queen's University in Canada, and theatre production at the Royal Academy of Dramatic Art in London. She was a Senior Reader at the Royal Court Theatre in London before joining the Schaubühne Theatre in Berlin as a dramaturg. She has worked with directors including Thomas Ostermeier, Benedict Andrews, Armin Petras, Simon McBurney and Ivo van Hove. She is also a translator of plays into German (Lars von Trier, Caryl Churchill, Lars Norén) and into English (Marius von Mayenburg, Roland Schimmelpfennig).

Keren Zaiontz is Assistant Professor and Queen's National Scholar in the Department of Film and Media and the Cultural Studies Graduate Program at Queen's University. In 2010, she saw her first Toneelgroep Amsterdam production, *Roman Tragedies*, at Festival TransAmériques in Montreal. Since then, she has published special issues on the cultural politics of festivals and mega-events for *Contemporary Theatre Review* (23.4), *Canadian Theatre Review* (164) and *PUBLIC* (53). She is currently completing two books: *Theatre & Festivals* and a co-edited anthology, *Sustainable Tools for Precarious Times: Performance Actions and Rights Emergencies in the Americas*.

Foreword

MY LIFE

Ivo van Hove

Plays are my life. My productions are autobiographies in disguise: they give me the chance to live life twice, in the real world and in the theatre. I discovered theatre while I was at boarding school. It immediately felt like coming home. A little world within the world of boarding school, a place where we would retreat on Wednesday afternoons to create a show which we would then present to the outside world at the end of the school year. Those shows were often political in nature – an opportunity to resist the strict world of a classic boarding school, governed by traditions, rules and laws. Breaking those rules without blowing everything up and being expelled from school was an art in its own right. I discovered that making theatre made me feel amazing. I found that I could express something of myself by working in that grey area between what is allowed and what is not allowed.

Our first productions at the beginning of the 1980s meant breaking away from dominant theatre traditions in Flanders. Some people were greatly opposed to our work, whereas others championed this change. And this is still very much the case now. In New York, they still call me a 'bad boy avant-gardist' and an 'iconoclast', because of the way I direct Molière and Ibsen. I love theatre that goes against the grain, that does not want to please, that *really* means something. This approach to theatre-making requires you to know your own worth and to stick to whatever artistic decision you want to make.

Our productions belong to my life. My life is my work, and my work is my life. Nothing of what we do is insignificant. Dora van der Groen, the *grande dame* of Flemish theatre, once told me: 'Ivo, you and theatre make a perfect couple.' I was only twenty-four then, but this is how theatre still feels: as a marriage, in good times and in bad times. Everything positive and negative that comes with it. I am at peace with this. When I am in the theatre, I feel completely like myself. Here I am!

In addition, I am now more than ever aware of the social importance of theatre. Even though art and society have their own dynamics, goals and resources, they truly are intertwined. If it is true that politics creates a society by means of considering and tolerating other people's ideas, then art engages with the exact same process; perhaps not in direct relation with society, but on a poetic level. Art is of vital importance to society, because it allows us to experience our deepest fears, frustrations and desires in museums, concert halls, theatres and cinemas. Compare it to dreaming: I am afraid of heights and, without fail, all my dreams end the moment I am about to fall off a bridge or cliff. It is a way to experience, to control, and to allow ourselves to coexist with our fears. Just like dreams keep us alive, art keeps society alive. Art purifies society. On stage, Medea's vengeful infanticide goes unpunished and Romeo and Juliet love each other unconditionally, so much so that they jump off cliffs like lemmings, preferring to die together rather than live unhappily apart. We go to our theatres to experience something that we either fear or covet in our daily lives. This is the most important function of art in every society.

At the same time, there is a crucial dividing line between politics and art. Whereas politics needs to concern itself with the order of society, art attends to chaos. Both are pivotal for survival; imperative for life. A failure to negotiate this dividing line has been obscuring the role not only of art, but also of politics over the last few years. Politicians from both right-wing and left-wing parties gnaw at the line which divides chaos and order. Today, politics are often driven by gut feelings, feelings of disquietude and anxiety, dissatisfaction about the presence of too many strangers, feelings of alienation in a globalized world.

In a museum, theatre or cinema, I want to immerse myself in chaos. I want to be confused, afraid, hopeful. Art can surprise and be dangerous, if it becomes a sanctuary, a place where you feel totally free. The artist needs to move and shock us in order to allow us to look inside our troubled souls. Art is timeless – it is allowed to, even needs to, be outside time. On the one hand, I advocate for the absolute autonomy of the artist. On the other hand, I realize that in a society in which many question whether living together peacefully is still a viable option, the theatre and other forms of art can play a crucial role. Art needs to address the big issues of today's society, including questions of identity, globalization, migration and multiculturalism. Today's big issues need to be visible on our stages, and the stage should not serve merely as a mirror but should give us access to what happens 'on the other side of that mirror.'[1]

Acknowledgements

We wish to express our gratitude first and foremost to Ivo van Hove, who welcomed our plan to edit this collection and made himself and his associates at Toneelgroep Amsterdam available to us for interviews and to source archival materials. Ivo also allowed us to publish a selection of his Director's Notes, which appear for the first time in print in this book, and agreed to put us in touch with some of his closest collaborators, who then went on to write some of the key contributions that make up this collection. Jan Versweyveld was similarly generous with his time: he kindly agreed to be interviewed and to curate the visual aspects of the book, personally suggesting the selection of his own production photographs, which now richly illustrate the volume. A note of thanks also to Mirthe van Merwijk, who proved utterly indefatigable in answering all our questions about, and facilitating access to, the archives at Toneelgroep Amsterdam, and to her successor, Kiki Meijerhoven, for helping with the final stages of the project.

We would like to acknowledge financial support from the Social Sciences and Humanities Research Council of Canada and from the English Department at King's College London.

Isabelle Groenhof, Samantha Carron and Celiese Lypka, graduate students at the University of Calgary, provided excellent research assistance at various stages of this project.

Many people helped in identifying key contributors so that this book would have the geographic and generic scope that it does. Our thanks to Linda Hutcheon, Clemens Risi, Marisol Fernandez, Anthony Wall, Christopher Balme, Peter Eversmann, Alexandra Sakowska, Margherita Laera, Ramona Mosse and Joseph Pearson. Our thanks also to Jenny Mollica (Head of Creative Learning) and Lauren Monaghan-Pisano (Creative Learning Producer) at the Barbican Centre, London for facilitating access to events and supporting materials to do with Barbican Box 2016–2017, an annual theatre education programme produced by Creative Learning, Barbican and the Guildhall School of Music & Drama. We are grateful to photographers, Philip Carter, Camilla Greenwell and Monika Rittershaus, for granting permission to reproduce their work. Sincere thanks to Frédéric Maurin for his generous assistance and support as we made the selection of suggested further readings.

We would like to thank Mark Dudgeon, publisher at Methuen Drama, for his early willingness to consider a book on Ivo van Hove as well as Susan Furber and Lara Bateman, editorial assistants, for steering us through technical and other requirements pre-production. We are also grateful to copy editor Paul King and project manager Merv Honeywood.

IVO VAN HOVE: AN INTRODUCTION

Susan Bennett and Sonia Massai

'Ivo van Hove is having a moment'[1]

Any theatre director who has productions, in a single twelve-month period, on stages in London, New York and Paris, as well as at international festivals such as the Brooklyn Academy of Music's Next Wave, The Holland Festival and the Taiwan International Festival of the Arts, is having a good year. But, for Ivo van Hove, his productions in these cities and festivals in 2017 were only the tip of his directorial iceberg. The Artistic Director of Toneelgroep Amsterdam (TGA) is at the helm of twelve company productions booked for the 2017–18 season in venues that include TGA's home stage (the Rabozaal at the Stadsschouwburg), the Kennedy Center in Washington DC, the Tokyo Metropolitan Theatre and the Adelaide Festival. And, in this same season, his work independent from TGA includes a revival at Chicago's Goodman Theater of his 2014 interpretation of Arthur Miller's *A View From the Bridge* (a Young Vic production, seen in London, New York and via the internationally distributed NT Live stage-to-screen broadcasts), with a new cast and a new production of Modest Mussorgsky's *Boris Godonuv* at the Opéra Bastille in Paris. A theatrical adaptation of Joseph L. Mankiewicz's 1950 film *All About Eve* (with Cate Blanchett in the Bette Davis role of Margo Channing) is planned for London's West End.

Of course, while this level of success is phenomenal and virtually unheard-of, van Hove has hardly been an overnight sensation. The Flemish director began his theatre career in Antwerp in 1981 with productions of his own works (*Germs, Rumours*) and his resumé lists considerably more than 100 productions since then.[2] Van Hove's 2007 *Roman Tragedies* – the six-hour, Dutch-language compilation of Shakespeare's Roman plays (*Coriolanus, Julius Caesar* and *Antony and Cleopatra*) – is perhaps the production that not only first brought him significant international recognition but also a flurry of scholarly interest as it toured over the following decade, yet van Hove had first directed Shakespeare twenty years earlier: *Macbeth* for the Antwerp company De Tijd. His much-lauded production of *A View from the Bridge* (which garnered ten award nominations and won two Oliviers, for Best Director and Best Revival, and two Tonys, also for Best Director and Best Revival) was only the latest in a long line of productions of American dramas, many of them staged in collaboration with the New York Theatre Workshop (NYTW). As Marvin Carlson has pointed out, '[a]fter winning a second Obie for his *Hedda Gabler* [NYTW, 2004], and at least grudging respect from New York theatre critics, van Hove had clearly established himself as a leading director, perhaps *the* leading director of the New York Theatre Workshop'.[3] Between his first dip into the American theatre canon in 1988, a production of Eugene O'Neill's *Mourning Becomes Electra* in the Netherlands, and *A View from the Bridge*, there are a dozen other productions of plays by American authors including Tennessee Williams' *A Streetcar Named Desire* (1994 in the Netherlands and 1998 at the NYTW), Susan Sontag's *Alice in Bed* (2000 at NYTW) and Tony Kushner's *Angels in America* (2007, TGA). At the same time, admirers of van Hove's theatrical work may not know that, in 2014, he directed an opera version of *Brokeback Mountain* (Charles Wuorinen's music, E. Annie Proulx's libretto) – a hotly anticipated première that brought 'representatives of more than 100 media outlets and more than a dozen opera companies' to Teatro Real in Madrid, 'an absolute record for opera in Spain'.[4] But this one production belongs on an equally long list of the operas he has tackled, starting with Alban Berg's *Lulu* (1999) and continuing with projects at many of Europe's pre-eminent opera houses.

The story of van Hove's journey to a place of prominence and reputation across international theatre and opera has been told often in the last few years. He was born in a village in Belgium in 1958 where most locals worked in agriculture or coal mining and where his father was the (not 'a') pharmacist. At eleven he was sent to a boarding school that might have been an unhappy experience except for the decision to join the school's theatre company (one of three designated activities for the students' Wednesday afternoons). His participation in the theatre option quickly became 'the best time of my life'.[5] After school, he headed to university to study law (his parents' idea), but in his third year transferred into a programme to study directing. He met Jan Versweyveld while a student in Antwerp and they have been life partners and theatre collaborators ever since. And if his parents were less than delighted with his choice of a career in the arts, they have surely been amply convinced by now of the merit of their son's decision, not just by the longevity and degree of his success, but also by the distinctions with which he has been recognized: an honorary doctorate from the University of Antwerp (2014), the Flemish Cultural Prize for Overall Cultural Merit (2015) and Commander of the Order of the Crown, one of Belgium's highest honours (2015). Van Hove, however, has his own distinctive take on the subject of his life as he suggests in the Foreword to this book and, as he put it to Rebecca Mead, 'My productions are my massed autobiography: if you look at all the plays I've done since I was twenty, you know who I am.'[6]

Ivo van Hove: From Shakespeare to David Bowie is intended to be an introduction to this 'massed autobiography' and, we hope, a starting point and sourcebook for others' studies both of his creative process and of the critical impact and influence of his productions. We hope that the book provides a generative context for van Hove's prolific output as our contributors illustrate and examine the exceptional breadth of directorial work. Each section presents a series of original materials and focused reviews that collectively aim to capture the range of subjects, styles and themes that the productions explore. Beyond the specific, however, there are interests that repeat across the different areas of his work – contemporary politics are certainly never far from a van Hove production, but it was striking, too, how many of our authors found in his work what Pamela Newton calls 'universal themes that speak to the ages'.[7] Love, for example, is mentioned frequently. Yet, at the same time as his productions seem ubiquitous and sought-after, they have not all met with sweeping acclaim. Reviews for his work in opera have been consistently mixed and some theatrical productions have been less than enthusiastically received (Paul Taylor asked that *Obsession* 'be filed with his pieces that don't really come off'[8]). And some are controversial: real-world videos of torture scenes deployed in Tchaikovsky's *Mazeppa* and the casting of a white actor (Hans Kesting) in the title role of *Othello*.[9]

The best theatre, of course, challenges those who make it and those who see it. It was our own experience of the style, complexity and intensity of van Hove's productions – the exhilaration in seeing them and the images and ideas that lingered long afterwards – that brought us to collaborate on this project and it was no surprise to find that so many others shared an enthusiasm to try to put into words what van Hove does in his directorial practice. We thank them for their generous contributions to this book. We have, too, come to recognize the importance of collaboration in van Hove's own process – the longevity of his working relationships (with companies, with technical staff, with actors, with producing theatres and festivals). He has the benefit of a full-time repertory company in Amsterdam where 'he casts by fiat, assigning actors to play characters',[10] no doubt a product of knowing their individual strengths as well as seeing their development over time, but elsewhere he has collaborated with a veritable 'A' list of artists working on stage and off: Cate Blanchett, Ruth Wilson, Annie Proulx, Saoirse Ronan, Anne Carson, Jude Law, Mark Strong, Philip Glass, Ben Wishaw, Patrick Marber, and David Bowie among them – a measure that others value what he brings to their own creative process. Described through our conversations with van Hove and his

Figure 1 *Enobarbus (Bart Siegers),* Roman Tragedies, *external of Stadsschouwburg, Amsterdam (2012).*

partner Jan Versweyveld and in a conversation between Halina Reijn (a member of TGA since 2003 and frequently seen in van Hove's productions) and Ruth Wilson (who worked with van Hove for the first time in the 2016 production of *Hedda Gabler*), what follows is an account of that process.

Ivo van Hove in conversation with Susan Bennett and Sonia Massai (January 2017)

SB   Can we start with you describing how you choose a project that you want to direct?

IvH   It has changed over the years, but now a decision is made a year or two years before – sometimes even longer – and it starts with a decision about the text. For me it's always the toughest decision in the whole process because you have to know that you will still be interested in it in two years' time. The choice of a text is always very impulsive, an intuitive thing, a love affair. Sometimes it's something someone proposes and it lays there for ten years and then I remember it. Sometimes it's very specific. But most of the time, it's an open field. *The Fountainhead* is a good example. Ayn Rand's novel was given to me by an associate working on *Roman Tragedies* in 2007. On opening night, he gave me the pocket edition of the text – 700 pages – and wrote on the first page, 'Ivo, YOU have to read this NOW!' I didn't know Ayn Rand nor *The Fountainhead*. And, against all odds, I started to read it, and then I couldn't stop reading: it is a page-turner with huge theatrical possibilities. It took several years to get the rights and when we eventually did, people [in my team] started to read it and said, 'Ivo, you cannot do this.' They thought that the text was politically very sensitive. But when I know I want to do something, I'm hard to stop.

After the text has been chosen, there are two parallel groups that meet and develop the work. One is concerned with dramaturgy in the traditional sense and the other with what I call the visual dramaturgy with Tal [Yarden, video], Jan [Versweyveld, scenography and light design] and me as its core. I'm the only one who works in both groups. And for some plays, the visual language is at least as important as the words. For example, our production of *The Damned* (2016) is extremely visual.[11] The text is only 50 pages long: we could read it in an hour and 5 minutes but the production runs for 2 hours 15 minutes.

We look at each project and see what it needs, but every process is somewhat different.

SB   How long do the two parallel streams work on a text in preparation for rehearsals?

IvH   With each project I like to think, develop, rethink for at least a year. With *Obsession*, it was designed last summer and we start rehearsing in March [2017], although we had been talking about it for much longer. But we have many different projects happening at the same time, of course. I like the slow-cooking pre-production process.

SM   How do you prepare the scripts for your productions, particularly the Shakespearean 'epics' – the six-hour *Roman Tragedies* and the four-hour *Kings of War* (his 2015 compilation of *Henry V*, the three parts of *Henry VI* and *Richard III*)?

IvH   Based on our vision for the production, my dramaturgs do the first cut and then I cut further during my rehearsal time. In the case of *Roman Tragedies* there was one dramaturg for each of the three plays and I oversaw everything. In the case of *Kings of War*, it was the same process so one dramaturg had to deal with the three plays of *Henry VI* and to make sense of them for performance in 70 minutes. A different dramaturg prepared the texts for *Henry V* and *Richard III*, which were more straightforward, but, of course, they presented their own challenges.

SB   Do you like to return to a text you've already worked on? You directed *Hedda Gabler* in 2004 at the New York Theatre Workshop and the following year in Amsterdam, but returned to it for the National Theatre (NT) and, on this occasion (2016), with a new translation of Ibsen's play.

IvH   In the early days I didn't like to return to a production, but now I think of it as revisiting a house you know very well and looking at it with new eyes. With my production of *Hedda Gabler* for the National, we started with the set from the earlier productions and during rehearsals took things away – it felt like a cleaning up. Working with English actors for the NT production, I thought it would be great to have a new text and Patrick [Marber] wrote a version that suited the concept. Today we don't need all the exposition that is typical in an Ibsen play and Patrick created a twenty-first-century play, not a nineteenth-century one.

SM   Some features are common to your productions – for example, an audience always arrives to see the set and the actors already in place.

IvH   The strength of theatre is that everybody knows that it is a virtual reality, but at the same time our job is to make you forget that. So the stage world doesn't start with the first line from an actor. Over the years we have developed a few basic principles and one is that the set, the world, will always be visible when the audience enters. This allows the audience to construct their own fantasies about what this world is before the action begins. In *Hedda Gabler* [at the NT], Hedda is already on stage and the music is John Cage's 'Suite for Toy Piano' – the audience starts to think about what is happening here.

SB   Would you say that music is one of the signatures of your productions?

IvH   Music and sound. In the last 15 years I've used it a lot. I was inspired by my idol, the French director Patrice Chéreau.[12] He was known for his spectacular opera productions and amazing theatre. He directed *I Am The Wind* at the Young Vic. He used sound in such an emotional and atmospheric way and that's what I learned from him.

SM   And your use of video? Is that to offer the audience more complex perspectives on the action?

IvH   Video is an extra instrument that the twentieth century gave us and it needs to be used carefully. We use it to bring the emotional life of the characters closer to the audience, but not to beautify the production or just to create effects. We also use video to show moments that could not otherwise be staged. In *Kings of War*, long sequences of the production take place in corridors that are invisible to the audience, but they are captured by live cameras. Another reason why we use video is to create subjective worlds on stage. In *Lazarus*, video provided the mental landscape – it allowed spectators to look into the souls of the characters. This level of access to the world of the characters would have been impossible without video. Our philosophy is: if there is no compelling reason to use video, we don't.

SB   How does your process for directing an opera differ from what you do in theatre?

IvH   I was fortunate that the great Belgian opera administrator Gerard Mortier[13] was appointed to the Théâtre de la Monnaie in Brussels [1981] and he brought the most exciting people working in opera to its stages and I was able to see so many great productions. I came late to directing opera, however, as I refused for a long time. I didn't feel a strong urgency to take on the projects that we had been offered before Alban Berg's *Lulu* came along, and that was an offer that I couldn't refuse. Later came *The Macropulous Case* by Janáček and I felt at home working with these fabulous scores and stories. I discovered very early on that, as a director of opera, one has to accept that there has been a director before you: the composer. Alban Berg, Wagner – they are great dramaturgs. I learned to find opportunities for personal expression within the limitations of a musical score. I study the scores thoroughly with musical dramaturgs. I brought my experience in directing actors to working with singers in an opera, and I took what I learned about music and sound from opera back to my work in the theatre.

Crystallizing the vision

Van Hove and Versweyveld have developed a highly personal and yet thoroughly collaborative creative process over the years, which combines their distinctive vision for each of their productions with the input of the large number of collaborators they regularly work with, including video artist Tal Yarden, composer Eric Sleichim, dramaturges Peter Van Kraaij, Bart Van den Eynde, Jan Peter Gerrits and Alexander Schreuder, and members of the permanent company at their headquarters in Holland (TGA). When van Hove and Versweyveld partner with other institutions for their ambitious co-productions, or when they work with a different group of actors, they ensure that anybody who is unfamiliar with their way of working is brought up to speed, so their approach to theatre-making travels with them.

The trademark clarity of their productions, along with their stunning acoustic and visual distinctiveness, the inspiring use of the performance space and the raw and visceral quality of the acting, are the result of the process that van Hove and Versweyveld have honed since they first met and started working together in the early 1980s. It is certainly unusual for a director and a stage designer to have worked so closely together for such a length of time, but it is also unusual for a director to work as closely with other key members of the creative team from the very early stages of the creative process, while keeping a firm grip on the initial, core vision for each production. The short period devoted to rehearsal – typically only three weeks with the actors in full costume, on set, and off-book from day one – is another basic principle in van Hove and Versweyveld's practice.

Jan Versweyveld in conversation with Sonia Massai (February 2017)

SM Ivo has explained how textual dramaturgy and visual dramaturgy go hand in hand as you start developing an idea for a new production. Can you tell us a bit more about this early stage of the creative process?

JV   We follow no fixed formula: every project stems from a new encounter with new textual materials and circumstances. But everything generally starts with reading and studying a text. I then create an open document, where I sum up my ideas about the essence of the text, what the text means to me, or the timings for opera, and, of course, the visuals. Everything goes into that document. Tal Yarden, our 'go-to' video artist, shares this document, when Ivo and I decide that the production will involve video, since we never have a design first and then decide to add video. In fact, if we use video, that's because video is integral to the design from the very beginning. The composers get to see this document too. It's a shared document; it's the skeleton of a production, gathering everything about the production that is not already in the text. So we start involving all our collaborators from this early stage. But, as a designer, I don't offer choices. The moment I start thinking about a text, there is often an image that forms itself in my head; and that image is where the production will stem from. It's still a very general vision; it is not crystallized, but it is there. Then Ivo crystallizes it, by developing and directing this general vision into a fully-fledged production. So our creative process is collaborative from the very beginning, but the focus stays firmly on that first core idea.

SM   Does this early stage of the process involve deciding where and how the actors are going to move on your stage?

JV   Yes, and even more so since I started photographing the actors, because I have become aware of the fact that the actors need to feel comfortable in the spaces I create for them. The feel of a set for an actor is crucial. I always think, 'Would I want to live in this space?' or 'Would I want to spend time in it?' The space I create can be a horrible world, but it still needs to feel that it fits in with our overall vision for the production, which we then share with the actors.

SM   Does your training as a painter feed into your set designs?

JV   Yes, of course. Take the set of *Hedda Gabler* as an example. Hedda's world is not a nice environment; she hates it, in fact. But it is, and must be, highly defined: so the quality of the light is part and parcel of that world, and I guess my attention to light has to do with my painting and my photography training.

SM   Has the advance in stage technology changed the way in which you work?

JV   No, it has not changed the way I work; for me using new technology is an organic process. I am curious about projectors, cameras, light sources. I can be inspired by new technology, but I am also happy to use traditional technology. I also use technology that

Figure 2 *From left, Reverend John Hale (Bill Camp), Betty Parris (Elizabeth Teeter) and Abigail Williams (Saoirse Ronan, background),* The Crucible, *Walter Kerr Theatre, New York (2016).*

was not meant to be used on stage: I for example work with sources used to light up the outside of buildings, when I want a strong, brutal type of light.

SM   How would you describe your stage designs? Is there a defining quality to them?

JV   Very few of my designs are not contemporary, but I am not sure I would call my settings contemporary. I would call them 'new realities', because they bring into being a world that has not existed before and may never exist. I also often mix up time frames. My settings are rarely hugely high-tech. The house in *Hedda Gabler* could for example recall the 1920s. But my settings are never mimetic. Even the war room in *Kings of War* might resemble Churchill's war rooms, but it is not meant to re-present that specific space on stage.

'In rehearsal with Ivo van Hove': Halina Reijn and Ruth Wilson, in conversation (June 2017)

HR   Did you know Ivo's work before you played Hedda?

RW   Yes, I had seen some of his shows – *A View from the Bridge*, *The Crucible*, *Antigone* – and they were so different from anything I had seen. The acting was raw and free. In that moment I knew I wanted to work with Ivo. I had already told the National Theatre that I was interested in playing Hedda, and when Ivo's production of *Network* for the National Theatre was postponed, Ivo suggested reviving one of his productions and he chose *Hedda Gabler*. I completed filming on a TV show in early November. This gave us a mere three weeks to rehearse. The National Theatre never rehearse for less than five. However, three weeks is enough for Ivo; in fact, three weeks is often longer than it needs. Ivo rehearses from 11 am to 4 pm and he was away for three of those precious days. And yet, by the time the show opened, I felt more relaxed and more prepared than ever before.

HR   Did you learn your lines beforehand?

RW   Yes. I was told to, and I was off-book by the time we started rehearsing.

HR   After working with Ivo for so many years, I find it difficult to work with other directors, who sit and talk at the actors, for longer than it seems necessary, about thoughts and ideas that often seem irrelevant to what we are doing.

RW   Yes it often feels like pointless avoidance of the work that really matters and it can be extremely frustrating.

HR   Ivo and Jan relate very differently to their actors: they arrive on the first day of rehearsals fully prepared and they will of course stop if you have questions but, other than that, they have a very clear idea about what they want to do with the show.

RW   But their vision and their preparation then give actors freedom. They give you very strict guidelines that have to do with how you physically inhabit the space. I feel that most of Ivo's direction is physical rather than emotional and that his style of directing helps actors explore their emotions freely. So Ivo would tell me – 'Right, now staple the flowers to the walls' or 'Curl up in a ball as if you had pain deep inside your stomach' – and I modulated my emotions around those directions. If one of us asked 'Why?' Ivo would answer 'I don't psychologise'.

HR   Ivo's process liberates actors from thinking in psychological patterns. Ivo and Jan had already come up with the idea of getting you to staple flowers to the walls of the set, but they do not tell you why and when you do it, you have to find your own answers.

RW   Yes, and the answers are so much more original, because you need to find them yourself. I remember the first day of rehearsals, when Ivo simply asked me and Rafe [Spall] to play a scene. I felt awkward and frightened, because with Ivo you basically start a full-tech on day one with the entire creative team watching you. So Rafe and I stood up and started playing the scene from the page, as it were, and Ivo said 'No, no, no: you over here, you over there, and you on your knees'. I liked the constrictions; they made me more creative.

HR   Only a strong actor takes kindly to being directed so fully. I have seen actors over the years, with no previous work experience with Ivo, looking and sounding absolutely outraged at being directed so meticulously.

RW   Ivo is so direct he can come across as quite brash.

HR   **And some actors may feel that he is not interested in their creativity, but that's quite the opposite.**

RW   I really like his ideas and felt relieved, actually, to find out that I was not expected to stand by a wall and look depressed, like some sort of ice queen. I liked what Ivo and Jan wanted to do and so I went along with it.

HR   **Were you scared or embarrassed at any point?**

RW   No. Well, I was scared in a good way. Big dramatic and iconic moments like the burning of the manuscript scared and thrilled me in equal measure; I was not sure what I was going to do with it, or what Ivo was going to ask me to do. It was also a scene we didn't rehearse until our first run through. Terrifyingly he told me to 'Just make theatre'. It felt in that moment that he trusted me to come up with something honest and truthful, he was asking me not to over-think it or try to prepare, just do what comes instinctively in the moment. I remember watching Hans Kesting, as he played Richard III in *Kings of War,* when he started galloping around the stage with a carpet on his shoulders, elated by the prospect of getting closer and closer to securing the crown, and I thought, 'That's what Ivo meant by "making theatre"'. I wanted to do that; I wanted to have that moment in *Hedda Gabler.* So after the first 'Blue' moment ['Blue' by Joni Mitchell], he said, 'Right, go and do something with the blinds and the flowers'. And I trashed them! Ivo then said, 'No: that's the next "Blue", not this one!' But from that moment he knew that I was entirely prepared to let go. I knew he had given me license to play and he realized then that I was going to embrace it. Did you have that moment with Ivo, when you started working with him?

HR   **I first saw one of his productions, Alban Berg's *Lulu,* when I was thirteen years old. I loved the production and Lulu, who is wild, sexy, strange and funny, ugly and beautiful all at once, became my role model. I already knew that I wanted to be an actor back then, but my mother, who took me to see *Lulu,* did not want me to work with Ivo because he was so radical. She thought that his theatre was dangerous, a bit like rock-and-roll. So I joined a different company first and when I was playing Lulu for them, Ivo came to watch the show. He never talked to me then, but I was reminded of how badly I wanted to work with him. I felt immediately at home with Ivo when**

I started working with him, because, unlike my other director who was very invested in Stanislavsky and method acting, he would never tell me how I should feel and why; also Ivo is not interested in judging characters or the moral message of any given piece. Ivo does not have a method or a philosophy as such; he is interested in creating a world within which he allows his actors to explore their emotional responses to situations. And he never judges you for what you find, even when what you find comes out of the darkest recesses of yourself. And his approach is addictive for actors once they have got to know him.

RW   He gives you the space, the freedom and the trust to do whatever feels right to you within the confines of his vision. I cannot explain exactly why I felt so liberated, but I did. And I enjoyed his directions: they were physical and imaginative, as when he said to me, as we were rehearsing the final sequence in *Hedda Gabler*, 'die like a fish'. That felt amazing because I knew exactly what he meant. There were also moments on the stage when I did not understand what Hedda was doing. But, strangely, I liked that feeling. In other shows I would have beaten myself up for not knowing what my character was doing at any particular moment and why she was doing it. I believed, and of course much of this is true, that if I knew the motive of the character's actions then the audience would understand it too. But Ivo creates drama out of questions, not answers. He believes you don't have to explain everything; in fact in life you can't.

HR   That's why for an actor to be in one of Ivo's productions is like being part of a work of art. Instead of striving to shine as an individual actor, building on your personal reputation, you feel part of a larger, organic work, and that feeling is liberating. I guess one can compare that feeling to a religious experience that involves losing yourself into something bigger than your own ego. With Ivo you'll also often play roles in ways that alienate audiences, but pleasing audiences becomes secondary.

RW   He also takes away from you the responsibility of having to know everything, and of telling the story in a conventional way that people understand. At some stage I said to him, 'I get the relationship with Lovborg, I get the relationship with Brack, I get the relationship with Mrs Elvsted, but I don't get the relationship with Tesman – I can't get my head around it'. 'Exactly', he said, 'and it is the most real relationship because of it'. As a result, his work feels truthful, more truthful than in any other versions of *Hedda Gabler* I have seen. He deconstructs the play and, by doing so, he shines a light on all the key moments.

HR   He is like a surgeon, or an anatomist, who lifts the heart out of the body for you to look at. And it is not a pretty sight! In *Hedda Gabler*, you moved inside this huge set, with hardly anything on it, wearing a skimpy nightdress most of the time.

RW   Yes – there were hardly any props on stage, the set was not a warm, cosy space. The piano, the guns, the flowers, and actors were isolated from each other, almost in a spotlight.

HR   His background in performance art makes his work feel completely real in an artificial situation. Ivo and Jan don't like fight instructors because they make fights very safe, and everyone keeps at a safe distance from each other. But their work is the opposite of safe: it feels raw and naked.

RW   Performing in Ivo's productions is never about range and acting. When actors try and put on an accent, he tells them not to. Even in *A View from the Bridge*, all actors were encouraged to use their own accents. In *Hedda Gabler*, Kyle Soller originally spoke with a British accent, but Ivo asked him to play in his own voice. So Tesman became American and with that Soller had a whole new angle on that character.

HR   Acting, pretending, is of course a lot of fun for actors, but working with Ivo allows you to experience being fully caught up in an artificial situation by exploring the very real emotions triggered by it. And that is why the combination of the psychological realism practiced in mainstream theatre in the English-speaking world with Ivo and Jan's ability to confront you with the fully formed vision of alternative worlds works even better than within the Continental European tradition inspired by Brecht, whereby actors switch registers and modes of delivery in order to get in and out of character. And that is probably why Ivo's approach to making theatre is now finally proving so popular with audiences in the UK and the US.

While this book is focused on van Hove's directorial process and the critical reception of the wide variety of work he has undertaken, it is important, too, to acknowledge his role as Director of TGA. The company and its theatres have become an internationally significant site of, and incubator for, original dramatic productions. TGA has invited and staged work by some of theatre's most innovative directors – among them, Katie

Mitchell (Jean Genet's *The Maids*), Simon Stone (*Husbands and Wives*, based on Woody Allen's script; *Ibsen House*, based on some of Ibsen's lesser-known plays; an adaptation of Euripides's *Medea*), Luk Perceval (a stage adaptation of Hugo Claus's *The Year of Cancer* and *Disgrace*, based on J. M. Coetzee's Booker Prize-winning novel) and Robert Icke (a contemporary adaptation of Sophocles' *Oedipus*). TGA also fosters the work of 'directors of the future' through their TA-2 platform, run in cooperation with Toneelschuur Producties (Haarlem) and Frascati Producties (Amsterdam). There have been ten productions since the collaboration started in 2007 with three of those transferring to the TGA mainstage.[14] Among the young directors who have staged productions at TA-2 are Thibaud Delpeut, Eric de Vroedt, Julie Van den Berghe and Maren E. Bjørseth. TGA also has a commitment to provide 'business leadership, sales, marketing and administration' for other creators such as Adelheid|Female Economy.[15] In other words, TGA has become a vibrant creative hub under van Hove's leadership, one that has put Amsterdam firmly on the 'theatre city' map. These varied roles and ambitions among TGA's ventures have their roots in van Hove's experience with the Holland Festival, which he ran from 1998 to 2004.

Our volume sets off to offer a book-length, critical account of all the roles and ambitions that have defined van Hove's work with TGA and beyond. It also charts the evolution of van Hove's work, as it has come into contact with a phenomenal range of other companies, artists and producers, who have in turn left a mark on it. Van Hove himself speaks eloquently about how directing opera for some of the leading opera houses on Continental Europe has affected his approach to directing theatre. We include in this volume reviews by leading opera critics for a range of these productions. Various other contributors similarly highlight other aspects of van Hove's work that have changed and are changing in ways that this volume can only begin to outline. As well as sparking controversy for his direction of female roles (the focus of Ruth Wilson and Halina Reijn's conversation included in the 'Directing the Classics' section), van Hove's original and, at times, surprising approach to race and colour-blind casting emerges as another focal point of interest in several essays. Worth highlighting here are the casting of Hans Kesting as a white Othello (see essay by Massai in 'Directing the Classics') and the sustained colour-blind casting of John Douglas Thompson as Brack in *Hedda Gabler* at the NYTW in 2004 and Chukwudi Iwuji as Lovborg in *Hedda* at the National Theatre in 2016–17 and in the roles of the priest and the policeman in *Obsession* at the Barbican in 2017 (see essays by Skantze and Sanders in 'Creation, Adaptation, Direction'). Our volume, in other words, captures a prolific director at a crucial stage in his already long career. We believe his work promises to continue to shock and surprise, to challenge and enlighten, if not necessarily to entertain, reassure and please all.

Section One

Directing the Classics

CANONICAL ICONOCLASM

Sonia Massai

Ivo van Hove's productions of the ancient, early modern and modern European classics routinely elicit extreme responses. But even those who describe his approach as 'taking stylized wrecking balls to a host of classic plays'[1] find his work theatrically breathtaking and uncompromisingly original.

It is not innovation alone, however, which makes van Hove's bold theatrical revisions of the classics distinctive. In fact, the very notion of 'the classics' implies revival and reinterpretation and is historically linked to the emergence of the figure of the director as a powerful creative force. Several world-leading directors have indeed built their reputations on radical reinterpretations of the classics, and of Shakespeare, more specifically: for example, Peter Brook's *A Midsummer Night's Dream* (1970), Giorgio Strehler's *La Tempesta* (1977) or the Wooster Group's *Hamlet*, directed by Elizabeth LeCompte (2006), to name but a few. So how do van Hove's uniquely innovative productions of the classics intersect with, while departing from, the work of earlier and contemporary game-changers, like Peter Stein, Robert Lepage or Thomas Ostermeier?

This opening overview focuses on three distinctive qualities of van Hove's approach to the classics, which can help us understand his work in the context of other innovative directors and theatrical traditions, and ends with a brief account of the different perspectives offered by the contributors to this section of the book.

Jan Versweyveld describes the striking settings he creates for van Hove's productions as 'new realities',[2] effectively capturing their immersive quality. Versweyveld's design does not simply do away with naturalist clutter. Inspired by Jerzy Grotowski's minimalist aesthetics, Brook's famous imperative 'we must open our empty hands and show that really there is nothing up our sleeves . . . only then we can begin'[3] has not gone unheeded and minimalism has become *de rigueur* among even the more moderately minded contemporary theatre makers. However, Versweyveld's design is also specific to each work, so that each of van Hove's productions of the classics takes place in its own intensely distinctive space. Van Hove's productions therefore derive additional unity of vision through Versweyveld's design: as explained in the Introduction, textual and visual dramaturgy are central to the creative process from its very first stages, when van

Hove's role as director and Versweyveld's role as designer overlap as they decide what lies at the very core of a classic play and how text, space, sound and choreography can be made to converge to realize their vision for it.

Van Hove's productions are also thoroughly informed by Versweyveld's use of light and colours. He was training as a painter when he met van Hove in Antwerp in the early 1980s, and he readily admits that his sets are painterly, because he draws on his skills and interests in the visual arts. His 2016 set for *Hedda Gabler*[4] had a signature quality to it, in being made up of light and space. During most of the production, a cold shaft of white light traversed from large French windows stage right a bare, immense room, with a piano as its focal point in the middle. The lighting changed only at very specific times, when the stage was plunged into semi-darkness, except for a beam of deep blue light that rose from underneath the walls surrounding the stage. The sudden switch in lighting suggested a world elsewhere, possibly the life that Hedda wishes for herself but that remains firmly beyond her reach. The overwhelming effect of some of these moments was heightened by Joni Mitchell's 'Blue', and the lyrics – 'Underneath the skin / An empty space to fill in / Well there're so many sinking / Now you've got to keep thinking' – blended seamlessly with Hedda's sense of emptiness and isolation. These moments – what van Hove describes as the rare silences in Ibsen's text – constituted the visual and acoustic make-up of Hedda's world and conjured a 'new reality'. This 'new reality' was neither (or not only) Ibsen's stifling nineteenth-century Norway, nor (or not only) the type of hell conjured by Mitchell's song; it was rather a layering of the performance space that challenged Hedda to acknowledge the emptiness underneath her skin, as the room that enclosed her was momentarily transformed (see Plate 1).

Even when the worlds forged by van Hove and Versweyveld for their revisionary take on the classics are unusually detailed – the war room at the beginning of *Kings of War* (2015) is a case in point – they are never meant to reproduce specific locations. Although Churchill's War Rooms were effectively conjured by Versweyveld's design, the brightly lit white corridor, visible through a central opening back stage and regularly captured by live video feeds projected on to a screen above the main stage area, undercut any attempt to read that space mimetically. The interplay between the war room and the corridor, between live performance and live video feeds, transformed the space into an uncompromisingly theatrical world in its own right (see Plate 2).

Only much earlier on in his career did Versweyveld localize his stage designs. In *'Tis Pity She's a Whore* (1991), for example, he decided to arrange the stage into several levels resembling the architectural structure of early modern town houses in Parma, Italy, where the play is originally set. The use of a ceiling-high wall, placed down stage, left little space for the actors to move about freely, forcing them instead to negotiate their movements carefully and self-consciously, thus suggesting the societal constraints imposed on their characters. With most of the cast simultaneously on stage and 'hiding in dark alcoves, or propped up against the wall,'[5] this early production beautifully conveyed the overwhelming sense of entrapment generated by social conditioning and the equally disorienting impact of incest, which collapses social space as it attempts to challenge it.

Despite its effectiveness, Versweyveld regards his choices for this production as marginal to his practice, because rather than *recreating* locations, even in a very minimalist and symbolic way, as he did in this production, he has since then committed to *creating* 'new realities' that are deeply familiar – much like the conference centre-like space in *Roman Tragedies* (2007)[6] – even while they are utterly other. So the conference centre-like space in *Roman Tragedies* becomes hybrid and un-localized as members of the audience sit on it, surrounded by actors, cameramen and multiple screens showing recorded footage and live video feeds. The detailed settings of *Roman Tragedies* and *Kings of War* are therefore neither entirely minimalist nor entirely abstract, but they share an intensely focused and yet un-localized quality with the worlds that Versweyveld creates with van Hove for all their productions.[7]

Their 'new realities' are also distinctive because they often extend to encompass the entire venue and the audience within it. In *Roman Tragedies*, audience and cast intermingle on stage and Enobarbus delivers his famous speech at the end of *Antony and Cleopatra* – 'Be witness to me, O thou blessed moon' (4.9.10)[8] – outdoors, having left the stage and the venue followed by a small video crew (see Figure 1). By extending the performance space to encompass the theatrical venue and the streetscape beyond, van Hove and Versweyveld pry classical plays open for their audiences to experience them as raw and relevant from within, as if they were unfolding, quite literally, all around them.

Even when the extension of the performance space to include the theatrical venue is less obvious than in *Roman Tragedies*, it is achieved just as effectively through the explicit staging of the theatrical gaze. In *Kings of War*, for example, Hans Kesting's Richard III delivers his final soliloquy – 'Soft, I did but dream' (5.3.179) – sitting with his back to the audience. Staring at his own image projected onto the back of the stage, which is now totally dark, Richard watches himself morph into the ghostly semblance of his victims (see Figure 3). At this moment in the production, the darkness and the camera work unify Richard's and the audience's sensory experience of a world that is and yet is not, where 'nothing is, but what is not' (*Macbeth*, 1.3.142). Similarly, in van Hove's production of Molière's *The Misanthrope* (2010), a screen separated the actors from the audience,

Figure 3 *Richard III (Hans Kesting),* Kings of War, *Stadsschouwburg, Amsterdam (2015).*

positioning the audience as self-conscious viewers, or voyeurs (see Figure 9). The glass structures that subdivided the stage in van Hove's productions of *Othello* (2003)[9] and *The Taming of the Shrew* (2005) into indoor and outdoor spaces also aligned the audience with onstage characters, as the latter stared at Othello and Desdemona in their bedchamber, barely screened by semi-transparent drapes, or at Bianca, reclining over a piano in Baptista's house, as she indecently solicited Lucentio's attention (see Plates 3 and 4).

The 'singularity of purpose'[10] and the acoustic, visual and almost sculptural quality of van Hove and Versweyveld's immersive, installation-like worlds, 'forged out of nothing but focus',[11] are the latest and most significant development of a well-established tradition of innovative directors that stretches back to Edward Gordon Craig's experiments to create a new theatrical language that would encompass 'action, scene and voice',[12] or even further back to Richard Wagner's notion of *gesamtkunstwerk*, or 'the total work of art'[13] that draws from, and comprises, different art forms.

Another recurrent feature in van Hove's reinterpretation of the classics is his understanding of character, which he likes to explain by borrowing Amin Maalouf's notion that identity is 'the sum of all our allegiances'[14] to specific religious or political beliefs, to our professional vocations, our sexual inclinations, our national or ethnic roots, or to new and elective homelands. This understanding of character is best

Figure 4 *From right, Othello (Hans Kesting), Desdemona (Karina Smulders), Iago (Roeland Fernhout) and Emilia (Janni Goslinga),* Othello, *Stadsschouwburg, Amsterdam (2012).*

illustrated by van Hove's choice to cast Kesting as Othello (see Figure 4). Why a white Othello? The language in this production retained its original, virulent brand of hate speech against Othello's racial otherness, as voiced in the play by Iago and by Brabantio, but by casting a white actor to play Othello van Hove challenged his audience to wonder whether the outcome of Iago's plot would have been just as devastating had Othello rooted his sense of self in a different aspect of his subjectivity – for example, ethnicity or class. Kesting's Othello, in other words, pointed out the risks involved in privileging one of our many affiliations over others. Or, as Maalouf puts it: 'We should be encouraged to accept our own diversity, to see our identity as the sum of all our various affiliations, instead of as only one of them raised to the status of the most important, made into an instrument of exclusion and sometimes into a weapon of war'.[15] Race may be the most important determinant of our sense of identity, but, as van Hove intimates, any time we choose to identify primarily with any of our multiple allegiances we do so at our own peril and to the detriment of others.

This notion of identity is of course linked to recent changes in the way we live, travel and communicate with each other. Air travel and, most of all, digital media, connect us with each other across national, linguistic and cultural borders. 'Isn't it a characteristic of the age we live in', Maalouf asks, 'that it has made everyone in a way a migrant and a member of a minority? We all have to live in a universe bearing little resemblance to the place where we were born ... Many have left their native land, and many, though they haven't left it, can no longer recognise it'.[16] Prompted by similar insights into subjectivity and character, van Hove approaches canonical characters like Othello not as trans-historical and universal types but as a multiplicity of identities cobbled together in a way that we have come to recognize as more life-like than the psychological realism associated with Romantic and post-Romantic theatrical traditions.

Kesting's Richard III in *Kings of War* is a stunning illustration of this understanding of character. Kesting delivers all his monologues (except the last) to a large mirror downstage left. No other character takes the slightest interest in the mirror; Richard, by stark contrast, self-fashions before it. As a result, we are given to watch him reassess his sense of self, as he transforms from a bloodthirsty warlord into a brutal tyrant. This understanding of character is radically different from how other contemporary directors approach classical characters like Richard III. In Thomas Ostermeier's production (2015), Lars Eidinger's Richard III, for example, bursts on to the stage fully formed as a confident, malevolent deceiver, who seduces the audience even before he successfully woos Lady Anne in 1.2. Kesting instead constructs Richard on stage, in response to the events that led to his coronation and then to his fall. The raw, visceral quality of van Hove's canonical characters is heightened and made distinctive by this highly effective and inherently theatrical conception of the self. Also telling is a comparison with the 'anti-intellectual' methodology championed by other leading directors. Declan Donnellan, for example, encourages his actors 'to meet the world as it *really* is, not as we intellectually perceive it ought to be' (my italics).[17] Far from suggesting that classic characters are timeless universals, best grasped intuitively, van Hove shows us characters who construct themselves before our very eyes, in real time, and in response to the specificities of the 'new realities' designed by Versweyveld for their productions. Hence the urgent immediacy that seems to propel his characters into existence.

This approach to character emerges most clearly when van Hove discusses it with actors who do not belong to his long-standing ensemble at Toneelgroep Amsterdam. Both van Hove and Ruth Wilson have related how they approached the process that led to Wilson's exceptional interpretation of the title role in *Hedda Gabler*. During a brief pre-production meeting with van Hove, Wilson asked how she should start preparing to play this daunting role. Van Hove urged her not to think of Hedda as a specific person, as having a specific identity, and to try and respond instead to what happened on stage. At a platform at the National Theatre in London on 31 January 2017, van Hove went on to explain that directors 'tend to want to create unitary characters' in the name of an obsolete notion of psychological realism.[18] Since actors directed by van Hove start rehearsing off-book, in costume, and on set, they can afford to leave behind them their own personas or their own preconceptions about what any one character might be all about, and respond instead to how their characters develop within the unified, painterly, acoustically and visually layered alternative realities that Versweyveld designs for van Hove's productions. To all effects, they step into a 'new reality' and need to respond instinctively, on their feet, to it and to the other characters who inhabit this alternative world with them.

At an earlier platform at the National Theatre on 23 January 2017,[19] Wilson had also talked about how her Hedda developed in rehearsal and throughout the entire run of the production itself, and how she needed to find her character every night, as the character continued to change in performance, as opposed to being discussed and agonized over in the rehearsal room, reaching the audience as a finished product. In the rehearsal room, there was no talk about Hedda's psychological make-up; rather, van Hove would suggest what stage action might help Wilson respond to the unfolding interactions with the other characters. As a result, Wilson's Hedda came across as surprising, despicable and moving; she was electrifying because she was genuinely mercurial, at once merciless and manipulative but also damaged and profoundly sympathetic. 'Hedda is the most liberating thing I have done on stage', Wilson concluded.

Ironically, this conception of character is much closer to an early modern understanding of identity and to early modern theatrical practices than later Romantic and post-Romantic ideas about the self and how one goes about representing characters on stage. Identity in Shakespeare's time was 'in crucial ways prosthetic', as Will Fisher puts it.[20] Clothing and accessories, like handkerchiefs and codpieces, hair and beards, were all regarded as divisible, detached or detachable, and yet integral parts (or props) through which identity was materialized and made visible on- and off-stage. This understanding of identity was reflected in, and reinforced by, theatrical practice: rehearsal periods were minimal and actors worked from, and memorized, their own parts; like van Hove's actors, their early modern predecessors needed to learn how to respond to each other in performance, on a stage that had no realistic setting, but, like Versweyveld's alternative worlds, was brought into sharp focus by a few, key props. Eyewitness reports and archival evidence suggest that this understanding of character and the theatrical conventions within which it was embedded did not preclude deeply emotional responses. Van Hove's productions have similarly shown us, time and time again, that his deeply theatrical, if not exactly prosthetic, understanding of character can be as emotionally powerful as it is intellectually challenging.

The third distinctive element in van Hove's approach to the classics is his lucid and painstaking reworking of the text of the play. The theatrical language that informs van Hove's productions aligns him with what the Germans call *regietheater*, or what the English-speaking world has come to recognize as a distinctly European brand of 'director's theatre'. However, van Hove routinely describes himself as a 'text director'. Given his reputation for 'taking stylized wrecking balls' to the Western canon, he retorts that he is not, in fact, 'the kind of director who puts the text aside and starts fantasizing images'. On the contrary, he stresses that his only reference is the text. 'I do drive everyone crazy', he adds, 'because I question every line and, in an opera, every note. Why is that line there? Why this crescendo there? I want to know the why behind the text. Every text needs an interpretation. It needs to be taken care of. To be looked at.'[21]

Unlike most experimental directors, van Hove does not 'question the authority of the literary text as the gauge against which [his] stage productions are to be measured', as Maria Delgado explains about Calixto Bieito's style of theatre-making.[22] Text provides the backbone of van Hove's productions: 'I don't read a text, put it aside and start thinking about images. Images and interpretation come from old-fashioned research. I read a text over and over. I talk about it. I've given total fidelity to every text I ever did.'[23] One must be mindful, though, that giving 'total fidelity to every text' does not translate into an absolute loyalty to the letter of the text. Van Hove cuts and splices the text back together in ways that seemed unimaginable before his epic Shakespearean cycles. *Kings of War*, for example, reduces *Henry VI, Part 1* to a brief sequence (*c.* 150 lines), in which the mourning for Henry V's untimely death is followed by Suffolk's wooing of Margaret of Anjou. Even the most radical cuts, though, are carried out to enhance van Hove's interpretation of the text, and, paradoxically, they often improve, rather than sacrifice, clarity. The excision of Margaret from the fourth act in *Richard III*, for example, when she memorably teaches Queen Elizabeth 'how to curse' (4.4.117), foregrounds the role of the Duchess of York to great theatrical and dramatic effect. When Richard kneels at her feet, she embraces him, but while the Duchess's body language suggests that most recognizable and moving of gestures, a mother holding her own child in her arms, she in fact destroys Richard by cursing him. This Richard is not destroyed by Richmond in battle, or by Margaret's curses, or by the visitation of the ghosts of his victims; this Richard is destroyed by his own mother.

Similarly effective is the precision with which van Hove re-imagines the Shakespearean text as powerful stage images, which allow him to fulfil his artistic imperative of giving a text 'total fidelity', while not feeling compelled to perform the text in its entirety. *The Taming of the Shrew*, for example, evoked the language of the play on several occasions. Hélène Devos delivered Bianca's lines, 'Good sister, wrong me not, nor wrong yourself, / To make a bondmaid and a slave of me' (2.1.1–2), while strapped with black bin liners to a chair. The physical violence in this production exposed the symbolic violence of Shakespeare's language, which pervades the fictive world of this play, so much so that Katherina's shrewish qualities simply mirrored the loutish behaviour of all the other characters around her (see Figure 5). Another arresting stage image illustrated van Hove's sensitive reading of the text of the play. When later in the same scene Katherina is introduced to Petruchio, she rolls out a fridge and climbs inside it, thus pre-empting Petruchio's pun on Katherina as Kate/cate, which would otherwise reduce her to a delicacy, or a consumable commodity (see Plate 4).

As van Hove puts it, 'images are language'.[24] The images he uses to translate the texts of a classic author like Shakespeare into stage action are unfailingly powerful and eminently memorable. The uniqueness of van Hove's direction, coupled with the visionary quality of Versweyveld's 'new reality' settings, makes for a kind of theatre that

Figure 5 *From left, Biondello (Stef Aerts), Hortensio (Dennis Rudge), Lucentio (Eelco Smits), Gremio (Leon Voorberg), Tranio (Alwin Pulinckx), Petruchio (Hans Kesting) and Baptista Minola (Hugo Koolschijn); in the background, from left, Katherina (Halina Reijn) and Bianca (Elise Schaap),* The Taming of the Shrew, *Stadsschouwburg, Amsterdam (2008).*

is not only genuinely innovative and experimental but also popular with large audiences, thus bridging the gap between the Barbican and the West End in London, or Theatre Workshop and Broadway in New York. In remaking the classics in his own very unique way, van Hove has achieved his life-goal, which is to make great theatre for a mass audience and not only for the initiated few.

The contributions in this section by Mark Lawson and Kate Bassett expand on some of the defining qualities of van Hove's stagings of the classics discussed above, by focusing on how a radical use of the performance space is coupled with sustained attention to the specificities of the text. Halina Reijn and Ruth Wilson reflect on the sexual politics that inform not only van Hove's revisions of the classics but also his style of directing. The next four essays shed light on the poetics and politics of place, and how van Hove's work has been produced and interpreted in four major locations: Joseph Melillo and Toni Racklin write about how they have produced, and developed audiences for, van Hove's work at the Brooklyn Academy of Music in New York and at the Barbican in London; Maja Zade focuses instead on her work with van Hove as a dramaturg at the Schaubühne in Berlin, while Laurens De Vos explains how van Hove's productions of the classics address local concerns shared by his audiences at his headquarters at the Stadschouwburg in Amsterdam. Finally, George Rodosthenous writes about *Antigone*, van Hove's main production of the ancient classics in recent years. Contributions are interspersed with extracts from van Hove's Director's Notes for most of the main productions discussed in this section.

HEDDA MEETS A BIG GUN

Mark Lawson

Theatre critics, through the privileged necessity of seeing so many productions, risk losing the crucial tools of the trade. The ability to distinguish the exceptional is threatened because – after a run of three mediocre shows – the fourth, merely by being above competence, can seem remarkable. And the spotting of originality may be compromised by the fact that, across a long career of theatre-going, every possible sort of content and form can come to seem *déjà vu*.

It's possible that a third risk is seeing so many productions by an exceptionally inventive director that originality becomes expected, discounted. But – on three nights in London across two years – work by Ivo van Hove reassured me of still being able to recognize the tremendous. From *A View from the Bridge* at the Young Vic in April 2014, through *Kings of War* at the Barbican in April 2016, to *Hedda Gabler* at the National Theatre in December 2016, long-familiar plays were revealed anew without being traduced.

I have chosen to focus on van Hove's production of Henrik Ibsen's 1890 tragedy *Hedda Gabler*. Patrick Marber provided a new English version of the story of Mrs Hedda Tesman, daughter of the late General Gabler, whose guns she keeps in a drawer. Returning from honeymoon possibly pregnant but also probably unsatisfied, Hedda alienates her husband, a former admirer and an old school friend. Three deaths in the last act (one from old age, two suicide) create a body count of Shakespearean or Jacobean proportions. My choice of this entry among van Hove's credits reflects the extreme memorability of the piece: premièred during the last flaps of a calendar, it immediately became my theatrical highlight of 2016 and, writing seven months later, it has yet to be toppled by anything from the following year. Another – external – reason is that *Hedda Gabler* is the culmination so far of a particular geographical strand in the director's CV. Van Hove's national identity is one of the most fascinating aspects of his work. From the Belgium of his birth and the Holland of his professional home base, van Hove's most frequent and fruitful dramatic excursions have been to the Greece of theatre's creation (*Antigone*), the England and Rome of Shakespeare (*Kings of War*, *Roman Tragedies*) and the America of Arthur Miller (*A View from the Bridge*) or Tony Kushner (*Angels in America*).

A striking number of the flags on the map of van Hove's imagination, though, come from Scandinavia through his re-imagination of stories by Ingmar Bergman (*Scenes from a Marriage/Cries and Whispers* and *After the Rehearsal/Persona*) and Jon Fosse (*And We'll Never Be Parted*). Indeed, as Ibsen was a crucial influence on Miller, *A View from the Bridge* can also be included. But anyone assembling a smorgasbord of Nordic drama should have Ibsen as the centrepiece and van Hove achieves this with his *Hedda Gabler*, a play famously staged by another van Hove lodestar, Bergman, at Stockholm's Royal Dramatic Theatre in 1964. This production also seems to me increasingly key because it addresses and rebuts what might be called 'the van Hove Problem': the perception by some of the director's detractors that he prioritizes image and sound at the expense of – and even disrespect to – the text.

This critique has recently been given heat by media coverage of a comment made by the British dramatist David Hare in an interview for Jeffrey Sweet's book, *What Playwrights Talk About When They Talk About Writing*.[25] In the final exchange of their conversation, Sweet pays Hare a compliment about his State of England trilogy. The dramatist accepts the praise but goes on:

> Now we're heading in Britain towards an over-aestheticized European theatre. We've got all these people called theatre-makers – God help us, what a word! – coming in and doing director's theatre where you camp up classic plays and you cut them and you prune them around. And all that directorial stuff that we've managed to keep over on the continent is now coming over and beginning to infect our theatre.[26]

Hare doesn't name names and Sweet provides no date for the conversation, although internal evidence (the director Mike Nichols has recently died, Hare has 'just worked'[27] on *Behind the Beautiful Forevers*, which opened at the National in November 2014) would seem to place it in the first half of 2015, when one of the highest-profile shows in London theatre was van Hove's *A View from the Bridge*, transferred to Wyndham's from the Young Vic.

Certainly, in the minds of most readers of the remark, van Hove would struggle to escape the sweep of Hare's generalization, not least because the other leading British-visible proponent of the style that the playwright seems to be decrying is not European but South African: Yael Farber (*Miss Julie*, *The Crucible*). Perhaps perversely, Hare subsequently worked with Robert Icke, one of the English directors most influenced by the cinematic look and underscored sound of van Hove, on an adaption of Georges Simenon's novella *The Red Barn* (National Theatre, October 2016). It is not clear whether this experience changed the sourness of his contribution to Sweet. However, in the context of the argument Hare started, van Hove's *Hedda Gabler* at the National is fascinating because it challenges any simple divide between director's and writer's theatre or period and modernized versions of classics.

Patrick Marber, introducing the published text, intriguingly reveals the instructions that van Hove gave him:

> He sketched the set design on a scrap of paper and then asked me to write a script that could work for a modern-dress production in an almost empty space but that could, in theory, be performed in period costume on a realistic set. I should not

'update' the text nor use slang. I was permitted to edit the original and occasionally re-order lines of dialogue but no further liberties were encouraged.[28]

This does not sound like the mission statement – camping up and cutting up and pruning – of the un-named Hare-raising directorial auteur. The sketch Marber mentions presumably showed the thin strip of mostly bare stage – van Hove's theatrical vision tends, in cinematic terms, towards the wide-shot – containing a piano and sofa, and two elements that became vital to the stage-pictures: a fire inset into the floor, in which Ruth Wilson's Hedda burns Lovborg's book-baby, and long-stemmed flowers, which Hedda thrashes against floor and walls in a dance-trance of violence against natural beauty and perhaps also her own nature.

Otherwise, the stage-picture is minimalist. The script seems to contain one in-joke about the 'almost empty space' for which van Hove asked Marber, when Lovborg says, in reference to his latest book: '[P]ut it on a shelf for show – when you have one!'[29] But, if van Hove and Marber reject Ibsen's stage directions, with his paragraphs of demands for specific late nineteenth-century home furnishings, their approach is otherwise respectful of the meanings of Ibsen's play or, more precisely, the 127-year ambiguity over what it might be saying or showing.

Far from camping up the work – or imposing an overbearing vision on it – van Hove, Marber and Wilson are true to it. The only loss from the updating to an unspecified present-day 'city in Europe' is that we cannot share the shock of nineteenth-century audiences at Mrs Tesman remaining Miss Gabler both in her mind and in the play's title: it is now standard for married women to retain their family name. It is also unclear why a contemporary Hedda felt compelled to wed a dull academic at a time when her options would include not marrying at all or marrying a woman.

The time-shift, though, does not reduce the play's power as a psychological study. Director, writer and actress honour the unnerving elusiveness of the personality and purpose of Hedda, who seems compelled to get close enough to people that she can hurt them and drive them away. While the independence of Ibsen's Nora in *A Doll's House* (a play on which I'd love to see van Hove and Wilson collaborate) has become progressively more attractive to audiences in a culture shaped by feminism, Hedda can seem increasingly distant and irritating in her contrasting spirit of dependency: three men by whom she wanted to be wanted – her father, Lovborg and Tesman – escape her in various ways. A key line, as she schemes to become significant again to Lovborg, is given by Marber as:

For once in my life I'll have power over another.[30]

It's a pivotal sentence, crisply expressed. And, irritatingly for denigrators of theatre supposedly led by visual directorial diktat, Marber's text is always rewarding when heard or read. Here is Tesman comparing his own academic record unfavourably with the ideas in the next book being planned by his academic rival, Lovborg:

> **Tesman**   I feel like a dinosaur.
>
> **Hedda** (*bored*)   Yes, well.[31]

And now Judge Brack's reaction to Tesman's invitation to drop in on Hedda when her husband is working on a book with Mrs Elvsted:

> **Tesman** (*consulting notes*)   ´Brack will visit you.
>
> **Brack**   Of course I will! Every evening. Trust me, I will occupy her. Fully.[32]

Compare these exchanges (by Marber from a literal translation by Karin and Ann Bamborough) from the supposed era of director's theatre with the equivalent dialogue from a period when classics were generally in the hands of academic translators. For example, in Michael Meyer's 1960 script, published in various Methuen Drama editions over the last fifty years, the contrast between the minds (and possibly, by implication, bodies) of Tesman and Lovborg runs:

> **Tesman**   Amazing! I'd never think of writing about anything like that!
>
> **Hedda**   No. You wouldn't.[33]

And here is Meyer's pass at the moment in which Tesman effectively steers his wife back into the path of Brack:

> **Tesman**   I'm sure Judge Brack'll be kind enough to come over and keep you company.
>
> **Brack**   I'll be delighted, Mrs Tesman. I'll be here every evening. We'll have great fun together, you and I.[34]

Marber's economical metaphor about intellectual extinction and the insidious image of Brack physically occupying Hedda (prefaced by that disingenuous 'Trust me') make, in both cases, the text from the supposed era of director's theatre far superior to the lines in the time when words were supposedly more respected.

It's true that, for Anglophone theatregoers, there can sometimes be a textual problem with van Hove's Shakespeare, where the helping text projected for non-Netherlanders is an English translation of a Dutch adaptation of Shakespeare. So, at the April 2016 performances of *Kings of War* at the Barbican in London, theatregoers reaching what was clearly Henry V's speech before Agincourt were surprised to hear the warrior king refer not to 'gentlemen in England now abed' but, according to the surtitles, 'nobles who aren't here'.

It was also jarring, in the same production, for Richard III to speak some of Macbeth's most famous lines. But I have never seen a van Hove production of a classic text that the writer of the original text could have argued was not respectful and revelatory. Shakespeare and Miller would surely be intrigued and pleased by his renovations of their texts. And, although Ibsen notoriously liked things his own way, his ghost would be wise to recognize that, in van Hove, the Belgian whose creativity is so often unleashed by Scandinavia, he has found an impeccable interpreter.

PLAYING FEMALE ROLES IN THE CLASSICS

Halina Reijn and Ruth Wilson, in conversation (June 2017)

HR   Some prominent German actresses have described Ivo and his work as anti-feminist. Ivo came up against a lot of resistance especially at the beginning of his career, while I think he is actually a feminist. He thinks he is not a feminist, but he quite obviously is!

RW   He most certainly is!

HR   And I am too. He could not have made me do *The Taming of the Shrew* otherwise – and we did not shy away from the violence in the play in our production.

Figure 6 *Hedda Gabler (Ruth Wilson), Brack (Rafe Spall) and Berte (Éva Magyar)*, Hedda Gabler, *National Theatre, London (2016).*

RW   Yes, I agree. I never felt that he exploits women. Some reviewers accused him of exploiting his female actors in *Hedda Gabler*. But that was a very reductive way of reading specific moments in the production, including, of course, the infamous 'tomato juice' sequence (see Figure 6). That moment must be read in the context of Ivo encouraging my Hedda to be as brutal, dangerous and cruel as I wanted her to be. So when Hedda is on the receiving end, the brutality has to be equal, if not more so, in order to push her over the edge.

HR   And of course we are still living in societies where women are oppressed. So why lie about it? Put it on stage instead! And Hedda kills herself precisely because she cannot cope with having tomato juice poured all over her head. Otherwise she would choose to live!

RW   Quite. And the timing of our production made it even more harrowing. [Donald] Trump had just been elected President, despite his 'grab women by the pussy' boast. Then we had the Women's March [on 21 January 2017]. This production and its themes felt more resonant than ever. I realized how vital this play was and not because the production was misogynist: on the contrary, it was demonstrating how misogyny is entrenched in our society, and how even the most powerful of women are vulnerable. As you say, 'let's put it on stage and let people freak out about it!' The production really angered many people, but that is what art is designed to do: make people think and feel. They were angry that I, as an actress, was being exploited and abused. I was never exploited or abused. In that moment Ivo had made them connect to a deep truth about the play and about society.

HR   There are still women who say to me, 'Ah, but he hates women', but he is actually showing the mechanisms that inform relationships between people. Also, in the classical plays we have done with him, the women are of course especially oppressed, but he will always encourage you to look for the core strength of the characters and he will always seek to ask questions about what he puts on stage.

RW   Not to mention *Roman Tragedies*, where the female roles are extraordinary.

HR   Yes, and, of course, he switches the gender of some of the male leads so he provides a platform for rethinking about women in powerful roles.

RW   One should also consider the calibre of the women who work with him.

HR   Exactly! Chris [Nietvelt], Marieke [Heebink], or Elizabeth Marvel: these women are powerhouses in our world, and at all levels, really.

RW   We are not cowering dolls – we are all raging feminists, in fact! And we would not all be attracted to this director, his methods, and the materials he chooses to work on, if there wasn't something urgently truthful about it all.

HR   I would say that Ivo is fascinated by power relations, and not only between men and women, but also between and among men, and his interest in sexuality is closely linked to his interest in power more generally, including power in private institutions like marriage. *Scenes from a Marriage* is like a war zone. I think he is fundamentally fascinated by the contradictions and complexities within any individual, the blend of gender roles, and, for women, the whole range of roles, from the princess who is waiting to be rescued to the soldier. What I like about working with Ivo is that with him I can embrace all these roles and without shame.

RW He never judges his actors so you can afford to explore every facet of yourself. And this freedom is particularly important with a character like Hedda because the contradictions and the complexities are central to it. When I first read Hedda, I felt there was one dominant register. Ivo is not interested in this simplistic understanding of character and wants his actors to reveal the entire range of tones and colours associated with any given character. With Hedda, he said 'you need to convince all the other characters that you are who they think you are'. If you don't, her manipulation is too obvious. And what made Hedda really interesting to me is that she really believes that she is the different people she is to the other characters. She needs love, she needs recognition, and so she will do whatever it takes to get that validation. This approach makes the character so much more dangerous: you can play her at one moment as a child, then another moment as a friend, a lover, or a wife. Ivo recognizes we all have the capacity to be all these things and he does not judge you for it.

HR That's because he doesn't see people as characters. He does not believe in character. He believes that everybody is anybody or can be anybody, if circumstances change.

RW And, by not believing in character, he takes the responsibility of becoming consistently some other, one-dimensional individual from you.

HR That also applies to one's reputation, to what comes with stardom. Ivo takes away the pressure of living up to your own artistic persona. As he always puts it, our work is about making art; it is not about you, or me; it's about fearless story-telling and this understanding of theatre-making comes across very strongly in the rehearsal room, where his passion for theatre-making takes over completely. And the intensity of the rehearsal process means that his actors often quite literally collapse, physically and psychologically, because the exploration of the emotions that the world created by Ivo and Jan requires is so raw and genuine. Rehearsing with Ivo is a little bit like performance art.

RW I certainly had this moment while rehearsing Hedda, the first 'tomato juice' moment.

HR He did tell me, because he was worried about you.

RW   Yes the pressure was on; I had flown straight from another job into rehearsals. We only had three weeks and I was playing Hedda Gabler at the National Theatre! I also thought that I might have to go back to New York for a few more days of filming. Thankfully, that wasn't the case, so the last week of rehearsal took place as scheduled. Ivo always rehearses chronologically, so, as we were coming to the end of rehearsals, we were also coming to the end of the play. I hadn't really put much thought into the death scene or the final moment of humiliation. I knew it would be challenging and I had heard rumours about tomato juice but I had wisely put it out of my mind. As it happened, we didn't get as far as the 'tomato juice' moment. Ivo directed Rafe Spall (Brack) to take off his jacket and whip my back with it. I started sobbing and I could not stop. I hated the fact that I could not stop, because I had never cried in rehearsal before. We tried the scene again, but I simply had to get off the stage. But then I realized that what had happened was directly connected to how free I was feeling in the rehearsal room. Only by taking down a lot of barriers could I have made myself so vulnerable. In playing Hedda I had felt empowered, Ivo had encouraged that at every step, suggesting that she is in charge, in control. So when Brack demeans and humiliates her, takes away her control, takes away her choices, he is destroying her. I was in that moment having a very physical and emotional reaction to the whole experience of the play and this particular process and in that moment I found clarity. On other shows I would have held it all in, or I would have dealt with later and as a result I may never have really understood the intention or nature of that scene. With Ivo I was instead able to release it and use it. When I got to do that scene once the show had opened, I did not feel as overwhelmed as the first time we rehearsed it, but I was able to draw on what I experienced back in the rehearsal room.

HR   In *Shrew*, in the taming scene, when Petruchio [played by Hans Kesting] takes Katherina back home and starves her, I was wearing next to nothing, I was sleep-deprived, abused, disoriented, and in the rehearsal room Ivo said to me: 'Now pee, just stand on the table and let it all go.' Of course, we used special effects, but I remember the first time we tried it I walked out, as Hans was licking the water off the table – that was Ivo's idea of Petruchio surrendering, once he realized that Katherina has hit rock bottom.

RW   Did you feel humiliated?

HR   Yes, I felt what Katherina was feeling. That moment marked a turning point: she is at the lowest point of her journey through the play, but by coming up with the suggestion that Hans should lick the water, Ivo and Jan make it clear that Petruchio is now surrendering to her. They read the play as being about two people, who have absorbed the brutal qualities of the world they live in, and reach out to each other through brutal power play. Ivo and Jan's ideas are startling, challenging, but so very effective at least partly because no one dares to push the boundaries of what is regarded as acceptable and decorous as much as they do.

A HUMAN BEING IS ONLY A HUMAN BEING: THOUGHTS ON IBSEN'S HEDDA GABLER

Ivo van Hove (Extract from the Director's Notes)

The beginning of the play is striking. Two older women talk about a newlywed couple who are still in bed. They discuss the house that has been furnished for the couple while they were enjoying their honeymoon. They discuss codes of behaviour because the new woman of the house happens to be a woman of high descent: she's the daughter of a deceased general. Her husband is the sweetheart of the women. They could never have imagined that he would marry such a beautiful woman, desired by every young man in the city. On top of marrying Hedda, he'll be appointed at the university. Reasons all over for happiness. The room is filled with flowers to welcome the newlyweds after a long, deserved honeymoon. Who knows, maybe there'll be a baby in a few months' time.

However, this scene is steeped in a funereal atmosphere. It's autumn. Berte, a maid, worries about her new situation, the new house, the new mistress she's to deal with; she's afraid she can't cope with these new conditions. She is sad about leaving the house of Julia Tesman, who lives with her sick sister, Rina. For Berte to be a maid and help Julia with the intense care for her sister and George was her lifelong dedication. Berte and Julia try hard to hold on to a time that is disappearing. They are prepared to adapt but their total altruism only serves one goal: to keep the status quo unchanged. A society where the norms and values of the middle class reign supreme, where people live according to a socially accepted routine, where everybody controls everybody else and scandals are disastrous, a society where there's a strict division between men and women and where everybody has to walk on the same path heading to the same destination.

For Berte and Julia, their George is the living proof that living up to these rules is rewarding. George has become an adult, married a fantastic wife and will have a wonderful career. To preserve this delicate balance Julia plants Berte in George's new house, as a guardian. This is the life everybody should live. A life with no extremes, where people care for each other, where there is warmth and tenderness, where girls become women, where women deliver babies and become mothers. Mothers who are expected to maintain the home as a walled garden, a place where the husband can find refuge after his adventures in the world outside. Women should purify their homes; they are like angels who are full of love for the children, their homes and domestic duties. The life Julia Tesman believes everybody should live is ordered – men read books and become intellectuals. It is a world where a house is a home. This is how this play starts: a perfect day in an almost perfect world.

Hedda enters the stage. As a hurricane she whirls through the house. The curtains should be closed, the flowers removed and her own old piano moved to the inner room because it is totally displaced in this setting, arranged by the Tesman family. Hedda is unhappy and she shows it; she is unscrupulous and merciless as she does not discern or mention a reason, a cause for her unhappiness. When Tesman's aunt is gone, insulted, Hedda admits that she exaggerated and will make it up to the good willing aunt. But she won't make great efforts to do so. Later she'll tell Brack, 'I have these sudden impulses. And there's nothing I can do about it. . . . I can't explain why'.[35] Her revolt doesn't provoke changes, it is pure emotion; it is hysteria in pure form. Her revolt is not based upon an inspiring vision on life, on the future. Quite the contrary!

One should ask: why did she marry Tesman when her whole behaviour towards him is one of disgust and loathing? But another important question is: why did Tesman marry Hedda Gabler? The answers are terrible, horrifying, because Hedda and Tesman are opportunists in matters of love. She married him because she 'danced herself to a standstill', she says to Brack. Hedda is not young anymore, she's almost thirty; her father has died and left no money at all. It's now or never. She's addicted to luxury and Tesman seems prepared to give her all she wants. At the same time she remains a respectable, because married, woman. And what's even more important Tesman allows her to lead the life she used to live, dominating as a man everybody around her. Tesman has also his reasons to marry her: all but love, a marriage of convenience. For him the marriage with Hedda Gabler is a social event. Everybody in town will envy him. In his notebook Ibsen states that Hedda knows she's only a social trophy for Tesman.[36] It is remarkable that he didn't marry Thea. I think that's because she was only a governess. For Tesman Hedda is important for his career.

Tesman and Hedda's match is simply a bad, loveless marriage, a cover up in society and they believe they can get away with it. But Hedda is totally unfit to play the role of the housewife. She sees no meaning at all, after her honeymoon, in this daily routine of domestic duties. She is deeply unsatisfied, but never reflects on this. Hedda Gabler is not a Sylvia Plath who struggled with the same needs and obstacles but wrote wonderful poems, read books, married an intellectual who allowed her to be an intellectual, an author, not a mother or a wife. Her diaries are a reflection on her wishes, her needs, her depressions. Hedda has no talent, no fantasy. There is nothing she could develop in order to escape this boredom. She's addicted to material things, and if she doesn't get what she wants, she simply destroys.

It took me some time before I started to understand that hidden inside this demonic Hedda burned an enormous need to live, a real urge. Hedda wants to live but not the life of a woman (of the nineteenth century) but the life of a man. Her problem is that she doesn't undertake anything to reach this goal. She locks herself up in her homely prison, hoping that a lot of people will visit the house and talk about the fascinating life outside. She fantasizes about Lovborg having vine leaves in his hair. She fantasizes about Brack's bachelor parties. With Tesman she has a masochistic man that she can beat up once in a while and, when Tesman reminds her at the end of Act One that she's financially totally dependant, that she is just a woman, she takes a pistol and threatens to shoot.

The bourgeois heroes of Ibsen's plays always have a dream of freedom, of total independence but their dreams turn out to be pipedreams. There's always a reason not to make the final choice: there is always family, marriage or society (fear of public scandal). A human being is only a human being. That's what Ibsen wants to show us. In his notebook he wrote: 'In this play I didn't want to treat a problem. My intention was to depict human beings, their moods and their fate in a specific society under specific conditions'.[37] One shouldn't forget that *Hedda Gabler* was written ten years after *A Doll's House*, where Ibsen had an intense need to be a partisan to Nora and to make her decide to leave the man that treated her as a doll, making her dance the tarantella. *Hedda Gabler* is not a play in favour of women's rights; it is about a provincial, middle-class world where everybody (as described) has to live according to rules, because this way you have the best life there is. But this way of life also becomes monotonous. It's hard to deal with this monotony. And if one can't accept the rules one can only die.

Ibsen is not interested in writing suspenseful stories – he writes about crises of the soul, about a woman who wants to escape this smothering monotony. *Hedda Gabler* is an almost scientific description of an inevitable suicide. I think it is important to understand that in order to get to the core of this play we have to accept that *Hedda Gabler* is a play, not a piece of realism. The house seems to be a house but is a prison where all characters are in turn the guards, the oppressors, the prisoners, the victims. Nobody (not even Brack) has the role of the witness; everybody is totally involved in this life in prison. Ibsen turned this nineteenth-century room into the world, into our existence. Theatrically we should be able to show the world behind the world of things. Hedda's house has a table, a sofa, a stove, a piano, but these objects are signs of a veiled world of emotion or of the world she's bored with. The piano, for instance, is her only tool to express herself emotionally. Immediately in the first act she announces the removal of her piano. She'll remove it to the inner room, which will become her nest, where the portrait of her father still dominates. In Tesman's world she feels displaced, homesick. The whole play can be seen as a step-by-step removal of Hedda Gabler from this world. It reminds me of the central image of *Peer Gynt*, the peeling of an onion, discovering that there is nothing inside.

Eventually, right before committing suicide, unseen by the audience, Hedda plays a wild dance tune. It's her last cry, an ultimate expression of an enormous urge to live. But my opinion is that *Hedda Gabler* is a suicide play. When Hedda has destroyed everything, Tesman and Thea are united in a spiritual marriage, and Hedda is almost raped by Brack, she can only commit suicide. I am convinced that suicide is in Hedda all the time. This talent for destruction is not something that is provoked by her marriage, Brack's blackmail, or Lovborg's failure to live the life of a Dionysian god. Destructive forces have always been inside Hedda. Talking about Thea she says: 'She had that irritating hair she was always flaunting', and 'I think I shall set fire to your hair after all'.[38] It's very clear that, as a young girl, Hedda resented everybody who was happy or beautiful or content. *Hedda Gabler* is a play about destruction leading to suicide, the ultimate destruction of oneself. The first act ends with Hedda showing Tesman the weapon, the third act she shows Lovborg how to use it (see Plate 5), and in the fourth act she uses it against herself.

Only Thea and Tesman seem to find a balance between the ridiculousness of our existence and the meaning of our existence. They break the rules of society. They break with their husband or wife and find a vocation. They break the barriers of family, marriage and society to give meaning to this life. They are capable of delivering a virtual child, a book about the future. Up to that moment children were killed. The book-child of Lovborg and Thea has been burned and Hedda kills her unborn child by killing herself. Life can only be meaningful as a compromise. But Ibsen, old and wise and without illusions, more scientist than author, shows this insight to us not as a happy ending. Hedda and Lovborg with their lust for life are dead. The greatness we all expect in life seems to be impossible; some people can't live with the compromise. Ibsen shows us people like ships on the ocean in the middle of a hurricane. There is no future but there is life. We better accept it.

To make this play work theatrically, we have to forget about Scandinavia and the end of the nineteenth century. Our *Hedda Gabler* is set in a loft in Manhattan. The play starts in a still empty, unfurnished apartment. We witness Hedda alone with her piano. It struck me that Ibsen has Hedda alone on stage quite a lot; these are her moments to express her inner pain: she clenches her hands, plays with pistols. Then the Tesman family moves in and all the other characters start the invasion. And Hedda starts destroying the enemy, evolving on a road towards suicide. In Hedda we witness this cry. We see how she chooses the negative way, the destructive way to deal with crisis. In *Hedda Gabler* we witness a person committing suicide, we witness the clock ticking, we know the inevitable will happen. *Hedda Gabler* is not a drama about a middle-class society in the nineteenth century, nor a drama about the conflicts between man and woman, but an existentialist play, a search for the meaning of life, unsympathetically, seeking the truth.

New York City, 9 August 2004[39]

IVO VAN HOVE STAGING SHAKESPEARE: WORLD ENOUGH AND TIME?

Kate Bassett

Ivo van Hove has been dubbed contemporary theatre's most celebrated exponent of 'maximal minimalism'.[40] This essay mulls on some ways in which that oxymoron and other paradoxical features operate in his acclaimed Shakespeare productions.

Working in tandem with Jan Versweyveld, his Toneelgroep Amsterdam (TGA) scenographer and life partner, van Hove often presents Shakespeare's plays in strikingly bare contemporary settings. *The Taming of the Shrew* is set in what might be a converted modernist warehouse: concrete columns; white walls and a sheet-glass chamber a way upstage in which we see the wealthy Signor Baptista's mini-skirted daughters, Katherina and Bianca, initially mewed (see Plate 4). Another glass cabin, to house the General's new bride, Desdemona, is perched under a scarred brick bulwark in *Othello*. In van Hove's *Kings of War*, the wartime bunker of Ramsey Nasr's Henry V and his suit-wearing entourage is palatial in size, but panelled in unpainted MDF, with scant furnishings pushed to the edges.

The aesthetic austerity – which may include a nod to the disused buildings that van Hove and Versweyveld pioneeringly occupied for their early productions as avant-garde, Antwerp art-college graduates – feels akin to today's ex-industrial 'found spaces' on the recession-hit theatrical fringe. Thereby, TGA visuals come across as persistently subcultural. Seeing the troupe's productions programmed at kudos-endowing, world-class venues such as London's Barbican, upmarket punters have also come to embrace the bleak-chic look.

One might think that sounds superficial, but the visual importance should not be underestimated, especially when a troupe is performing internationally in Dutch. Beyond that, what's artistically profound is how van Hove and his design team – discussing options for over a year prior to production – find expressionistic and symbolic correlatives for the emotional states and the ethos in which a play's characters are caught. This is the equivalent of an astute poet's similes. A sea of empty space surrounding a character can poignantly suggest his or her loneliness, powerlessness or spiritual destitution. A sheet-glass cabin, besides making feminist issues of confinement and escape conspicuous, intimates that people are being regarded as wares when the suitors, striking deals with Baptista, ogle his daughters' chamber like an Amsterdam prostitute's *kamer* window. Meanwhile, spartan and scarred architectural brutalism intimates a contemporary but harsh, not wholly civilized society by which a dramatis persona might be damaged and/or which they might themselves embody – whether that's Nasr's explosive Henry V; the paternally disfavoured and (van Hove suggests) sadomasochistic Katherina; Othello; or Roeland Fernhout's desperately, dangerously messed-up Iago. A lone punchbag hangs from a chain downstage in *Othello*, not actually pummelled but coupled with the amplified sound of boxing at curtain-up. That concisely establishes a barracks gym setting and denotes a whole ill-boding culture of macho competitiveness and violence – a fine instance of van Hove's mature work fusing the realistic and significantly stylized with assurance.[41]

To return to his visuals, *Roman Tragedies* is pointedly far more crowded. This multimedia epic, performed sans intermission, lasts up to six hours. Much of the stage starts off crammed with over a dozen rectangular sofas. Facing in different directions, on stepped floor levels, amongst clocks telling various worldwide times, they look like a faintly Cubist vision of a conference centre-cum-TV studio complex, or tessellated swanky apartments. This calls attention to other 'Cubist' qualities inherent in what the audience is watching. Converting three plays into one, van Hove presents a government system going through permutations: upper-crust Coriolanus scorning the Republic's demos; populist Julius Caesar assassinated for autocratic tendencies; puritanical Octavius terminating the bohemian dominion of Antony and Cleopatra. Modern costuming also means we are 'seeing triple', watching characters sourced from Plutarch, envisaged by a playwright from Elizabeth I and James I's time, dressed like today's big shots.[42] Being polyvocal, drama quintessentially presents manifold perspectives, and van Hove additionally plays nuanced games with the geographic/emotional distance and divisions between people. In *Antony and Cleopatra*, for instance, enemy camps are non-naturalistically located on a single sofa – their scenes overlaid.

Roman Tragedies set is studded with numerous screens to boot. The players, live-filmed, proliferate on those screens, which additionally flash up images of Trump, JFK et al. in the manner of a news telecast, ticker display messages scroll out Roman Empire headlines as well. This 'maximalist' aesthetic has its difficulties, being distracting or even discombobulating. Yet van Hove is surely aware of that. His update of Shakespeare's political histories pointedly reflects how we today – hooked up to 24-hour multichannel media – are bombarded with incoming 'narratives' about world leaders.

This production feels like a sociological experiment as well, regarding liberty, democracy and participation. It is, along with *Kings of War*, a study of power and leadership, and those issues extend to audience-involvement when those watching *Roman Tragedies* are invited to move on to the stage. This is politicizing, turning the punters into amassing plebeians, cheek by jowl with Shakespeare's global rulers. Yet the 'emancipation' isn't maximal, everyone being marshalled at key points and obeying the unwritten rule of keeping mum (albeit tweeting is allowed). Van Hove's further acknowledges people's proclivity for disengagement, wryly and pragmatically placing a refreshments bar onstage.

As for the draw of flickering screens, this can leave the flesh-and-blood actors disregarded. Yet in terms of upped emotional involvement versus alienation effects, the results are interestingly complicated if, for instance, you view the onstage characters/actors from the stalls, then from centimetres away, then on a small screen, then on a gigantic one. Elements that look dispassionate can prove startlingly moving too. Each fatality in Rome's unlovely wars is registered, onscreen, by a harshly lit aerial snapshot of the sprawled corpse, plus the deceased's full name and dates of birth and death – almost everyone losing their life shockingly young.

Sometimes the TGA actors will sustain an anti-dramatic style for a long stretch: truly damped-down naturalism and Shakespeare rendered conversational. Van Hove's textual cuts further excise, for example, the action-hero battle scenes in *Coriolanus'* Act One and the 'comic relief' of *Henry V*'s braggadocio, Pistol. Those cuts arguably render Shakespeare more accessible, not less enjoyable, ousting anything like bombast and passé jokes, but expunging is, undeniably, reductive. Van Hove's history cycles are less socially panoramic than the originals, less Bruegelesque. Some journalists have even described him as an 'iconoclastic bad boy' taking 'wrecking balls' to classic plays.[43] Van Hove himself remarks, of his early 1990s production, 'With *Hamlet*, I made the mistake of doing the whole text!'[44]

However, he emphasizes that he is, in fact, 'very respectful'. As with his design plans, he spends at least a year discussing a script and sending lists of tiny questions to his dramaturgs about interpretation issues.[45] This is close reading, more in tune with, say, RSC traditions than avant-gardism. Moreover, he explains his policy of winnowing. 'From *Hamlet* I learned a lot', he says. 'There are too many side-lines. I made the mistake of making every subplot as important [as the main plot] . . . You have to make choices.' Perhaps what's thrilling is that this director demonstrates both sensitivity and – in daring to pick out weaknesses in the Bard – bravura.

Streamlining can positively produce clarity of line, a memorably *lucid* reading, and another van Hove trademark is clear overarching structures, bringing symmetries into sharp relief. He has Nasr crescendo from very muted to near-fascistic ranting in both Henry V's famous, imperialist speeches, 'Once more unto the breach' and 'St Crispin's Day'. Then, most surprisingly, the actor mirrors that, once more, in a comically diffident then boorish commandeering of Princess Katharine – inverting the conventional romantic categorization of the wooing scene.

Within that triplication, van Hove, manifestly, understands that variation is a desideratum. His ensemble pace their delivery through speeches, scenes and whole strings of plays with honed modulations in tempo, volume, mood and style. Quiet stretches can also be interrupted, physically, by flashes of raw violence, riskily unchoreographed brawls. Thus van Hove's corps manage to be technically rigorous and liberated, brilliant at detailing and at marathons, clear and complex, immensely flexible. Embracing otherness is, of course, an actor's métier, but van Hove's ensemble achieve this in a multitude of ways. And on top of that is the 'Cubist' effect of a cast member doubling in a single production and transforming into multifarious personalities in the revolve of their repertory programming. So, each individual contains multitudes: minimal and maximal.

THE TAMING OF THE SHREW

Ivo van Hove (Extract from the Director's Notes)

Padua, where *The Taming of the Shrew* takes place, is described as 'the pleasant garden of great Italy' (1.1.4). Here, young men on the brink of adulthood come to study virtue to know happiness. Padua as a temple of the Renaissance is an oasis of culture to prepare oneself for a balanced – and thus happy – life. A life that is governed by laws and rules which everyone follows. A life in which sons follow their fathers' footsteps and daughters take over the roles of their mothers. Stability is the norm and the way to happiness.

Another way that leads to happiness is money. Wealth determines to which class one belongs and status leads to power. When Baptista must choose between two prospective husbands for his youngest daughter, the wealth of their fathers is the deciding factor. Baptista is a merchant, who ranks relationships according to their material worth. Every father turns out to be a merchant. The wealthiest person is also the city's most powerful man. People who have money can afford to hire employees and servants. There is even a hierarchy among these servants. Rewards depend on accomplishments. Society is ruled by economic principles in Padua.

Unsurprisingly, this chimera is flawed. The sons want to break the rules set by their fathers and their daughters want to become women as well as mothers. The employees would like to be employers occasionally. The carnival is the perfect solution for this problem.

Once a year, everyone is allowed to give in to their cravings. During the carnival, the ordinary man is king. Everyone dresses up to become someone he or she always longed to be. All rules are suspended. For a short period of time, complete chaos reigns supreme and people indulge in excessive eating and drinking. Carnival is a celebration of all carnal pleasures, but it only lasts for a couple of days. After carnival, everyone is expected to restart following the rules in a society ruled by fathers and wealth.

In this social stronghold, a miracle takes place. The final sentence of the play claims that "'Tis a wonder, by your leave, she will be tam'd so' (5.2.190). What is this wonder? The miracle is that two people, who seem to have nothing in common with each other, eventually get together. Katherina is Baptista's elder daughter and is believed to be a shrew – a woman who has a sharp tongue and who does not obey without questioning. Baptista is a widower, who expects that his daughters will take over the role of their [deceased] mother. His younger daughter, Bianca, behaves dutifully and Baptista sees her as an ideal daughter. Katherina, however, does not feel loved, talks back, and is seen by her father as the black sheep. Her shrewish behaviour stems from the lack of attention not only from her father, but also from every other man in Padua. Bianca, however, is adored by her father and by all men. Katherina transforms this lack of love into negative energy, which alienates others even more.

Petruchio is an orphan. His mother died a long time before the play starts and his father, a wealthy businessman named Antonio, has also recently passed away. Petruchio now travels around the world looking for happiness. He thinks he can find that happiness by marrying a wealthy woman. But he secretly longs for a woman who will do whatever he wants – a woman with whom he can become one person. This is not simply a whim – it is something he desperately needs. When he meets Katherina, who rejects him, they clash. He fights for his life, and she simply does not want to get hurt by anyone anymore. In three successive declarations of love, he makes it clear to her that he can see through her shrewish act. He whispers to her that "'Twas told me you were rough, and coy, and sullen, / And now I find report a very liar; / For thou are pleasant, gamesome, passing courteous, / But slow in speech, yet sweet as spring-time flowers' (2.1.238–241). When he takes her to his home in the country, far away from society and its strict rules, the 'miracle' happens. Petruccio's home is bitterly cold. The servants are regularly beaten and seem savage. In this barbaric world, Petruccio and Katherina fall in love – a love between an executioner and his victim, between master and servant, a love that breaks all boundaries. She kindles the executioner in him and he hurts her body by not giving her food and her spirit by thwarting her own very wish or desire. By breaking everything, something new is created: a relationship between equals. When Petruchio claims that the sun is actually the moon (which is complete nonsense), Katherina gives in and claims: 'Forward, I pray, since we have come so far, / And be it moon, or sun, or what you please. / An if you please to call it a rush-candle, / Henceforth

I vow it shall be so for me' (4.5.12–15). Katherina has found the only man who complements her, the only one she can spend her life with. And Petruchio has found the only woman he can spend his life with. All of Padua's citizens believe it to be a 'miracle'.

The Taming of the Shrew, however, is not a love story, but a play that clearly criticizes society. Padua is a city which holds on to archaic values and where no one focuses on the future. Padua presents itself as a paragon of tolerance – a city with a rich academic life and highbrow culture. However, these all turn out to be forerunners of modern marketing strategies. . . . Pretending to be tolerant and civilized, Padua is a corrupt society in which the end justifies the means. The goal is acquiring wealth and, to acquire wealth, Padua organizes the annual carnival where everyone can fulfil his or her dreams of another and better life. The story of Petruchio and Katherina in fact reveals that people need to accept and respect who they are in order to truly live in harmony with others. The relationship between Petruchio and Katherina is highly improbable. Nevertheless, they marry. Their kiss proves that they are completely and deeply connected. They embrace the truth of life and accept that it is ugly, crude and disruptive. For them, life is always a carnival. Life *is* anarchy. The norms and the values that shape Padua's society are only in place to secure economic interests. It is a world of owners without ideals. It is a world in which children obey their parents.

At the beginning of the final act, Petruchio tells Katherina: 'Prithee, Kate, let's stand aside and see the end of this controversy' (5.1.55–56). It is at this point that Petruchio and Katherina, along with the audience, are given to watch what life is really like in Padua. We see how Lucentio and Bianca enter a loveless marriage in order to meet the expectations of their fathers and to abide by the rules of their city and their society. The marriage, which took place in secret, is legalized by their parents. We see how a teacher, who, as per his profession, is responsible for educating the younger generations, has become a fraud. What can you expect from children who are raised in this environment? No matter the costs, the fragile balance is kept in Padua. Katherina and Petruccio have abandoned this society. In the final act, they do not seem to speak anymore – they only kiss.

Translation by Isabelle Groenhof

STAGING IVO VAN HOVE AT BAM

Joseph V. Melillo

Over the course of my 34-year tenure as Executive Producer at Brooklyn Academy of Music (BAM) I've had the pleasure of presenting Ivo van Hove's work six times. Audiences have been engaged from the beginning and, although the name of this section is 'Directing the Classics', I think it's important to note that Ivo's first few productions at BAM were not of classic works, at least not in any traditional sense. Van Hove first came to BAM with *Opening Night* (Next Wave Festival, 2008), a screen-to-stage adaptation of John Cassavetes' 1977 film about an aging actress rehearsing for a new play. The production involved an onstage camera crew whose close-ups of the action were projected onto a large overhead monitor; it both introduced and exemplified van Hove's inventiveness to our adventurous audience, who responded with great enthusiasm. *Cries and Whispers* (Next Wave Festival, 2011), adapted from Ingmar Bergman's 1972 film about the final hours of a fatally ill woman, featured the same magnifying techniques.

What these works have in common with the exceptional (and durationally significant) Shakespearean productions that came next – I'm speaking of *Roman Tragedies* and *Kings of War* – is something that may seem overly simple. With all of these productions, the work begins, and ends, with Ivo and Jan. I will attempt to offer some personal and professional insight into these two works specifically, but I'd like to underscore this seemingly simple point. When a creative partnership is as long and fruitful as that of these two men, a kind of alchemy of assurance occurs. No matter how challenging, unusual, or even abstract the directorial and scenic choices, there is a confidence that the audience can sense, and which makes them willing to follow these artists anywhere.

The same can be said of Toneelgroep Amsterdam (TGA), the Netherlands' largest repertory company, and one that Ivo has been directing since 2001. As much as Ivo and Jan are the co-captains of these extraordinary productions, it is these highly trained, deeply attuned actors that populate the worlds they have created. After working together for more than a decade, they are able to pull off feats of theatrical imagination that simply would not work with a 'new' cast. Van Hove has done masterful, memorable work without TGA, but I am so proud that BAM has become its US home, because it is not until you see his work with them that you can understand this remarkable artist in full.

Which brings us to *Roman Tragedies*, arguably the most technically complex production that Ivo has brought to BAM and, to date, the longest at 5 hours 45 minutes (no intermission!). This Dutch-language with English surtitles melding of unlikely Shakespearean bedfellows – *Coriolanus*, *Julius Caesar* and *Antony & Cleopatra* – was a thoroughly mediatized event with screens everywhere and live video feed and pre-recorded video at the very core of the experience. The audience moved at timed intervals and spent time both onstage and in the house proper, constantly moving in and around the action. The effect was something like being inside a twenty-first-century newsroom crossed with an ancient Roman amphitheatre. Again, I'd like to emphasize that our audience has followed Ivo from the beginning, and while *Roman Tragedies* creates a deeper level of immersion via technology than *Opening Night*, that earlier work prepared and taught viewers how to experience the latter. That is why it is so meaningful for an institution to build an ongoing relationship with an artist, because in the end what you wind up presenting and representing is an entire oeuvre rather than any individual production.

When Ivo and Jan present us with an utterly compelling theatrical reconsideration of a classic work, it is easy to think that what they are doing is 'radical'. But I would draw attention to what critic Ben Brantley wrote in *The New York Times* regarding van Hove's

Figure 7 Roman Tragedies *at the Brooklyn Academy of Music (2012).*

Broadway debut, *A View from the Bridge*: 'This must be what Greek tragedy once felt like, when people went to the theater in search of catharsis.'[46] I think this is an important point to consider in the context of all of his work. The innovative staging and unorthodox directorial choices are all in service of connecting to something deep and elemental in the audience experience.

Van Hove's stagings reflect a deep analysis of the text and strive to distil the central conflicts at play. He is fascinated by human behaviour and relationships in the context of great social upheaval – war, betrayal, death and disease. His use of mixed media manipulates the concepts of public and private space (very notably in *Roman Tragedies*, but throughout his body of work), offering the audience multiple prisms through which to view the story and its characters. With his more minimal stagings, he encourages his actors to take extraordinary liberties, aiming for performances that he characterizes as 'naked-soul acting'. Emotions that are usually left to simmer beneath the surface become alarmingly and unavoidably apparent. Cutting-edge technology is only deployed in the service of that most ancient *raison d'être* of the theatre, catharsis, as Mr Brantley rightly noted.

It is only such mastery of all the elements of the theatrical experience – text, design, sets, acting – that can produce a work like *Kings of War*, van Hove's most recent work at BAM. Ivo and Jan again took on the Herculean task of combining multiple Shakespearean works – *Henry V*, *Henry VI* and *Richard III* – into a single, evening-length whole (unlike *Roman Tragedies*, this production did allow for a single intermission). Catharsis is incidentally the exact word to describe the experience of watching *Kings of War*'s depiction of, as Brantley wrote in his review, 'a nation slowly cracking apart amid corruption, factionalism and political viciousness, as the oversize egos of would-be rulers collide with toxic trickle-down consequences.'[47] *Kings of War* came to BAM in November of 2016, as a gruelling election season came to a close but before the results of an election that upended all conventional wisdom.

More than one reviewer has alluded to television series like *The Sopranos* and *House of Cards* when discussing this production, emphasizing our cultural interest in spending time with 'cutthroat schemers'. Even more presciently, an April 2016 *Variety* review notes Hans Kesting's extraordinary turn as an 'utterly, awfully recognizable' Richard III: 'Kesting is, at first, as laughable as Donald Trump: an overgrown schoolboy, bursting out of his too-small blazer.'[48] The compression of the plays in service of a single study of political mendacity meant the excising of language and beloved characters, including Falstaff. A contemporary setting deploys van Hove's now signature screens, turning the throne room into a war room full of high-tech cartographic and surveillance equipment.

Productions like these, as even casual theatregoers know, are planned, rehearsed and created many years in advance. So how to account for the eerie experience of sitting in a theatre in Brooklyn on 6 November 2016 watching Richard III slowly morph from schoolboy punchline to 'a joke that's no longer funny'?[49] Perhaps the key to 'Directing the Classics' is realizing that there is no such thing as a 'classic' work after all. There are only texts awaiting the eye, ear and vision of an artist like van Hove to remind us that the past is more present (and prescient) than we could ever imagine.

STAGING IVO VAN HOVE AT THE BARBICAN

Toni Racklin, in conversation with Sonia Massai (March 2017)

SM   What prompted you to introduce van Hove's work to the Barbican back in 2009?

TR   Louise Jeffreys (Barbican Director of Arts) and I (Head of Theatre) went to the Avignon Festival in 2008. We were watching new work to consider it for inclusion in our international programme. The word on the street suggested that there was a genuine buzz about *Roman Tragedies*, but we hesitated to go and see it at first, because the idea of sitting through six hours of Shakespeare, in Dutch, was rather daunting. But we did go and we felt instantly and utterly captivated: we sat on the stage, in the auditorium, we moved around. We were particularly struck by the way in which Ivo breaks down theatrical conventions in order to make his audience feel so close to Shakespeare, so that we can see it with new eyes and hear it with new ears. The dialogue is in Dutch and of course there are English surtitles, but Ivo's directorial approach makes the work so clear and so accessible that one leaves the show feeling that they can almost understand Dutch, which is an extraordinary phenomenon. While still in the theatre, we both felt that the show would be in that small list of everyone's favourite, most transformative shows. Before the show had properly ended, while the audience was still applauding, we spotted Ivo across the stage. We approached him and we simply said, 'you must come to London'. And he did, with *Roman Tragedies*, in 2009.

SM   Was it difficult to make a business case for his first visit?

TR   It was hard to convey the significance of this show and why people should see it. But audiences did come and they did grow: it was only three performances, but by the end of the run, *Roman Tragedies* had already become a cult. Some people lie, to this day, about being at the show in 2009, because Ivo's debut on the Barbican stage has acquired the aura of a cornerstone in British drama.

SM   How comparable is van Hove to other international directors, especially in terms of potential appeal to UK audiences?

TR   One prominent feature that Ivo's productions share with other major European productions has to do with the distinctive quality of the acting generally associated with established ensemble companies, like Toneelgroep Amsterdam. We have brilliant actors in this country, and text and its delivery are very important, but directors and actors tend to come together only for individual productions. Ivo, like other European directors, has developed a long-standing relationship with his actors over the years. The unity of purpose that emerges from that relationship shapes the acting and is one of the defining qualities of their work. That relationship is forged and renewed each time through the pre-production process. Ivo is very active during the rehearsal process. Ivo's attention to each line in each scene has a forensic quality to it and each change is discussed and tested with the actors. It is the most astonishing process to watch. Ivo has said that, by the end of his short rehearsals – they start at 11.00 am and they are over by 3.00 pm – he feels exhausted, because he is so immersed in the process. And I think that the intensity of the work that Ivo carries out so thoroughly and so painstakingly with his actors then shows in the quality of his productions.

SM   How has your working relationship with van Hove evolved since 2009?

TR   Our relationship has grown and deepened. With Ivo there is a genuine synergy, a shared language that has developed through each of the projects we have worked on together. *The Antonioni Project* (2011) spoke both to Ivo's interest in cinema and to our cross-art programming, to our attempt to bring theatre, film, dance, photography and all other major art forms into conversation with each other within the space of the Barbican Centre. *Scenes from a Marriage* (2013) also highlighted a synergy between Ivo's theatrical language and the flexible use we often make of our spaces: this production subdivided the actors and the audience into three groups, but in such a way that each group could just about see and overhear the others, so that different scenes from the marriage overlapped and lent a fresh significance to the different stages of the piece. Once again, the design of the performance area allowed the audience to be so close to the actors, to share their space. That proximity in turn triggered one to think critically about one's own relationships! After *Scenes from a Marriage*, our audiences started to recognize the actors and the roles they had played on our stage started to coalesce into a sort of collective shared history. We then co-produced *Antigone* (2015). Juliette Binoche was working here a year earlier and she said to me that she wanted to work with an interesting director who would challenge her. Of course, I suggested Ivo. Then Ivo's creative team and our respective technical teams, along with Les Théâtres de la Ville, Luxembourg and Toneelgroep Amsterdam, gathered a group of British and Irish actors, alongside Binoche, and mounted this thoroughly international, thoroughly collaborative production, that opened in Luxembourg, then came to the Barbican, and then toured to Amsterdam, Antwerp, Recklinghausen in Germany, the Edinburgh International Festival and on to venues across the Atlantic – Brooklyn Academy of Music, New York; the University Theatre at the University of North Carolina; and the Center for the Performing Arts, Ann Arbor, Michigan. It was an ambitious tour and that continued for over a year. We then wondered how to take our relationship further. We were at that point rather preoccupied with the upcoming quatercentenary of Shakespeare's death in 2016. And it just so happened that Ivo was starting to think about how he could revisit the battle and the crowd scenes that he had chosen to omit from *Roman Tragedies* in another Shakespearean cycle, this time focussing on the English history plays. Ivo's initial idea developed into *Kings of War*, which seemed to us a most fitting contribution to our Shakespeare400 programme.[50] Ivo was at least initially reluctant to present *Kings of War* as part of the anniversary year programme, but we knew that there would be an appetite among our audiences for non-English Shakespeare, in all its 'infinite variety', performed in different languages and theatrical traditions. Audiences in the UK know that they can hear Shakespeare's language, delivered in all its epic splendour, on our stages by companies like the RSC. Or they can hear it at the Barbican, pared back, in the work of companies like Cheek by Jowl, or as Thomas Ostermeier, Yukio Ninagawa or Ivo tackle it. At the Barbican we feel that British theatre must open a window onto a range of international Shakespeares to allow audiences to take different insights away from each of them. We therefore decided to co-commission *Kings of War*. The next conversation between us and Ivo took place with our Creative Learning team: he had done master classes with young professionals but we wanted to take this type of work with Ivo further. That is when we started planning the residency, which involved reviving *Roman Tragedies*. We were curious to establish how differently the production would play with most of his actors being now ten years older than when it first premièred in 2007. We were also keen to find out whether our response to Ivo's work had changed since 2009.

SM   Do you think that our responses to his work have changed? And have the demographics of his Barbican audiences also changed? Has his profile, in other words, changed from Shakespeare fetish to household name?

TR   Audiences here for *Roman Tragedies* in 2017 were much younger. They are now more familiar with Ivo's work and they know what Ivo brings to Shakespeare and to ancient and modern classics. Our audiences aged fourteen to twenty-five have access to cheaper tickets and come for all the different art forms on offer at the Barbican Centre, as well as to our theatre productions. There are also new audiences who come to watch Ivo at the Barbican, having encountered his work through his productions of *Lazarus* and *A View from the Bridge*. The numbers of scholars, actors, critics and directors in Ivo's audiences have also grown exponentially since 2009, because he has become a reference. In their time Peter Brook and Pina Bausch influenced other artists; similarly, we are now witnessing how Ivo's work is cross-fertilizing the work of others.

SM   How is the rest of the residency going?

TR   We are looking forward to the opening of Ivo's adaptation of Luchino Visconti's *Obsession*. Jude Law had already been in conversation with Ivo about working together on a forthcoming project. When the project was first thought of, we decided that the cast would include Ivo's actors alongside British actors. Law is enjoying working with Ivo. I think the thoroughly collaborative quality of Ivo's rehearsal process was new to him. And of course we end the residency with an Ingmar Bergman double bill, *After the Rehearsal / Persona*. Once again, audiences will find the quality of the acting, including its visceral brutality, quite startling, its uniqueness stemming from that long and well-established relationship of trust that Ivo shares with his actors. I should end by mentioning Barbican Box, a project connected to the residency that has given school children and their drama teachers a chance to learn about, and to test, Ivo's approach to theatre-making.[51]

ROMAN TRAGEDIES: *'THE TIMES THEY ARE A-CHANGIN' (BOB DYLAN)*

Ivo van Hove (Extract from the Director's Notes)

Roman Tragedies is a polyphonic theatre piece in which opinions, perspectives and attitudes coexist. It is a piece of theatre that refuses to adjudicate who is right or what direction we should follow. Shakespeare did not choose sides either. His Roman tragedies are three plays in which politics and its processes are centre stage. Shakespeare allows people who believe in political ideals or movements to confront each other without bias or prejudice – and he shows how they succeed or fail in their political goals. He reveals the human side of politics.

What is politics? I believe that Hannah Arendt's simple yet clear suggestion that politics is the determining possibility of each individual to speak and act in the world and to make a new beginning answers this question.[52] She furthermore suggests that the person who only wants to speak the truth cannot be political, as politics always involves fighting for a certain cause.[53] Politics is therefore the antithesis of absolute truth. Truth is completely apolitical, whereas politics concerns what is achievable in the world. Truth and public policy are different worlds. Politics exist because of consensus, whereas the truth does not tolerate compromise. Politics can only exist if one believes that people can change. . . . The truth, however, exists because it does not change when people do. Politics and the truth are always at odds with each other. . . .

Belief in a society that can change is the origin of politics. Politics is the product of human endeavour, the work of people who believe that they can decide their own fate. Politics emerges when a group of people attempt to grasp a problem by talking, consulting and evaluating, and when they attempt to control the natural course of things. It is a network of opinions, which shows how, by means of consensus, things can change and how changeable, flexible, but also how gullible, people are. Typical of politics is that every consensus eventually comes under pressure and that joint decisions come to be questioned, criticized and repealed again and again. Politics is man-made and cannot be severed from the family and home – oftentimes the common good is influenced by personal interests. The challenge of these three plays is that they never take a specific stand and that they do not make an ultimate claim about what is the right and only way. By the way, Shakespeare never moralized in his works. Like Hannah Arendt, Shakespeare is convinced that truth and politics are at odds with each other. Politics leads to different people coexisting. Politics can connect people who have nothing in common, but it can also cause division between people who do not share the same opinion. Politics always involves a group of people, and not an individual.

Political Dramas This is the framework in which the show needs to be placed. It is not human psychology that occupies centre stage, but how people come to take a joint decision, a political murder, a civil war or war with another country. Agnes Heller wrote an insightful book about these tragedies in which she suggests that

> In the Roman plays … time is out of joint for some, but new times are triumphantly setting in for others. This is not because the new man appears at the end … but because new institutions replace the ancient ones. This is not the same thing as when a good king takes the place of a wicked one, or vice versa. The men who carry those new institutions on their shoulders, or who embody them, appear at the beginning of the three Roman political dramas and not at the end. *Coriolanus* begins with the establishment of the institution of the tribunes. They just enter time. In *Julius Caesar*, as well as in *Antony and Cleopatra*, Octavius – the *homo novus* of politics – will bring the work of Caesar to full fruition. 'Caesarism' will sweep away the ancient times. The very circumstance of basic political institutions are changing, and that the men who change them are present at the very moment a drama political struggle begins, is one of the main reasons for calling these three Roman dramas political dramas. . . . [54]

The Women in *Roman Tragedies* The role of women in history is another common thread, which links these three political tragedies together. The first woman is Volumnia, who raised Coriolanus by herself with military discipline, a woman with the heart of a man, who eventually manages to change her ideological fanaticism into a political and fruitful attitude towards Rome and her inhabitants. She convinces Coriolanus to choose harmony and to change his 'us versus them' ideology. Her tragedy is that she cannot be politically active herself and realizes her insights by proxy. In the same play, there is a second woman: Virgilia, the wife of Coriolanus. Both Virgilia and Coriolanus clearly entered this marriage out of love, but Coriolanus refuses to show his love in public. Private and public need to remain separate. Inherently, *Coriolanus* takes place in the public sphere. Virgilia's love has no chance of becoming political. Her near-silent presence with her son and mother-in-law in Act Five is the image of family, its (biological) roots, and leads, among other things, to Coriolanus's change of heart. In *Julius Caesar*, two women also play a decisive role. Whereas Virgilia's love was reprimanded, let alone acknowledged, in public, Portia challenges her husband Brutus. She does not tolerate that she cannot be part of his train of thoughts. She does not want to spend only her free time with him; she wants to be part of his entire life. Brutus does not accept Portia's demands and, thereby, risks his own marriage because of his commitment to higher political ideals. Simultaneously, we witness the first true public love relationship. When Calphurnia asks her husband to stay at home and not to go to the Capitol, he listens to her. Julius Caesar loves Calphurnia, cares for her, and stays at home for her – even though he believes that she is overreacting. It is almost as if the hidden relationship between Virgilia and Coriolanus was finally given a chance to become public and, thus, has political power. And Cleopatra definitely has political power. She is the queen of an ancient empire with rich traditions and is herself worshipped by her subjects as the new goddess Isis. Cleopatra is Egypt. Her power seems to be a mirror image of Volumnia's power. But Cleopatra manages to bring her personal and political personae together in her role as a leader and leads out of passion and a firm faith. In this respect, she is unlike Fulvia and Octavia, two less important goddesses and the two Roman wives of Antony. Although Fulvia is only mentioned by other characters – she herself never appears on stage – she has much influence. Out of spite, she encourages internal rebellions and Rome seems to dissolve into chaos. When he finds out that Fulvia has passed away, Antony realizes that he has gone too far and decides to return to Rome in order to restore stability. Octavia also plays a political role. Octavia is Octavius's sister – they are very close and he loves her very much. The irreconcilable differences between Octavius and Antony are resolved through a political marriage between Octavius's sister and Antony. In this way, Octavia comes to symbolize national unity.

There are, of course, other common threads. We can read Aufidius, for example, as an early proponent of the pragmatic policies, which bring Octavius much success [later on in the cycle]. Both Coriolanus and Julius Caesar are murdered because of political reasons; we observe that Antony's advisors are his friends, just like the conspirators in *Julius Caesar*. All three plays feature politicians who believe in debate and politicians who believe in conflict. Wars are continually waged for different reasons. All these similarities show the importance of staging these three plays as an *opus magnum*.

In our production, we want to highlight the political mechanisms that lie beneath the surface of the plot rather than a linear historical narrative. At the level of the story, you can see the plays as the laborious establishment of the Roman Empire. Accordingly, *The Tragedy of Coriolanus* anticipates the birth of a great empire, as a play that reveals how people, politicians and soldiers cannot let go of their ideologies and how the expansion of political power by the patricians was halted by the tribunes who wanted more attention paid to domestic affairs. *The Tragedy of Julius Caesar* takes place when democracy reveals its weaknesses in the face of a great, charismatic leader. And, in *The Tragedy of Antony and Cleopatra*, Octavius manages to establish a great imperial kingdom. Simultaneously, the establishment of this globalized world requires wars, murders, broken marriages and lost friendships. The production will be staged as a big conference about politics, in which case studies are presented to the audience: how do politicians act when people are complaining about austerity? What are the possible consequences of a war? What is a good reason to go to war? Can you defect to the enemy? What happens when a democratically chosen leader is suspected to seeking power for power's sake and for personal aggrandizement? Can we allow political murders? All characters and scenes illustrate these questions and dilemmas, so in our production the participants in the conference will continuously be confronted with new political problems, in which they need to fully immerse themselves and which the characters they play need to resolve. The production will be non-stop and it will mirror world politics, which has become 24/7. The doors of the theatre will remain open to ensure that every visitor can take a break whenever he/she wants to. Perhaps he/she might miss a decisive monologue or a political murder, which will change history, but this is what happens in real life. *Roman Tragedies* is a production of incessant debates and decisions, which will become like politics itself.

Los Angeles, April 2007
Translation by Isabelle Groenhof

STAGING IVO VAN HOVE AT THE SCHAUBÜHNE, BERLIN

Maja Zade, resident dramaturg, in conversation with Sonia Massai (March 2017)

SM Can you please tell me a little bit about how you worked with van Hove on these two productions and if your work with van Hove reflected your usual practice with other directors or if you had to adjust your practice to suit his approach to 'directing the classics'?

MZ No director has the same practice as another director so there is always a period of getting to know each other and figuring out how best to work together. Also, the phrase 'directing the classics' makes it sound as if van Hove had a blueprint that he applies to every classic text and of course that's not the case – he makes a point of responding to each text in its own merit and tries to get to the core and essence of that text. Having said that, the two productions he did at the Schaubühne, Molière's *The Misanthrope* (2010) and Marlowe's *Edward II* (2011), shared certain features: a very stylish, very cool, modern world created by Ivo together with Jan Versweyveld, a world that is perhaps more influenced by film than by other theatre productions. In both shows we used translations of the plays that weren't completely modernized, so there was an interesting contrast between the modern world in which the actors moved and how they were speaking, a contrast that reminded the audience that they were watching characters and situations conceived in the past but still relevant in the present. As a result, the past was like a distant shadow behind these productions, which, in turn, opened a space where one could question what had changed, or if anything had changed, in how people live and behave.

SM Were there any other major interventions, besides the decision to use partly modernized translations, which were specifically aimed at adapting the original texts to the new worlds that Ivo and Jan created for these two productions?

MZ No, even with *Edward II*, which we set in a men's prison, we didn't adapt the dialogue to the set; we kept it in the original because we thought that provided an interesting friction.

Figure 8 *Edward II (Stefan Stern) holding Gaveston (Christoph Gawenda)*, Edward II, Schaubühne, Berlin (2011).

SM Ivo's productions cut classical texts, sometimes quite radically, while showing a sustained engagement with the text and even with the nuances of textual detail. Was this the case with these two productions? Did you feel that these productions shed light on some aspect of the original texts that more conventional productions overlook?

MZ I think there's a difference in theatre traditions between Britain and large parts of the continent here – my feeling is that with classic plays the text exists, it can be read in its entirety on the page, and what I want is for a director or an artistic team to come along and to illuminate that text for me for the present. What is the relevance of *The Misanthrope* or of *Edward II* for us today? Do they illuminate our present-day relationships, politics, etc. So it's through that filter that Ivo's productions shed light on the plays, that he manages to make classic plays seem relevant again, to make them speak to us directly. What I found most interesting about *The Misanthrope* is Ivo's take on Alceste's dissatisfaction with society, with human relationships, as directly linked to modern technology: Alceste feels that virtual interactions via Facebook, Twitter, etc., are fake and superficial and devalue human relationships. In the case of *Edward II*,

Figure 9 *Oronte (David Ruland) and Celimène (Judith Rosmair),* The Misanthrope, *Schaubühne, Berlin (2010).*

I would say that moving the play to a prison makes you look at power structures in a new way, in the sense that you see that structures of power are always linked to the worlds in which they take place, inform them and in turn are shaped by them.

SM   How did you interact with the other members of the creative team and with the actors during the production process and rehearsal? Were changes made to the script once rehearsals had started?

MZ   While of course Ivo is the driving and defining force behind his shows, he is also a very inclusive director: he is happy to listen to everyone, he also trusts people to do their jobs and to do them well, so it's not unusual for him to talk through a scene with a dramaturg and to then say, 'you go and talk to the actors'. And yes, of course, although we went into rehearsals with a prepared script, there are always changes that happen as you go along where you find that a scene isn't quite tight enough or a line isn't clear enough, or passages of text that in rehearsals turn out not to be even necessary.

SM   What would you say were the most arresting and memorable features of these two productions and why?

MZ I think both shows were very beautiful to look at: visually they had great clarity, paired with performances that were quite raw and emotional. It's an intriguing pairing that I think runs through all of Ivo's work, not just the Schaubühne shows, and in that sense offers a kind of meta-commentary on the condition of modern life, where emotion and warmth are often stifled and repressed. Ivo manages to get a very high emotional level of intensity from the performers, which is no small feat. This skill, I think, comes from his style of directing: of all the versions of a scene that an actor tried on a particular day, Ivo expects him or her to pick up from the last version on the following day and to continue pushing forwards. In a sense this direction sounds simple, but he's the only director I know who does that, and it took some time for the actors in our company to adapt to this – they're more used to trying out things at greater leisure, slowly searching for the right path, whereas Ivo has an unusual degree of clarity about what he wants and where he wants to go, and expects the actors to take a lot of responsibility and to keep pushing forwards.

SM **Did the shows fit in with the rest of the programming at the Schaubühne during their respective seasons or did they come across as quite different from in-house productions or productions directed by other visiting directors?**

MZ At the Schaubühne we deliberately don't programme 'seasons' in terms of a particular subject matter or theme. We try instead to get the best directors with very definitive aesthetics and styles, basically the people who we think are currently the best directors out there. So yes, Ivo's productions were different, but so were everyone else's.

CHRISTOPHER MARLOWE'S EDWARD II

Ivo van Hove (Extract from the Director's Notes)

The play is a drama about a weak king, who is driven by only one passion: his love for Gaveston, a man of lesser nobility. Edward gives himself totally to his lust. As a welcome gift, he overwhelms Gaveston with noble titles. Against this, the nobles revolt because they lose their prerogatives and Edward is stripped of his power and everything that goes with it. The play is the story of a monarchy in crisis. What precipitates the crisis is not the monarch's homosexuality, because there were many homosexual kings and rulers before him, and in Marlowe's time homosexuality was seen at best as capricious, at worst as sinful, behaviour rather than something that determines a person's identity. The king's downfall stems from his granting of titles to men of low birth, such as Gaveston and later Spencer. In the face of favouritism against class privilege, the status quo must be restored. But not at the cost of anarchy, allowing an uprising to replace legal rules. Saddam Hussein got a trial before he was hanged. It's called modern civilization.

We situate this royal drama in a prison, a world of criminals. We indicate that the prison and its structure, validated by violence, are a metaphor for our world. A prison is a law-regulated form of lawlessness. The philosopher Giorgio Agamben calls this a 'state of exception'.[55] He noted that modern democracies formulate laws according to this principle of 'states of exception', whereby violence can be legitimately used. The clearest example is Guantanamo Bay, where even torture is permitted. At any time, exceptional circumstances may be invoked to use violence. It is 'the sign of the system's inability to function without being transformed into a lethal machine', says Agamben.[56] This permanent state of exception is a dark mirror of the new political legitimacy on the planet. In *Edward II*, we see that our present democratic world is organized like a prison, a 'state of exception'. Our rules border on the boundary with violence and death. In *Edward II*, we show an anti-world, a world of criminals, which, in all its extremity, is very similar to our world, where the line between legality and lawlessness has become blurred.

The film *Un Prophète* [*A Prophet*] (2009, directed by Jacques Audiard) shows a similar anti-world in a very accessible way. The film tells the story of an adolescent, who disappears behind bars as a petty thief. Prison is a school and it transforms him into a top criminal, trained and connected with an extensive network of fellow-criminals. Perhaps most troubling are the absolute legality and lawlessness that blur into each other in Audiard's film. Gang structures with rival gangs thrive inside the prison walls and are hardly affected by bars in the way they communicate with the outside world (to control their 'hinterland' and the domestic supply of drugs, weapons, etc.). More: prisoners and prison guards are an inextricable network, where it is unclear who monitors and controls whom, what the law is and whom it represents. Rules and taboos of criminal gangs and legality and illegality in the community clash as if enclosed in an impenetrable fencing area. Only an experienced and cunning strategist can navigate this area without getting lost in such a morass. That's what the protagonist learns and he benefits from this 'state of exception'.

Prince Edward is silent and unobtrusive but he is also a diligently observant student in this school of power and violence. He learns every confrontation and will show that he has learned his lesson, when everybody else least expects him to. Like the protagonist in *Un Prophète*, he is finally the new king.

Leicester, the prison guard, is the representative of society. He must guarantee maintenance of order. But daily life in this 'state of exception' of the prison has affected him. In him we see the most ultimate form of violence and power. Leicester is low-status in the outside world. The intimacy of Edward's cell is his *hortus conclusus* ['enclosed, walled garden'; historically, monastic cloister garden, hence 'private world' or 'microcosm' – eds]. He can freely entertain and overwhelm his victim, because he has absolute power over life and death. Accordingly, Edward completely surrenders to him. In 2001 Armin Meiwes slew and partially ate Bernd Juergen Brandes [this murder took place in Rotenburg, Germany – eds.]. Shocking was the discovery that the conscious and fully cooperative Brandes had sought this death. In an interview, Meiwes explained that he had spent time on the Internet searching for a victim, but that all other candidates ultimately were dropped because 'it was essential for him to find a victim who would fully assent to be killed and cannibalized'. Through Brandes's complete surrender, Meiwes ate his lover and victim, bit by bit bringing him closer to him. Killing and eating Brandes gave Meiwes a 'soulmate'.

Marlowe's *Edward II* holds a dark mirror up to a world, where power is associated with violence, because man is inherently violent.

SIGN OF THE TIMES: THOUGHTS ON MOLIÈRE'S THE MISANTHROPE

Ivo van Hove (Extracts from the Director's Notes)

The Misanthrope is mostly considered as a critical description of a dying world. I think it looks at the beginning of a new way of living together. In both cases *The Misanthrope*, as most plays by Molière, should be considered as sociological, a research of and critical look at society today.

When I first read the play it struck me that a family – a father, a mother, brothers and sisters – were absent. The characters of *The Misanthrope* constitute a new kind of family of semi-detached people who abhor the idea of sharing home and household, preferring to keep their bank accounts and friends separate, and share time and space when they feel like it. These characters live a 'liquid' life, as the Polish sociologist Zygmunt Bauman calls it. In different books with titles like *Liquid Love*, *Liquid Life* and *Liquid Fear* he describes 'the risks and anxieties of living together, and apart, in our liquid modern world'.[57]

There is one character in the play who doesn't share the beliefs and lifestyles of the liquid people: Alceste still believes vehemently in the old-style 'till death do us part' marriage. He believes in a job for life, he believes in true friendship and in the existence of absolute truth. It is the conflict between a liquid society and a society of social cohesion that is central to *The Misanthrope*.

Of course in the seventeenth century Molière wrote a critical play against the morals of his time with Célimène as the icon of that perverse social attitude and Alceste as the excessive, but rightful enemy of society as it existed. For Molière there was a possible positive outcome, which he presented in the character of Philinte, a modern man, who believes in moderation, compliance and tolerance. Alceste is only destructive; his attitude and views lead to isolation and anti-social behaviour. In the eighteenth century Rousseau, who hated the play, saw in Alceste's attitude a plea for truth and sincerity, ridiculed by Molière. He considered Alceste as a true heroic alternative to the vices of a corrupt society.

It is the strength of a true masterpiece that it has the capacity to let us have a glimpse behind the mirror of the present times. We have to accept the challenge Molière presents us with in *The Misanthrope*. We have to take sides! In the twenty-first century, the central problem of *The Misanthrope* is how to live together in a society where long-term relationships are almost non-existent. Life in big cities is regulated by mobile phones and the Internet, we cocoon ourselves in a web of calls and messages that make us feel part of society and make us feel good because we feel connected all the time. In cities everybody is always on the move and our mobile phones make us feel the sole stable point in this universe of moving objects. This feeling of virtual proximity has a shadow side: virtual distance. Proximity no longer requires physical closeness and physical closeness no longer determines proximity. How many times do we see two people sitting together during a personal meeting or a dinner making a phone call or sending a text message to another person? To be open to all possible contacts in the world is to be king of our lives. Another side effect is that these contacts tend to be short and shallow, too shallow to condense into bonds. Homes are no longer places of intimacy, but places where we live together apart and household members can live side by side with their computers. We live in a world of Internet-dating because it is easy to press delete, perhaps the easiest thing in the world. The Internet is anonymous; dating is possible without any repercussions.

Relationships without risks, without sadness, without pain, without plights seem to be the new utopia. This world of virtual relationships is open, flexible and free. It is a world of possibilities where the nature of relationships itself has changed drastically. There are no commitments for life and people have no bonds. The danger of a liquid society is that it treats people as objects of consumption. We can consume each other as long as we like the product. Relationships exist as long as they represent value for money.

The American philosopher Kwame Anthony Appiah believes that we can deal with new collective identities, new families: 'We have to bridge our differences based on race, gender, sexuality, religion and nationhood. We can't live isolated; we have to think in a universal way. Reasonableness has to accommodate competing beliefs and behaviours without polarizing the differences between them.'[58] I think this could be the hopeful message of *The Misanthrope* today.

New York City, 22 August 2007

STAGING SHAKESPEARE AT TONEELGROEP AMSTERDAM: POLITICAL MURDERS AND BACKROOM POLITICS

Laurens De Vos

Maybe more than the murder of Theo van Gogh two years later, the assassination of politician Pim Fortuyn, in 2002, blew away the foundations of the consensus model that had been praised in the Netherlands as the only way forward in politics. Suddenly, a couple of bullets had blown up the Dutch idyll. What is more, as Fortuyn was shot in the car park of the national broadcast company, the whole country could follow live streaming of the politician's body drenched in blood, surrounded by ambulance staff trying to resuscitate him.

Five years later, Ivo van Hove's *Roman Tragedies* (2007) uncannily brought home to the Dutch public this political murder. As in many other productions, van Hove resolutely brings the past to the present, setting the Roman plays in a contemporary Western environment that bore references to both a television newsroom and a UN convention room, a clean and cool scenography that was vintage Jan Versweyveld. No Roman togas and sandals, but tight suits, neckties and glittering shoes. Footage from twentieth-century news events, such as the murder of John F. Kennedy, brought in reality. So did the political murders of Coriolanus and Julius Caesar. They were encircled by their adversaries and eliminated, after which a bird's-eye view snapshot of the body was projected on a large screen, which 'reminded audiences in the Low Countries of the assassination of the Dutch politician Pim Fortuyn'.[59] Moreover, political deaths in the public space also appeared in another guise; upon hearing that Antony, whom he has betrayed, has nonetheless sent him his belongings, Enobarbus (played by Barry Atsma) becomes hysterical and – torn by pain and remorse – runs out of the theatre building. As he is pursued by a camera crew, we can follow him live on a screen, and it is there – on the square and streets outside the Stadsschouwburg that are so familiar to us in this other universe called reality – that Enobarbus kills himself. With these interferences of the public domain in the theatrical fiction van Hove enhances the realness of Shakespeare's plays.

Van Hove, in other words, refrains from the simple strategy of introducing reality on the stage – it also happens the other way around. By breaking through the frame of the theatre and occupying the public domain Atsma leaves behind some of the fictionality of his character and presents Enobarbus as one of us, ordinary people. *Roman Tragedies* played with the involvement of the audience throughout. With the exception of *Antony and Cleopatra*, because of its more private nature, spectators were asked to sit on the sofas onstage, while some of the actors playing the tribunes were dispersed among the other spectators in the auditorium. When Coriolanus was being accused by the tribunes, the audience involuntarily became the Roman people taking sides and deciding on the development of the plot. They fulfilled the same function in *Julius Caesar*, yet at the beginning of the last of the Roman tragedies about love and geopolitical strategies, they were summoned away from the stage. In this environment of power games there is no room for the voice of the people to be heard.

Set in what could have been a newsroom, *Roman Tragedies* was an explicit comment on one of the most popular television programmes of the decade, *Big Brother*, where a group of people is locked up in a house and followed by cameras day and night. The Dutch format was subsequently sold all over the world. Everything that was taking place onstage was recorded on camera and live projected on a big screen; the imprisonment by the camera's lens was even extended outside the theatre, as when a crew followed Enobarbus onto the streets as mentioned above. There was no escape from the all-seeing eye of the cameras. Everything that is normally hidden from view was now exposed; the theatre – literally the place from where to watch – became a 360-degree world with apparently no backside. We could constantly follow who was in the cybercafé[60] that both actors and audience could visit, we had a view of the make-up table where actors and actresses put on and off their masks like television stars. We could not only follow the fierce political debates and even parliamentary fights but also the backroom politics where Coriolanus was being put under pressure and the murder of Caesar being plotted by Brutus and his companions. In a tsunami of images, the idea was pressed upon the audience that the smallest detail was visible and registered. The audience was even granted transparency with regard to the future. Of all protagonists who are destined to get killed, a light board indicated how many minutes and seconds they had left before their death, so the audience could uncannily 'predict' when Caesar, Brutus, Coriolanus or Mark Antony would die.

Yet the mere choice of where one decided to sit down on the stage countered this illusion of the all-seeing and omniscient perspective from the very start. And that the bombardment of media images can be equally manipulative was shown by Mark Antony, who in his famous speech to the people of Rome grabbed the cloak of the murdered Caesar and held it before the camera's eye to underscore his argument, thus deliberately using multimedia to bring to the fore his particular truth.

With *Kings of War* (2015), van Hove continues to analyse the dynamics of power. Some of the aforementioned elements could also be recognized in this history cycle. Rather than uncovering the universality of power, in each of them van Hove identifies another aspect of power. Whereas Henry V (Ramsey Nasr) is a smart, strategic but also just leader, the weak Henry VI (Eelco Smits) has no spine, no courage and is easily deceived by his plotting advisers. The limping Richard III (Hans Kesting), big birthmark on his face, is portrayed as a cool, calculating and cynical powerbroker.

Versweyveld created an underground bunker as the headquarters of the king, behind which a white labyrinth led to nowhere but this bunker and the centre of power. This maze was, as in *Roman Tragedies*, the setting of conspiracies and manipulations. Here again, what was going on in this labyrinth could be followed by projections on a video screen. A cameraman recorded everything live. But the audience also saw footage of the outside world, of the atrocious consequences of war. Images of Prince George and fake telephone calls by Richard III to Obama, Putin and Merkel drew the parallel to today's geopolitical theatre. It enhanced the clash between the real world and the isolated, alienated world of politics. New media show us – and the kings – what is going on in society, but at the same time cut us, and them, off from it. Van Hove presents us with this increasingly shrinking world that his protagonists occupy; at the end, Richard III is left entirely on his own on the stage, while the screen continues to project footage of his enemies outside plotting conspiracies against him.

Shakespeare is no recently discovered domain for van Hove. Back in 1987 he stepped forward with a remarkable *Macbeth* for his then-company De Tijd in Flanders. Although the Flemish author Hugo Claus had taken care of the translation into Dutch, van Hove's production was strongly informed by Heiner Müller's *Macbeth* adaptation. This should not have come as a surprise; just one year before, van Hove had staged *Russian Opening* by the German playwright. The unstoppable, blind progress of violence is the common denominator that characterizes the director's productions from this period. His collaboration with Jan Versweyveld was already established by then. On both sides of the stage were big, metal theatre machineries such as stage lamps, wind machines and sound boxes. Because of the light flashes and wind that they generated, the magical world in which the witches dwell was stripped of the natural lyricism generally associated with the foggy and eerie world of the Scottish highlands. Instead, it was replaced by an unrestrained, industrialized apparatus. Van Hove staged Macbeth as a human being who has increasingly less control over a system that exceeds him enormously. Inversely proportional to its growing power, Macbeth became increasingly smaller in an environment in which he tried to keep upright. Exemplary for this loss of self-control was the image of Macbeth, played by Lucas Vandervost, on a majestic Belgian Heavy Draft horse. With his misplaced sword and crown and his naked upper-body van Hove's Macbeth came across more as pathetic rather than as tragically evil.

TWO RIVAL QUEENS CAUGHT IN A MUSEUM: MARY STUART

Laurens De Vos

After looking at what an ideology of egotism may look like in *The Fountainhead* (January 2014), with Friedrich Schiller's *Mary Stuart* (December 2014), a co-production of Toneelgroep Amsterdam and the Flemish Toneelhuis, Ivo van Hove turned to the question of how emotionally engaged a political leader should be. His production was informed by Martha Nussbaum's concept of a 'decent society' in her book *Political Emotions* where she calls for justice and love in political leaders.[61]

Even before the death of Mary Stuart, Queen of Scots, the country seems in mourning. After nineteen years of imprisonment, Schiller's tragedy begins with the moment when Mary's execution becomes imminent because of the increasing danger that she poses to Elizabeth's throne. In van Hove's very stylized interpretation all characters, both queens included, are dressed in black, as if death were already looming large in court and country. The scenographical setting by Jan Versweyveld is dominated by dark colours; brown, grey and black alternate with the changing scenes.

But maybe this is less a production about queens, despite Mary and Elizabeth's Renaissance-styled and heavily decorated costumes in the final act, than about two women trapped in the roles they have to play. The tone is set from the beginning: in the first scene, Mary (Halina Reijn) demands to meet Elizabeth (Chris Nietvelt) face to face, because only as an equal can she be tried. She thereby explicitly refers to her position as a queen, but also as a woman. However, in the first two subsequent – and parallel – scenes, it becomes clear that while Mary is literally imprisoned, Elizabeth is also metaphorically chained to the expectations that come with her role as queen of England,

Figure 10 *From left, Elizabeth I (Chris Nietvelt), Mary Stuart (Halina Reijn) and Leicester (Hans Kesting); in the background, Kennedy (Katelijne Damen),* Mary Stuart, *Stadsschouwburg, Amsterdam (2014).*

both in political and in marital issues, amidst numerous opposing recommendations and admonitions from her advisers.

Consisting of horizontal and vertical lines Versweyveld's décors are always minimal, sober and tight, but spacious and grandiose at the same time. *Mary Stuart* is no exception to this artistic poetics. The stage is less deep due to the advanced brown rear wall, thus contributing to the claustrophobic atmosphere of imprisonment of both dungeon and palace. In the wall we can distinguish the contours of a double door, which, however, never opens until the moment Mary is facing her execution. At that moment she holds both doorknobs and takes a deep breath, after which the wall becomes transparent and the door theatrically slides open, sweeping the queen to the other side of the wall. The sliding doors make a full circle though, bringing Mary back to the fore, until she eventually disappears after the third round, analogous to the three blows necessary to sever her head from her body, as we are told in the next scene.

Van Hove's production was characterized by a highly stylized and ritualized performance that seemed set in an environment that resembled that of a museum. The only props in this wooden-like setting were two minimalist steel benches, and a huge frame with vegetative decorations surrounded the stage. Indeed, the actors often seemed characters out of a painting. In each scene, with every movement, van Hove placed his actors to suggest a pictorial composition. In their silenced, slow gestures they sometimes almost became *tableaux vivants*. Similarly stylized was the courtship dance performed by Elizabeth and Aubespine, the French ambassador, to the electronically modified sixteenth-century music 'Passe et Medio' by the Antwerp composer Tielman Susato based on keyboards and violin.

Even the more dramatically charged moments testified to a serene, subdued atmosphere. Realizing that he has failed in his attempts to rescue Mary, Mortimer takes off his jacket, kneels down to say a short prayer, hangs his jacket over his head and, tightening the sleeves around his throat, strangles himself. His prayer was addressed to Mary, and it is with this deliberate merger of the Mother of God and Mary Stuart that the deification of the queen begins. Right after Mary is executed by being swept to the other side of the back wall, we see her figure in the dark ascending to heaven, as a Catholic martyr. Subsequently, strongly opposed to this sublime image, a voice from the dark recounts the gory, prosaic details of her execution; the executioner needed three blows to kill the queen, then only grabbed her wig when he wanted to hold up her head. The production premièred in December 2014. Most probably unintendedly, motifs such as martyrdom and beheadings struck a shivering chord with the audience, as the world had come to know the executions of Islamic State in the Middle East, American war correspondent James Foley's beheading in August 2014 following and preceding many others.

More fundamentally, however, this production is yet another stage in van Hove's analysis of the dynamics of leadership that he explored earlier in *The Fountainhead* and that would lead up to his *Kings of War* the following year. Elizabeth is torn between the execution of her power and her sense of justice, between personal feelings and political interests, between her own desires and the will of the people. Moreover, as the most powerful person, she is, paradoxically, the one who is manipulated, lied to and betrayed the most, even by her own entourage. This does not mean, though, that she is being portrayed as a naïve leader who does not understand politics; we are given a sample of her Machiavellian hypocrisy when she shifts responsibility for Mary's death to the messenger Davison and her advisor Lord Burleigh. In Leicester we find the incarnation of the cowardly sidekick, who is constantly hedging his bets until it is eventually too late to rescue Mary. The outcome is not a very uplifting one: Elizabeth, in historical, ornate costume, has been reduced to a queen, a hollow icon deprived of her womanhood and personality. Leicester has fled to France, and her most reasonable advisor Shrewsbury resigns. Mary may be dead, but Elizabeth is left all alone. There is no sparring partner for her last dance, which ended the production. Here, too, we are given a preview of how *Kings of War* will end: Richard III in his war room, abandoned by everybody.

IVO VAN HOVE'S ANTIGONE: *A CONTEMPORARY UPDATE*

George Rodosthenous

Ivo van Hove has committed *hubris*. Days after stating that directors should not engage with Greek tragedy if they do not have a strong vision about the chorus,[62] his own production of *Antigone* did not ultimately manage to incorporate the chorus in an organic way. In an interview with the editors of this volume, van Hove explained that the chorus was the main reason why he does not direct the ancient classics more often.[63] His preference would be to have a very large chorus and that is not always possible, not least for financial reasons. But van Hove and his designer Jan Versweyveld constantly talk about the ancient classics as they prepare productions of early modern and modern Western classics. Those discussions about the ancient classics often have an impact on what van Hove calls the textual and visual dramaturgy of their productions (*A View from the Bridge*, and especially the ending, is a good example here).

His own initial intention for the chorus in *Antigone* was to be re-imagined as archivists and double as the main characters; this works as a dramaturgical device, which is also closely reflected in the set design. Duska Radosavljević aptly describes the set design as

> a conceptually sophisticated and visually simple platform (with a hydraulic opening for a grave), against a backdrop used for the show's own film projections (with a cut out sun in the centre). The platform is connected with the backdrop through a single bridge facilitating a sense of limited connectedness between the private and the public as well as moments of precariousness … The set design is

ultimately an installation within which the central conflicting forces of the play itself play out.[64]

The set also includes filing cabinets of the archives under the main platform. In his programme note, van Hove writes that the chorus 'try to come to terms with the deeper struggles of humankind, of society. The set is their archive. The play is their search, thoughts, emotions, and reflections. Somewhere a clock is ticking. When a chorus song starts, the clock stops and time stands still. The chorus songs slow down the tragic events and we reside with them in the subconscious of the society of Thebes.'[65]

Many other directors, including Emma Rice in a much more populist version of *The Bacchae* (2004), have managed the doubling of chorus members as main characters very successfully, while van Hove seemed to struggle to marry the two. In a year when his fellow European *enfant terribles* were reworking and adapting Greek tragedy – Jan Fabre in the 24-hour marathon *Mount Olympus* focused on the excesses of the body with Dionysian abundance and Romeo Castellucci in his revival of *Orestie* recreated a nightmarish vision of visual cryptic ambivalence – van Hove remained faithful to his own vision of a clinical, cold and hypnotic production, where naturalism prevailed

Figure 11 *Antigone (Juliette Binoche)*, Antigone, *Grand Théâtre de la Ville de Luxembourg (2015).*

within an atmospheric and domesticated setting. As I write elsewhere, in order to make a modern adaptation more contemporary '[t]here can be specific focus on the more domestic aspects of Greek tragedy: the relationship of a father and his son, brotherly love, incestuous undertones ... This reinforces a more voyeuristic approach to the Greek tragedy and its links to our voyeuristic society.'[66] I will therefore focus on the father–son relationship in this production of *Antigone* and its naturalistic approach to Greek tragedy.

When approaching *Antigone*, most directors focus on the juxtaposition of justice and injustice, burial and non-burial, the Gods and the State. The highlight of van Hove's version is, in fact, the father–son scene, the moment where Haimon questions his father Kreon about his plans for Antigone. For van Hove, there is always one central character or relation at the core of all his productions, and he always expects his actors to connect with it by means of what he describes as 'naked-soul acting'. In order to understand this further, I interviewed Samuel Edward-Cook (Haimon) about his process and the director's approach to naturalism. He commented on silence, the use of Daniel Freitag's sound and the emotional layering required to achieve van Hove's vision for this play:

> The naked soul acting comes, I suppose, from Ivo's passion for total naturalism. He allows you the time within a scene to really draw up the deeper darker emotions you are required to touch upon. The power of silence within a scene also adds to this. There is also usually some sort of underscore or soundscape accompanying the scene, which adds another layer or emotion and allows you to access that naked soul more naturally.[67]

This was clearly evident in the building up of the tension between the father and the son, which resembled to a cockfight, or even the moment where two boxers prepare pre-fight. I was fascinated to find out how Ivo works within the rehearsal room to extract these performances from his actors. Ivo's immediate positioning of the text 'on its feet' has a strong impact in 'activating the scene' with minimum textual analysis. In *Antigone*, the scene was organically created amongst the director and the two male protagonists, as Edward-Cook explains:

> The father–son relationship between Haimon and Kreon was very much a collaboration among the three of us. Ivo's process usually begins with a read-through of the scene followed by any questions we may have. Ivo will then explain his interpretation of the scene and then we will put it straight on its feet. Ivo does very

little textual work in the rehearsal room and prefers to *activate the scene* as soon as possible. For this particular scene, Ivo wanted to focus specifically on the strong bond between Haimon and Kreon, which is, then, dramatically broken by the end of the scene. . . . Ivo's simplicity with this scene allowed myself and Patrick O'Kane the freedom to, really, explore that relationship.[68]

For Radosavljević, the father–son scene is 'an exquisitely visceral vignette between Patrick O'Kane's combustible Kreon and Samuel Edward-Cook's humble yet heroic negotiator Haimon. In the choice between love and duty, Haimon, in other words, aims for a synthesis of both.'[69] Also uncanny is the way in which this scene reflects the first six of the eight stages of the healing of the father–son relationship, as described by Shawn Katz: 'Awareness of Satisfaction and Pleasure in Relationship'; 'Appreciation and Gratitude for the Relationship'; 'A Sense of Trust and Safety'; 'Emphasis on Family, Sharing and Emotional Availability'; 'A Recognition of the Unavoidable Nature of Life's Struggles'; 'A Minimum of Unhealthy Projection and Personality Traits of Reconciliation'.[70] Kreon accordingly welcomes his youngest son Haimon: 'are we still friends,'[71] he jokes. Van Hove works with the physical placement of the actors in the space to provide symmetrical reflections of their relationship. The 'Appreciation and Gratitude for the Relationship' stage is done in close proximity:

good attitude, son
good heart in your chest
a father needs a son to back him up
this is why men beget sons
to harm their enemies and honour their friends
some children are useless
some are just trouble
and who would disagree
this makes people *laugh at the father*[72]

They sit together. He teaches his son. The son calmly listens. The physical proximity is replaced with physical distance, when we hear Haimon utter '[I] do not know how to / say you are wrong'. They sit on opposite sides of the stage. Haimon explains 'yet I could not would not do not know how to / say you are wrong'. Then Haimon approaches and sits with him on the 'couch'. The son hugs his father (a Judas Kiss perhaps?). He continues, 'for a son to be proud of his father / a father proud of his son / what could be better'.[73] And kisses his hand.

The roles here are reversed. This is what Eric Miller calls 'rethinking of one's roles as father and son'.[74] Haimon gives his father advice, 'let go your anger, father',[75] but the child's advice upsets the adult. There is an unhealthy projection about the future from both father and son:

Kreon   thou canst never marry her this side [of] the grave

Haimon   then she'll die and take another with her

. . .

Haimon   if you weren't my father I'd say you'd lost your mind'[76]

And at that point Kreon pushes his son onto the floor. Haimon's disobedience has disturbed the balance and ended the process of reconciliation. The father and son relationship is now scarred forever. Mark Morman and Kory Floyd remind us that 'fathers who play a direct role in parenting their sons help to raise individuals who subsequently are better able to resolve conflict, who are more caring and better able to share intimacy. . .'.[77] This is not the case here, as Haimon shouts back:

never no never
if I am near she will not die
and you'll not see my face again, ever
rage on, madman[78]

The consequent fight of Kreon with Teiresias is prophetic,

a corpse for a corpse
the life of your only begotten child
. . .
not long now
there will be wailing of men and wailing of women
there will be tumult of cities and hatred against you
dogs and birds and body parts and stench[79]

Beside the father-son scene, there is another moment in this production that deserves close analysis as it goes right back, full circle, to van Hove's treatment of the chorus. After Antigone dies, Juliette Binoche reappears as chorus and gives the 'citizens / there is no stanza of human life that / I would praise or blame' speech.[80] At this point, one might wonder whether she is a corpse speaking from an after-death dimension. She tells Haimon directly 'Haimon's dead'. And he responds, 'by whose hand'.[81] This treatment of the chorus is effectively summed up by Radosavljević:

> [t]he individual vices and virtues of the protagonists are presented as being contained within all of us and, conversely, the crowd is presented as being a heterogenous collection of individuals rather than an anonymous mass. The lines chorus members speak are often allocated in such a way that they are complementary with the individual character-actor's overall function in the piece.[82]

And then, even more bizarrely, we get the second messenger speech describing Haimon's death to be spoken by Juliette Binoche's chorus member to Eurydike. As Sue Hamstead notes,

> [t]he only bodies displayed on stage by van Hove are those of Polyneikes and Antigone and both are brought on in the same way: by use of the trap door. This serves to relate the two of them in death most closely to each other. Kreon does not bring Haimon's body back with him, but when seated on the sofa in front of the stage, Kreon is briefly joined by the actor playing Haimon, who allows his head to be cradled.[83]

This intimate moment makes for an uncomfortable viewing and supports the idea of the complete inability of fathers to communicate with their sons in contemporary society.

Van Hove's contemporary updating of *Antigone* has given us access to the domestic issues of the tragedy and focused on the constant archiving of information that takes place in contemporary society. The ending, where the chorus resumes their positions – typing on their typewriters, organizing the filing cabinets and endlessly managing the flow of data – makes an acute observation that everything will soon be forgotten.

THE UNANSWERED QUESTION: HOW TO GET TO THE DARK SOUL OF ANTIGONE

Ivo van Hove (Extracts from the Director's Notes)

Antigone by Sophocles tells an ancient story about one of the remaining daughters of Oedipus, who refuses to follow the orders of her uncle Kreon, the new head of state.

Kreon has ordained that Polyneikes, who died in a cruel civil war with his brother Eteocles, cannot be buried because he is a traitor. After the war, with all its casualties, a new war of words begins with a short but razor-sharp sequence of scenes between Antigone and Kreon: an exhaustive, long, bitter but also passionate exchange between two opposite views on how to treat the dead, especially when they are deemed an enemy of the state. It is immediately clear that Kreon and Antigone share no mercy of understanding: as George Steiner puts it, their exchange illustrates 'the laying waste of stillness, of understanding heard, but not listened to.'[84] The result will be three suicides and a destabilized society.

The play is ambivalent and dark, modern and mythical: it is a tangled knot, a knot of thoughts, beliefs, convictions and emotions. *Antigone* is a play that leaves one with more questions than answers, a play as a great piece of art.

To delve into the deeper layers of the play we break open the climactic structure – with its unity of action, time and space – into an epic drama. It should feel like a ticking time bomb, a train that one knows will crash, yet at the same time it should be as slow as strangling by a boa constrictor. Breaking the conventions of Greek tragedy, we bring scenes on stage that would conventionally be played off stage or not exist at all. We show how Antigone buries her brother in a tender ritual. We see how Haimon wants to comfort Antigone. We see how Antigone is not able to love Haimon anymore, how she is stuck in her deep grief for Polyneikes, after the death of her father and mother. It is important to bring to the stage the scarred, deeply hurt, suffering and mourning Antigone. She is already emotionally and mentally dead before the play begins. We also show her suicide, the desperate but also serene loneliness of this ultimate action where she takes control of her own life.

Another way to turn *Antigone* into a drama of epic scale is with the chorus. They try to come to terms with the deeper struggles of humankind, of society. The set is their archive. The play is their search, thoughts, emotions and reflections. Somewhere a clock is ticking. When a chorus song starts, the clock stops and time stands still. The chorus songs slow down the tragic events and we reside with them in the subconscious of the society of Thebes. The chorus is constituted of senior advisors to the king of Thebes, but they also represent the people of Thebes. This latter idea will be our main focus, as our chorus will consist of a young man, a woman and an older man. Looking closer at the chorus songs, we see that they cover the whole intellectual and emotional scope of the main characters and of the play. The chorus listens, really listens to what Kreon, Antigone and others tell them. They listen and adapt their point of view accordingly. They are also empathic, they don't hide when they are moved or horrified. They are the way people should be. They can be critical, neutral, mad or sad. One thing they are not: hypocrites.

The chorus's journey starts with total support for the new political views of Kreon. When Antigone enters, they immediately empathize ('O you poor awful child of poor awful Oidipous'[85]). After the intense exchange between Antigone and Kreon, and later also Ismene, the chorus start to broaden their outlook and their awareness. They tell Kreon the gods are responsible for what has come to pass, that it is part of a long history of the haunted House of Atreus. It's as if they were digging into the archives of the city to make Kreon aware of the power of the gods. The balance between a man-made society and one dominated by the gods shifts even more when they describe the inevitable influence of Eros on Haimon. Haimon can't help being in love with Antigone and being blinded by this love. They even criticize Antigone when she compares herself to Niobe, a goddess: 'but Niobe was a god / born of gods / we are mortal / born of mortals'.[86] They come to a harsh judgement of Antigone, holding her responsible for disrespecting the gods and the laws of Thebes. She is 'too extreme'.[87] They turn their backs on her. But, as they are only human, unrest lingers and they dig even deeper into the archive of the city, bringing to memory the fate of three young women, or even a child that suffered terrible tortures because of the hubris of a parent. It's as if they were starting to remind Kreon that he is also only human and the gods could also turn against . . . him. They don't state it clearly, they are more surreptitious, but their message is clear enough for someone who wants to listen.

When Teiresias enters, they keep silent. They know he only comes when there is a real problem and that he speaks the truth, always. Teiresias lifts the play to another level. He states that this is not a battle between humans or between humans and gods, but rather a battle with consequences for the whole cosmos. And, what the chorus didn't dare to say or even think, he says to Kreon: '*the cause is you*'.[88] As stated earlier, the chorus began with the conviction that Kreon's new policies would bring necessary change for a better future for the tortured city of Thebes. Gradually they understand Kreon's idea of a man-made city outside the power of the gods. However the imprisonment of Antigone and, ultimately, the warning of Teiresias lead them to conclude: 'take advice . . . set the girl free bury the boy'.[89] But they also do something amazing on their own: they start to scream, to appeal to Bacchus for help. In a craze, they dance dervishes in an effort to purify the city. At the same time we witness the actual execution of Antigone's suicide, she ends her story herself, staging her own death, keeping control till the bitter end.

But the catastrophes are unstoppable; Kreon's effort to turn around his punishments comes too late. Teiresias was right again. The quick exit of Eurydike is another bad omen. She will also kill herself. The chorus is alone on stage when Kreon comes home to an empty house that is no longer a home. His wife Eurydice is dead; his two sons Megareus and Haimon are dead. Like Antigone, Kreon is 'alone on his insides'.[90] He has been driven by a sincere ambition to turn Thebes, his beloved city, into a better place and has failed because he made his first law the symbol of his new policy and his authority. In every scene he is given the chance to adjust his law but he can't. His inflexibility, his incapacity to think outside the box will lead him to his downfall, publicly and, even more painfully, privately. He is a broken man, who tried to make a difference and failed. The chorus's conclusion is that life is eternal learning, keeping the right balance between rational wisdom and respect for the irrational power of the gods. Kreon doesn't kill himself. He leaves the stage to go to the morgue where the body of Antigone is kept and, finally, embraces her.

Ismene is still on stage. Ismene is an intriguing character. She is not what she seems to be. She doesn't urge compromise. She asks Antigone to compromise so they can finally go on with their lives. Ismene has a firm and clear point of view, with all due respect to her brothers, her father and her mother, she has made the decision that it is time to end the string of dead bodies and never-ending mourning. She lights a match and sets the archive on fire. It consumes the whole past, the whole archive of Thebes, and thus creates the possibility for a real new beginning.

Among the ruins a tree begins to grow.

The Festival Performances of Ivo van Hove and Toneelgroep Amsterdam

'EVERYWHERE WE TRAVELLED WE BECAME THE CENTRE OF THE FESTIVAL'

Keren Zaiontz

To understand the global reach of Ivo van Hove's work and the ambitious repertoire he has directed as part of Toneelgroep Amsterdam (TGA), it is important to examine the role of the international festival circuit. While the name is eponymous with the city, theatre audiences often experience TGA *not* as a resident company, but as an international ensemble that has, since 2001, served as a kind of laboratory for van Hove's sprawling directorial vision. The history of the stage *auteur* who tours with an ensemble is inextricable from that of modern festivals. Storied productions such as the Living Theatre's *Paradise Now* (1968), Peter Brook's *Mahabharata* (1985) or Robert Lepage's *Seven Streams of the River Ota* (1994) each have their own unique touring histories to festivals and arts centres. These histories are attendant with what has become a stock narrative about the charisma of uncompromising directors, the dedication of ensembles to experimental performance, the anecdotes of spectators who persisted through durational events, and the division among critics who either lauded or opposed the work. All of these elements combine to create a *festival performance* – the *must see*, event-within-an-event show. Of course, much has changed from the *Mahabharata* to the present, as the larger currents of globalization have transformed West/East divides, shifting centre and periphery. Distinct theatrical interpretations rooted in productions that essentially annexed the culture of the non-Western other have, in part, given way to festival works that scrutinize the West's institutions and so-called masterpieces.

Building a repertoire that ranges from durational Shakespeare to the adaptation of popular novels and films, van Hove and TGA have contributed to the changing landscape of the touring production as a site where the West gazes back at the stories they tell about themselves. Most notably, festival performances such as *Roman Tragedies* and *Kings of War* literally move the audience up close to Shakespeare's texts by using multiple cameras and monitors and by encouraging spectators to move throughout the playhouse.[1] The adoption of monitors and mobility not only asserts the viability of the theatre as a communal site of deliberation in an era of dispersed connectivity, but that of the festival as a site that continues to shake up the usual ground rules of performance.

In the interviews that follow with Ivo van Hove and TGA's co-director, Wouter van Ransbeek, both independently talk of the festival as a space that reinvents theatrical convention and the stage–audience relationship. It is the promise of an *event* that has also established TGA as a reoccurring presence on festival stages. Van Ransbeek, who has been key to developing relationships with festival producers that set regional and global programming trends, discusses how TGA's epic productions have, in some instances, functioned as a gateway to the company's larger repertoire. These works, all of which are essentially 'tour ready', have often been pitched to programmers on the heels of a successful festival performance. Van Hove brings to the TGA touring productions his experience managing the Holland Festival from 1998 to 2004, while van Ransbeek has worked with the Vienna Festival and Germany's triennial Theater der Welt. The wealth of experience that van Hove and van Ransbeek have had managing, programming and producing festivals in continental Europe has been formative to the operations of TGA. In this section, they discuss how their respective backgrounds (and networks) laid the groundwork for building a resident company that tours van Hove's signature range of monumental and minimalist productions.[2]

IN CONVERSATION WITH IVO VAN HOVE (JUNE 2017): THE HOLLAND FESTIVAL

KZ   Can you speak to what the existing culture of the Holland Festival was like when you first assumed the role of manager? How did it compare to other performing arts festivals in Europe, and how did the Holland Festival change over your tenure between 1998 and 2004?

IvH   Traditionally, the Holland Festival is one of these great festivals where opera, theatre, dance, music and music theatre are presented. It belongs to the festivals established in Europe after the Second World War (such as the Edinburgh Festival), when culture was needed to make sure that we were still human beings, that we were going to resist violence, that we were going to be inclusive rather than excluding people. It has never been a real creation festival; rather, it programs things that already exist in the world. The festival was long a site for Dutch music including the wonderful ensemble-culture and smaller orchestras. It had always been run by someone with a music background – a manager or a composer. Before I joined the organization, the analysis by the supervisory board was that they needed more international theatre and a program that attracted younger people, so that it had a future and was not only part of the establishment. There was a feeling among politicians, society and the public that the festival had become a little old-fashioned. Enthusiasm had waned and there was a desire for change.

The tradition is that the Queen – or the King now – comes to open the Holland Festival. And people feel that's good, but let's also get out of the box, let's get a little bit more contemporary, more crazy! So, that was my mission, that's what they asked me to do: to program more international theatre and attract new audiences. And that's what happened. I did that immediately. I increased the number of theatre productions, but I also kept the balance with dance, music, music theatre and opera. But even the music underwent a change in direction because, traditionally, it had been the likes of composers such as Pierre Boulez and Karlheinz Stockhausen. Even though there was resistance, I opened it up to more popular work. For instance, in 2000, I did a big project with Brian Eno about Frank Zappa, in which we recreated his *200 Motels* (1971) in a new way. In 2003, we did a program with John Zorn, reuniting his band Naked City for one night, live on stage. When I first opened the festival it was a little bit too much change – there was a lot of resistance from composers and ensembles who felt that they owned the festival.

KZ   Why did you want to bring experimental art music onto the festival stage?

IvH   It was a different kind of music and one of my favourite questions at the time was, why is somebody who plays on an electric guitar less valuable than somebody playing a Stradivarius? In Holland, this was not done at the time – culture was strictly valued as an elite activity. I said 'no, we have to bring in the so-called "low culture" because that is the high culture of today and tomorrow'. So it was not only a program but a statement – of course, the program reflected that statement. And immediately, I attracted a lot of young people. I did the works that were presented in the opera house but opened it up to the public. Today it's very obvious because everybody does it everywhere, but I streamed the productions. This way we could show it to thousands of people who could enjoy Wagner in the open air in the park; people who never could have otherwise afforded tickets to go to the opera house. It was a huge success and it also opened up what they call 'high culture' to a broader audience. That, in short, was my mission: bringing high quality productions to as large an audience as possible.

KZ   And do you feel that the shaking up of the music program, updating it, is your most valuable contribution to the festival? Or is there one production or collaboration that jumps out at you as a highlight of managing the Holland Festival?

IvH   There were so many highlights, both theatre as well as dance and music productions. I programmed a lot of work by directors that audiences didn't yet know here at all. It was the end of the 1990s, early 2000s, I brought in Sasha Waltz & Guests, Meg Stuart, Thomas Ostermeier, Romeo Castellucci (I brought him three times – they hated it, but I kept on going!). I already knew there was a huge music theatre tradition hidden in Europe and I wanted the festival to showcase that new practice. We had plenty of that and, as I said, I worked to make opera as accessible as possible to the public, but I also wanted to open up space for music theatre works such as Heiner Goebbels' *Schwarz auf Weiss/Black on White* (1998) and Christoph Marthaler's very contemporary staging of *Die schöne Müllerin* (2003) (*The Maid in the Mill* song cycle by Franz Schubert, based on the poems of Wilhem Müller). My main achievement was bringing in a lot of new choreographers, new directors, new composers. They needed an international platform, and I knew they could fill the house, which they did most of the time.

KZ   What approaches did you carry forward from the Holland Festival to the management of TGA?

IvH   Before I managed the Holland Festival, I already had an international network that only increased during my time at the festival. I brought that international experience to TGA and since then we have travelled all over the world. Of course, a festival is very different from running a theatre company, particularly a repertory company. In a festival, you work during the year with a very small team – ten, twelve people – and then in the last month it becomes a big organization, with hundreds of people, and you 'attack' as I always put it, for three weeks, working day and night, day and night, day and night. It's like a guerilla action. With a repertory company, the dynamics are totally different: you work every day and you make consistent work every day. At the same time, the festival created a natural context for the work that I did afterwards with TGA, which is a project for the long term. Developing and refreshing an ensemble of fabulous actresses and actors, creating a body of work that we can keep playing. We always have thirty productions in repertory that we can perform. Some play for more than ten years. A festival is a very intense three weeks; a repertory company is a whole year and every day. Both are great!

IN CONVERSATION WITH WOUTER VAN RANSBEEK (AUGUST 2016): TONEELGROEP AMSTERDAM AND INTERNATIONAL FESTIVALS

KZ You wear multiple hats in your role as co-director of TGA. Can you speak about how you came into the role of creative producer for the company?

WvR I started to work for international festivals when I was twenty-two. I had just completed university when I took on the job of personal assistant to Gerard Mortier (1943–2014), founding director of the Ruhrtriënnale. Mortier was an ambitious manager and had a reputation for producing large-scale operas and musical works at centres like Théâtre de la Monnaie (1981–92) and the Salzburg Festival (1992–2001). In 2002, he was building what was then a new festival in Ruhr, Germany, and I came from Belgium (where I'm originally from) to work for him. I think it was my second day at the office that I met Ivo van Hove but, at that point, we didn't really have much contact. Following the Ruhrtriënnale, I moved to the Vienna Festival where I worked in a more curatorial capacity as a programming assistant. At that time, it was easily one of the most international festivals in the world. There was a lot of money, and we travelled. I saw close to 200 productions a year outside Vienna. Every other day I was on a plane going somewhere in Europe and beyond just to see theatre.

It was during my travels in 2003 that I first saw van Hove's work. I was completely blown away by *Scenes from a Marriage*.[3] My boss, general director Luc Bondy, had already worked with van Hove and we wanted to establish a closer affiliation, so we asked him to direct a remake of John Cassavetes' play *Faces* for the Theatre der Welt festival in Germany (2005). He came over for two months, I showed him around the city and we hung out, eating dinner together practically every night. A year later he called me and said, 'I've got a job for you.'

KZ   When you reflect on your role within TGA, what do you think has been your most significant contribution to the company?

WvR   First, I wanted to make the company international. Second, I wanted the company to act as a training ground for young directors. In Holland, as elsewhere, there is a big gap between the established cultural institutions and graduates fresh out of school. Traditionally, young theatre artists tend to form their own collectives and do smaller, more experimental work. The big theatres are often regarded as old-fashioned. When I look back on it, these two initial goals have moved to the centre of the company. And I have moved with it as co-director of Toneelgroep. Today, Ivo and I run the theatre together.

KZ   What does that look like in a day-to-day way?

WvR   I'm on the ground at the beginning of the process when we choose the repertoire, when we assemble the teams. There's the chief dramaturg Johan [Reyniers], me, set designer Jan [Versweyveld] and Ivo. We basically make all the decisions in a kind of open atmosphere about what we're going to do next. I'm also involved in the casting, and in establishing the general parameters for the production. Once the production starts, I step back. I'm not involved in rehearsals. Only at the end of the rehearsal process, in general, do I come in and watch the production with the dramaturge to offer minor feedback. I sometimes say my job is to maximize artistic output, to remind everyone that we are here to make art, and that is where our energies should lie rather than getting lost in the fine details of the production.

KZ   As co-director, you often work as a cultural broker, which has been key to the global success of the company.

WvR   I think I've always been very good at liaising between artists and producers. I have a knack for reverse programming, anticipating what might be appealing to other countries. I've acted as a liaison between programmers and the work of Ivo, translating the big ideas that we've developed together. Early on, we made a decision to concentrate on two or three spots in the world because we knew that, if we were programmed there, everyone would take notice. We were very lucky in that we had experience travelling on behalf of the Holland and Vienna Festivals. We could draw upon our networks and, importantly, we knew which festivals were willing to take risks and essentially serve as the avant-garde.

KZ   Which festivals, then, did you set your sights on?

WvR   It had to be a festival or a partner that was interested in establishing a relationship with us rather than simply staging a one-off production. (Of course, first we had to agree to one-offs, but our intention was to establish long-term relationships.) We concentrated on North America and Europe at the same time and started conversations with sites like Festival d'Avignon. Presenting Ivo's *Roman Tragedies* at Avignon in 2008 immediately led to our being programmed in cultural centres and festivals globally. For example, *Roman Tragedies* at FTA [Festival TransAmériques] was an immediate reaction of the programmer who saw it in Avignon. The Barbican was also an immediate consequence of us playing in Avignon.

KZ   I can see why programmers gravitated towards it. *Roman Tragedies* has all the markers of a festival performance.

WvR   It's significant that our first contact with programmers was an *event*. At the time, it was new to bring multiple works, side-by-side, in one production. Because it's six hours long, because it's the Bard on stage, because it's Shakespeare but different, everywhere we travelled, we became the centre of the festival.

KZ   Can you talk more about that aesthetics of eventness, because it seems like it is tied to bringing together – in the case of *Roman Tragedies* – a whole set of works. Here, avant-garde is not an event that unfolds in the margins but a blockbuster production.

WvR   A blockbuster that resembles a kind of Netflix series. *Roman Tragedies* is a good, real-time story with cliffhangers. Putting these tragedies together [*Coriolanus*, *Julius Caesar*, *Antony and Cleopatra*] said more about the construction of politics than could be contained in a single play. As a spectator, you're able to witness the trials of three

Figure 12 Roman Tragedies *at the Adelaide Festival (2014).*

Figure 13 The Damned *at the Avignon Festival (2016).*

leaders [Coriolanus, Julius Caesar, Cleopatra], and shoulder-to-shoulder, these three reveal more about the others than sometimes they do about themselves. Jan and Ivo are so aware about what's happening on stage, but also about how spectators perceive shows, and that's why they've experimented so much with moving the audience, letting them be onstage, offstage, letting them have the flexibility to leave the theatre and come back. A generation raised on surround sound will not sit in a theatre trying to understand an act that they would not engage if they weren't fully immersed. You have to adapt your set design. We included a lot of video to bring some aspects of the experience closer. That's what I loved about travelling to the US and Canada: they immediately picked up on the fact that our storytelling unfolds in a simultaneous manner; you will not be able to understand everything and it's not necessary.

KZ   **There is certainly a lot of latitude given to audiences in TGA shows.**

WvR   They [Jan and Ivo] understand that it's a dance between two parties and they can direct this dance incredibly well. And in a way, that's also why these festivals were drawn to the production. The main focus of festivals has always been the audience – how to get audiences into the hall, how to engage them, how to give them a different experience, particularly a different experience within the theatre. *Roman Tragedies* is both something we've never witnessed and completely resonant with an Elizabethan theatre culture in which spectators drank, shouted, watched their entertainments from the pit. All these cultural institutions where we've performed have had to deal with traditional repertoires, with Shakespeare, with Ibsen, with how to come to grips with the canon in the twenty-first century. Ivo and Jan can *do* classics, they can revitalize them for audiences, and they endow them with a different experience.

KZ   **Where do you go as a company after producing and touring something as iconoclastic as *Roman Tragedies*?**

WvR   For Ivo, it was very difficult. As a theatre maker, he was a bit lost for two or three years following *Roman Tragedies*. When you've done something that huge it's very difficult to go back to one play. What other people would consider an immense project suddenly seemed small. That's why we waited so long to do another Shakespeare trilogy, *Kings of War* (2015). The good thing was that after *Roman Tragedies* we had, in our repertoire, *Scenes from a Marriage* (2005), *Opening Night* (2006), *Angels in America* (2008).[4] *Roman Tragedies* allowed us to engage in a conversation about programming the next work. And we have continued to use this production and our larger repertoire to establish new partnerships. Six years after its debut, we brought *Roman Tragedies* to BAM [Brooklyn Academy of Music]. We knew we had a success on our hands, but we had to first gain an audience. Those very same ingredients that make a festival performance a success can also prove too tall an order for new audiences: it's six hours, it's durational, it's Dutch Shakespeare. If you're not a famous company, it's difficult. But once again, we were able to ride the wave of this production and establish ourselves as a sustained presence. *Roman Tragedies* led to the US première of *Kings of War* at BAM's Next Wave Festival (2016).[5]

KZ   It's interesting that the production has been a kind of gateway to your repertory system.

WvR   In this regard, the group of people that he assembled, working for fifteen years here, has shaped his body of work and the way he's producing theatre right now. The development of his theatrical language and technical innovations really happened here. He refers to TGA as his experimental laboratory. And, as I've been saying, from the start we've worked with a handful of festivals around the world to put our works into larger circulation, something that has only been made possible by our repertory structure. It's an incredible advantage to say to a festival or cultural institution, 'yes, we can bring the production we made last season'. It also means that Ivo has been able to continuously show his work. And if you're able to show an artist's work over a number of years, an audience will follow this artist, and will be able to understand what they are seeing as part of an oeuvre. You become more than a programming trend; you're something that's here to stay. That, I think, is what we have been able to do in France, England, New York and a bit in Australia. Now it's become normal for us to return to these sites every few years with something new, something different. We slowly built a presence for Ivo's work, which is much more difficult for UK and North American directors, because their productions often disappear after an initial run. And our international audience has gotten bigger and bigger. We have around 140,000 people that come to see our shows every year, including 50,000 spectators outside Holland.

KZ   I imagine this global reach has led to a fair share of co-productions.

WvR   And not just co-productions in Germany or France but also the US. We're now slowly approaching centres in Asia and Latin America. The 2008 economic crisis provoked a mental 'old regime' European crisis. Our co-production monies across the continent shrank; we had difficulties. So we moved outside Europe, which has kept us fresh and has also had the added privilege of keeping our attention fixed on stagecraft. During this period, I was travelling to cities like Seoul to discuss potential projects and my instinct was to pitch smaller, more cost-effective projects. At one point someone actually stopped me and asked that I not discuss the production details, but the vision for the project. I realized how much I had internalized this crisis mentality. Just a couple of seasons ago we brought *Othello* to Taipei as part of the National Theatre Concert Hall's biennial International Theatre Festival (2014) to mark Shakespeare's 450th birthday. This was a production that has been in our repertoire for over a decade, but we wanted to start with a piece that Taipei audiences could readily connect to. This year [2016] we're going back with *The Fountainhead*, and I think, now that we've laid the ground with *Othello*, there will be an openness to the production. In that way the repertory system helps us acclimatize new audiences.[6]

KZ   It's interesting how this back catalogue of productions can be used in a festival context to expand an audience's horizon of expectations, moving them into increasingly more complex and experimental work.

WvR   A festival should be a site where you create a context to present work which is not part of the normal, day-to-day theatrical landscape within a city or even a country. An injection that hopefully inspires the local theatre culture. Ultimately, we are very careful about what we bring and why we bring it, as we are typically invited once or twice a year, or every other year. If you make one mistake, you've cost a lot of money, and you're not going to be easily invited back. The result is that audiences won't see that next production of yours. Their sole judgement will rest on the one production.

KZ   I'm wondering – is that a common production model to have a repertoire of shows that you can then offer to festivals?

WvR   It's not unique to play repertoire, but it is unique to combine the structures of a touring and repertory company. The original companies in Holland were all touring organizations that travelled throughout the country and, in some cases, to theatres throughout the world. We reversed that. We had young international talent, and we wanted to become a kind of resident theatre in Amsterdam. That's why we built our new theatre here – we invested a lot in growing our local audiences. But we also still tour.

Everything is made to fit in containers. Even when we make a set, we immediately start itemizing every piece because when it goes abroad we have to provide a list to customs. So everything is built to be shipped and road ready.

KZ   So how does this tour readiness shape the way Jan and the company approaches its set design?

WvR   It's a paradox because I know no one who makes the type of big sets that typify many of our best-known works. Jan and Ivo are really known now for productions like *Roman Tragedies* and *Kings of War* with immense, complex sets. Even our smallest production, *The Human Voice* (2009), for example, includes an incredibly long window. It's one window, it's heavy, and creates a problem just about everywhere in the world it travels. In Italy, they had to open the roof of the theatre. So while we're prepared to tour, the set pieces themselves do not necessarily conform to standardized shipping practices. When we first discuss productions, we are not immediately thinking of its touring feasibility, but as soon as we make the decision to tour then preparations begin. This includes travel maximums. Everything must fit onto three trucks. Of course, we have to consider the financial practicalities of each production and whether it's possible or not to produce it. But, mostly, Ivo's productions are vast. They have wind machines, rain machines. This monumental scenography is part of the company's signature style.

KZ   Do festivals ever demand that you moderate your vision for budgetary reasons?

WvR   The funny thing is, it's much more difficult to tour mid-scale shows at this moment because people do not want to invest in that. The rationale is that, if you're going to invest in a co-production, then you want to see fireworks. But it's only possible if your way of telling stories is big enough. You need a big, epic story to tell something with power. Of course, sometimes a small story can be epic – I'm thinking here of our Ingmar Bergman productions.

KZ   Yes, I've seen *Scenes from a Marriage*, and it's remarkable how films, as well as novels, have been taken up by TGA as source texts for stage adaptations. Clearly, you have been able to adapt these texts on their own distinct theatrical terms.

WvR   If you consider the role of film and TV repertoires then you have to admit that more people have knowledge of screen than stage works. I mean, a lot of my contemporaries simply aren't familiar with Shakespeare's repertoire (they've never seen *Othello*, for example), but they know movies. Beyond the familiarity factor, films offer opportunities to revisit topics from a theatrical point of view. And, like any artistic mode, theatre has its own rules, its own form of storytelling, which has the potential to result in a more direct relationship with certain characters. When compared with narrative fiction filmmaking, the lack of realism in theatre makes for an incredibly powerful tool to re-imagine certain stories. Many of our film adaptations have had premières at festivals because, like the combined Shakespeare productions, it's often never been done. The uniqueness of these stage worlds, their eventness, is attractive to festivals.

KZ   **What do you think is the future of the festival given that audiences have this desire for adaptations, narrative combines (e.g., *Roman Tragedies*, *Kings of War*), and multiple entry points within the very apparatus of the theatre?**

WvR   For me, the real question is, will performing arts festivals even continue to have the same impact in the future? A lot of the bigger international festivals have an identity crisis on their hands. *What are we?* Established after the Second World War, they are no longer the kind of window into the other they once were, since the very notion of accessibility, and the staging of different cultures have themselves been reconfigured into a series of online searches. A young artist can google and have direct contact with an artist half way round the world, watching their work on YouTube. Today, you have a contingent of audiences who can travel, often relatively cheaply, to see our resident work here, so a lot has changed since the establishment of these post-war festivals.

KZ   **In what ways do you think that instantaneous accessibility you describe has shaped the contemporary festival landscape?**

WvR   One of the challenges of today's performing arts festivals is that they often show so much work that it's nearly impossible for everyone to see everything, so there is no real debate over the programming. Moreover, these festivals, and I count the Holland Festival among them, regularly promote projects *with*, and artists *from*, the city. The result is that almost every urban core has become saturated with the same types of events, which, as a spectator and programmer, can quickly start to wear thin.

KZ The criticism (for years now) has been that such work risks serving as a form of civic boosterism – a stage for promoting the city at the expense of the art.

WvR I think a core group of festivals have managed to balance these economic imperatives with rigorous programming. Festival d'Avignon remains a place where, if you present there, you will be sharing your work with an incredibly international audience; the FTA is a very important site for North America; if you go to the Adelaide Festival in Australia, then programmers from different parts of Asia will look very closely at your work. And it's a very small world. You travel to certain destinations knowing that all these programmers will be there. So you know that next year this particular work will be everywhere.

KZ Perhaps, then, the answer to the question of the 'future of the festival' is to resist a factory model of constantly pumping out new programming.

WvR It would be incredible to make a festival that only takes those productions that really stand out. Such a festival would remove itself from the race to be first and from the pressure to program an abundance of work, and it would start to model a more sustainable method of programming for audiences and organizations alike.

Section Three

American Theatre

IVO VAN HOVE AND THE ART OF HUMANITY

Joshua E. Polster

The Coolidge Corner Theatre in Brookline, Massachusetts was one of many cinema venues to present Arthur Miller's *A View From the Bridge* as part of the 2016 National Theatre Live's Encore Series. It was a broadcast of the Young Vic's 'magnetic, electrifying, astonishingly bold' 2014 production of Miller's play, directed by Ivo van Hove, about Brooklyn longshoreman Eddie Carbone's doomed entangled relationships with his wife, niece and illegal immigrant cousins.[1] The production, which transferred to the West End's Wyndham's Theatre, won three Olivier Awards – Best Revival, Best Actor for Mark Strong and Best Director for Ivo van Hove. It quickly caught the attention of Broadway, where it continued at the Lyceum Theatre and garnered 2016 Tony Awards for Best Revival and Best Direction. The *Independent* described van Hove's 'unforgettable' production as 'emotionally devastating', which was clearly on display at the Coolidge Corner Theatre, where there was a stunned silence in the audience after the film concluded with powerful poetic imagery and moving performances.[2] The devastated Carbone family, in their final moments together, desperately grasped each other in a primal and protective huddle as blood rained down upon them. Watching the production, as the *Guardian* aptly described it, was 'like watching a runaway train hurtle towards you and being unable to move'.[3] At the Brookline cinema, among the many admiring van Hove's work, was Obie Award-winning director Melia Bensussen:

> As another theatre director, I am inspired by his ability to really zero in on an idea or metaphor, as well as the thoroughness [. . . and] depth of pursuit of his vision, which I just admire enormously [. . . It] was very influential for me to see that ability to shape everything towards the idea. . . . I was intellectually riveted by this *View From the Bridge*.[4]

The production of *A View from the Bridge*, of course, was not the first time van Hove directed a US play in its country of origin. In 1999, for instance, he won the Best Direction Obie Award for New York Theatre Workshop's production of *More Stately Mansions* by Eugene O'Neill. In fact, New York Theatre Workshop has been van Hove's primary place of work in the United States, where he also directed, among others,

Figure 14 *From left, Catherine (Phoebe Fox), Rodolpho (Luke Norris), Marco (Emun Elliott), Eddie (Mark Strong) and Beatrice (Nicola Walker),* A View from the Bridge, *Young Vic, London (2014).*

Tennessee Williams' *A Streetcar Named Desire* (1998), Susan Sontag's *Alice in Bed* (2000) and Lillian Hellman's *The Little Foxes* (2010). In 2014, van Hove also brought his TGA production of Tony Kushner's *Angels in America* to the Brooklyn Academy of Music (BAM). Van Hove triumphantly returned to Broadway with another Miller play *The Crucible* at the Walter Kerr Theatre (2016), which was nominated for the Outer Critics Circle Award, the Drama League Award and the Tony Award for Best Revival. Most recently, TGA's production of Ayn Rand's *The Fountainhead*, directed by van Hove, was staged at the 2017 Next Wave Festival at BAM.

With his highly successful stagings of some of the greatest works by American dramatists, van Hove has emerged as one of the most important and sought-after directors of US plays. Indeed, as Marvin Carlson has noted, 'he has received more productions in New York than all of the other continental theatre directors combined, many of whom, equally important in Europe and elsewhere, have yet to be produced in New York at all'.[5] Van Hove has brought a power and personal intimacy to each of his productions that have given new life to older American plays and deeply moved audiences in unexpected ways. In conversation with Ben Whishaw, who played protagonist John Proctor in *The Crucible*, he discussed this interesting relationship between van Hove and his audiences: 'It's completely beguiling the way he's constantly moving the audience from detachment to intimacy ... He does such strange, sophisticated things with theatre – like no-one else.'[6] For van Hove, unlike the plays he previously wrote and directed, he learned to find this intimacy through the pre-existing work of others:

> What I have done before felt less personal when it was my own texts ... I discovered for myself that I could make personal work through the filter of old texts ... even in a text that [... was written] over 400 years ago or 50–60 years ago. I could tell even more about myself, about what I thought about the world, of people, of mankind by using a text by a good author.[7]

Some of these 'good authors', in particular, have been US playwrights like Eugene O'Neill, Lillian Hellman, Tennessee Williams, Arthur Miller, Susan Sontag and Tony Kushner. In each of these dramatists' work, van Hove found new and exciting ways to strip artifice and reach the core of the plays to better communicate himself and, in extension, the human condition.

It is interesting to note that this Belgian-born artist has become one of the most trusted directors of some of the most trusted American plays. It calls to mind a recent controversy brought up by African-American actor Samuel L. Jackson who critiqued the casting of black British actor Daniel Kaluuya as the protagonist for the US movie *Get Out*, which tells the story of an African-American man victimized by white liberal racism in suburban America. Jackson wondered 'what that movie would have been with an American brother who really feels that'. Mr Jackson's comment largely dealt with issues of race, but nationality played a significant part in it as well. 'Daniel', Jackson observed, 'grew up in a country where they've been interracial dating for a hundred years. What would a brother from America have made of that role?' There, indeed, are complexities and complications to this viewpoint, but, according to *Guardian* columnists Gary Younge and Joseph Harker, 'Is it a valid point? Absolutely.'[8]

Similar arguments have also been applied to directing, specifically the nationality of plays and their assigned directors. Can a Belgian director truly understand and, to use Jackson's words, 'really feel' the trials and tribulations of a Brooklyn longshoreman? How would American audiences receive such work? According to the Tony Awards committee and many theatre viewers in the United States, van Hove definitely 'got it'. Still, there is validity to this critical viewpoint, according to US director Melia Bensussen, who sees a curious trend toward assigning US plays to international over American directors:

> In a way, [the casting of an international director to a US play] is a mistrust of our own work (if I count myself as an American). We feel like it's important if it's done in an [international] style as opposed to an American vocabulary ... I think there should be room for both.[9]

In an interview David Lan, the South African-born playwright, social anthropologist and artistic director of the Young Vic, discussed his rationale and approach to bringing together the international director and his favourite Miller play *A View From the Bridge*:

> It happened because I admired [van Hove's] work and my job is to find the most interesting, adventurous, innovative, intellectually [and] artistically leading directors *wherever* I find them and invite them to come work with us [... Regarding] the point of view that only American directors can direct an American play ... I don't care about that stuff. I'm totally uninterested in nationality. I'm only interested in the ability of the director to communicate a play to an audience ... If we start doing that [having US plays directed only by US directors], we limit ourselves. The whole point about art is that anybody can speak to anybody.[10]

This is a significant point for those who believe in the importance of keeping art universal and accessible, especially in a dangerous political climate that spouts a necessity to build ideological and physical walls between nations.

One might still ask, though, what would an American director have made of *Angels in America*, Kushner's gripping portrait of life and death in New York during the start of the AIDS epidemic, as opposed to a European artist from a Dutch theatre company? This last query, of course, has an answer. American director David Esbjornson directed the compelling world première in San Francisco, American director George C. Wolfe won a Tony for his direction of the excellent 1993 Broadway première, and countless other US directors have had their turn with *Angels in America* throughout its long production history (and Kushner's play has also had highly successful productions by other international directors throughout the world, including Marianne Elliott's 2017 production at London's National Theatre).

Plays, when compared to movie scripts like *Get Out*, have greater opportunities to live beyond their première productions, and to express themselves in innovative and exciting ways when they are revived and revived with different casts and creative teams.

Movies do get reproduced, but not at the rate and range of theatrical texts, especially classics and well-received new dramatic work. This is one of the great strengths of theatre, as is the ability of plays to take on new meanings when in new hands – hands from different races, ethnicities, genders, sexualities and, yes, nationalities. Moving beyond a strictly American lens and providing international perspectives, such as from a Belgian director, allow US plays to engage in richer conversations – at home as well as abroad. It allows audiences, as said by van Hove, to better consider what these plays mean to each of them, to their unique societies and worlds. It creates deeper layers of signification, as well as universal resonances, without necessarily losing any of the plays' important particular referents. There is no need for an artistic face-off between national and international direction. As Bensussen said, there simply should be room for both.

Van Hove's production of *Angels in America*, for instance, provided one of several significant interpretations of Kushner's great work, and it was another huge success. 'This is in many ways', according to *The New York Times*, 'the most penetrating *Angels* that I've seen ... Mr. van Hove finds a universal heart that seems destined to beat, loudly and steadily, for as long as there is Theatre.'[11] Kushner, who attended a performance, agreed:

> I was absolutely gripped by it from the very beginning ... It had this feeling of being stripped to its absolute bare bones ... You can decide to make [*Angels in America*] more about politics than anything else, more about interpersonal dynamics, more about theology, or spirituality, and I've seen productions that do all of that. But Ivo's production was very much about the frailty and fragility of the human body. I found it overwhelmingly moving. And I left [the theatre] sort of floating on air, feeling like, this is what it's all about.[12]

Collected in this section are new scholarship and interviews on some of van Hove's most gripping work of American plays performed in the United States – *Angels in America, The Little Foxes* and *The Crucible*. They are a testament of the power of theatre, the importance of providing new international perspectives and, above all, van Hove's craft – his ability to cut through artifice to find the art of humanity.

THE LITTLE FOXES: *A MODERN MORALITY TALE ABOUT RESTRICTION AND GREED*

Susan C. W. Abbotson

In a 2010 production at the New York Theatre Workshop under the direction of Ivo van Hove, Lillian Hellman's *The Little Foxes,* largely divested of its Southern and period associations, became a parable for rapacious capitalism of the twenty-first century and a digression on the continued subjection of women. As Marilyn Stasio suggested, 'the ugly emotions so nakedly exposed by the directorial demolition job reveal a timeliness that is downright terrifying', and while van Hove allowed the women to speak out more freely in his production, they were also shown to be 'more exposed and vulnerable' in their clingy, sleek costumes, rather than the usual period dress.[13]

Instead of the usual turn-of-the-twentieth-century dining room and parlour of an opulent Southern mansion, the action occurred in a single, constricting, minimalistic box set of regal purple velvet designed by Jan Versweyveld, with walls against which actors literally bounced in anger and rabid frustration; each member of the family a powder keg of pent-up emotion, including Alexandra, Birdie and Horace, despite his infirmity (see Plate 8). As van Hove explained: 'The play raises the ethical problem of gaining prosperity through destruction. It describes also the devastating influences this has on the human psychology, on their private lives. Capitalism is a jungle, a struggle for life and has nothing to do with civilization.'[14] The coldness of the set, despite its plush coverings with skeletal chandeliers, a small, unused spinet and tiny footstool revealed the emptiness of this family's grasping – and they have trapped themselves in this box.

Within the box was another large box, centre stage, which emulated a mantelpiece with a gilt-framed, blank video screen above (where one might expect a family portrait). This began playing off-stage scenes, in the second act, such as Horace preparing to return and the family in their dining room. Instead of a fireplace, beneath the mantel was the ominous side-view of the rising white steps of a staircase. Rather than the expected melodrama, the audience were given front-row seats to a modern morality play about restriction and greed that ran for an intermission-less two hours.

It was not that van Hove eradicates Hellman's melodramatic moments, but rather that he leant into them, replete with dark, pulsing music provided by Thibaud Delpeut, to underscore the horrors about to be witnessed, the music rising at key damaging

Figure 15 *From left, Addie (Lynda Gravatt), Regina Giddens (Elizabeth Marvel) and Alexandra (Cristin Milioti),* The Little Foxes, *New York Theatre Workshop (2010).*

moments of action. Here was a family that 'preys together' rather than 'prays', and, like the Ouroboros, will hopefully end up eating its own evil tail; a fitting metaphor for a family so willing to destroy its own, though in their destructiveness they establish themselves as a continuing threat to others, and this was a threat about which van Hove was explicitly clear. 'A once civilized world became barbaric', he explained; 'Hellman shows us a family of predators, a new breed of industrial capitalists, driven by greed'.[15] It is a cycle of damage and violence from which he suggests it is almost impossible to escape, especially if black or female, although Alexandra is allowed a way out by the play's end – as she is shown exiting the closed set and walking away into the outside world on the screen.

Foxes depicts three Hubbard siblings, Ben, Oscar and Regina, who take on a Northern partner, Marshall, to build a new mill. The brothers need Regina's ailing husband, Horace, to contribute some financing, but he initially declines, recognizing that, while lucrative for the family, the deal will be exploitative to the town. Oscar persuades his son Leo to steal bonds from Horace to cover the shortfall, but when Horace discovers this stratagem, he decides to allow it as a way of punishing his wife, from whom he has been estranged. He and Regina argue, and as he relapses, she effectively allows him to die by refusing aid. With his death she now forces her brothers to give her a larger share. Their daughter, Alexandra, no longer able to stand her mother's machinations, and fearing she will end up as helpless as her alcoholic Aunt Birdie, married to Oscar, decides to leave.

Usually labelled a 'realistic melodrama', van Hove conveys his grander vision in his production notes, describing the play as 'Greek tragedy, a Shakespearean power drama and a chamber play'.[16] Under his direction it becomes all three. The sense of a modern tragedy lies in the play's mythic aspects: 'Think', he asserts, 'of the killing of the father coming home, think of the evil that continues from generation to generation, think of Alexandra as Electra, remaining loyal towards the father, Birdie being Cassandra . . . But most of all think of the fatal hubris of these characters who think they can control their lives'.[17]

The Shakespearean characteristics lie in how Horace can be envisioned as 'the dying king' who 'doesn't want to give up his kingdom', meeting his match in Regina, who having provoked his heart attack, 'does nothing and lets him die', and in the portrayal of innocent Birdie, 'victimized and destroyed by the men'.[18] The director conveyed this aspect of Horace by beginning Act Two in relative darkness, only bringing up the lights on Horace's entrance, where he is tended by Alexandra and Addie as if acolytes, Alexandra kneeling to remove his shoes, as they placed him on a throne-like chair, placed centre stage. Later, another throne was brought on from which first Ben and then Regina tried to win Horace to their side, a modern-day War of the Roses.

Foxes is also a chamber play with scenes, in particular between Horace and Regina, that 'could have been written by Strindberg or even Ingmar Bergman, they are full of pain, hope, harshness, bitterness, stubbornness, and revenge'.[19] Van Hove showed them as a couple, caressing and violently attacking each other, suggesting a marriage with 'too many scars to come together again'. Horace's intent becomes that of saving his daughter: 'He wants her to understand, in full scope, the terrible history of her family. Horace knows he will die soon, he also knows Birdie will never be able to escape, but he hopes Alexandra will have the courage to break with the past of the Hubbards. Therefore she has to know everything and be conscious of the sins and destructive forces of her family'.[20] As Horace's business suit was removed and he untucked his shirt, we saw his business persona unravel as he tried to divest himself of his old life.

Taking a scalpel to the script with the precision of a neurosurgeon, van Hove achieves that sculptural 'plastic theatre' sought by Tennessee Williams back in 1947 that would 'take the place of the exhausted theatre of realistic conventions if the theatre is to resume vitality as part of our culture'.[21] Hellman's missing dialogue was replaced with gesture, evocative sound and light, and other visual cues that more than helped carry its meaning and elevate it to a new and relevant commentary on our contemporary world. Characters paced across the stage, marking out their territory, sometimes circling behind the central structure, as if to rally their strength or composure when challenged, much like stalking wolves searching for an opportunity to attack. They formed distinct groups at the sides of the stage, moving centre to battle, as if stepping into a ring, sometimes breaking into physical violence.

Other times characters showed affection, with hugs and caresses, sitting together on the floor, animalistic in their movement as they crept on all fours or stretched out on the ground. For example, in Act One, after the deal with Marshall is sealed, filled with excitement, Regina removed her high heels, sat on the floor, and when Birdie joined her, placed her head in her sister-in-law's lap to be stroked as they gossiped; the two were clearly close. When her brothers returned, Regina crawled over to them on all fours, lying with legs apart as first Oscar and then Ben knelt between her legs in a pantomime of sexual assault, before sitting next to her. All in black, Regina, Oscar and Ben appeared as crows congratulating each other on their kill! Ben played with Regina's hair and stroked her arms, she lay on her front, and Ben lay next to her before crawling over her to listen to Birdie. When Ben and Oscar threatened to cut her out of the deal, they retreated to opposite sides of the stage, as Regina replaced her shoes and faced off against her brothers. As their tempers flared, she and Ben marched toward centre stage and shouted at each other face-to-face with a proximity that bordered on sexual tension. Though Oscar hung back here as the weaker of the brothers, he was less foolish than usually portrayed, and soon began to circle to find his opening. All three came together again with Ben's suggestion that he would leave his wealth to Leo and Alexandra, should they marry.

Where playwrights consider themselves akin to composers in the way they write their plays, van Hove is clearly a master conductor and has expedited his vision of *Foxes* with a skillful tune-up both visually and aurally, playing with the pace and changing a note or two for pointed effect. The careful incisions, sometimes only a word or two, subtly altered how we view certain characters, changes supported by a carefully chosen palette of colours in the costume design of Kevin Guyer. Sanjit De Silva as Marshall, shorter in stature and wearing a light grey suit that suggested his kinder soul, still flirted with a sexily dressed Elizabeth Marvel as Regina, and held his own against the black-suited and black-hearted Hubbard men who literally circled about him as Regina stood aloof. However, he lost most of his complaints against his family, and when kindly crouched to talk to Cristin Milioti's Alexandra, who was sitting on the floor, he came across as more decent than colluding. Regina was less involved in the deal, less able to control her family, and closer to Birdie and Alexandra, who stood well away from where men's business was being conducted. Several of Regina's nastier speeches in the play had been cut to make her more sympathetic, just as the eradication of Leo's more inane exclamations and some of his family's jibes against him made his character less the fool, and, consequently, darker. Oscar's manipulations of his son were cut; he simply beat his son into compliance.

The play began with Alexandra, centre stage, facing the audience while strident music pounded an alert. She dramatically turned to face the rear, then left, but this unscripted appearance established her centrality. Then the battle over her soul commenced. As Birdie, Tina Benko was pretty, slight and blonde, dressed in bright red against the sombre colours worn by everyone else, as if to mark her as a target. While capable of love, being effusive and affectionate when allowed, she constantly consoled herself with alcohol. Her self-esteem was so low that she appeared to invite the disdain of her husband, Oscar, played by Thomas Jay Ryan, who did not simply slap his wife, but punched her in the stomach, a repeated action to which she calmly offered herself. Van Hove described her as 'victimized and destroyed by the men. She is an innocent, with almost no will to fight them ... [but] although Birdie is a victim of the brutality of the Hubbards, she is also a passive bystander, doing nothing, drinking alcohol to escape the rough realities of life'.[22] Earlier, when Oscar was simply beating her with words, van Hove had their son, Leo, played by Nick Westrate, onstage to witness his father's treatment; he never interceded on her behalf, and was clearly learning how to behave just like his father.

Written in 1939 and set in 1900, *Foxes* can seem fairly dated, a nostalgic look at an unpleasant Southern family from the past. But van Hove stripped away most of the place- and time-bound references to truly universalize the play's message regarding the outcome of unfettered materialism. He explained, 'I think it is necessary to dissociate the play and this particular family from its historical context and focus on the dysfunctional family. This family is isolated, frozen in time, like animals running out of food, chewing each other up. They inhabit a once civilized, aristocratic world in decay, where people do not know how to escape. They became bitter, frustrated, cannibalistic'.[23]

The Hubbards are presented as a mass of desire, the 'foxes' of the title, based on a verse from the Song of Solomon, 'Take us the foxes, the little foxes, that spoil the vines; for our vines have tender grapes' (2.15), which Hellman used as an epigraph to the play. The Hebrew word translated here as foxes could also be jackals, which may have the better connotation in both playwright's and director's visions. Van

Hove described them 'like animals, [that] are driven by the instinct of killing; their life is an endless struggle of the fittest'. He then adds, 'The Hubbards behave like animals because they've been conditioned to act this way'.[24] The production showed the Hubbards' feral and brutal nature by having them crawl on the floor and lash out at each other as much as those outside their tight family circle. It is not just Birdie who gets hit in this production, but all the Hubbard siblings get physical with each other, as well as Christopher Evan Welch's Horace, and Leo and Alexandra – at one point Alexandra yelled at Leo and pulled his hair, for which he put her in a choke hold (while glaring defiantly at his mother).

It was moments like this that fully conveyed the core of the play, which van Hove based on Addie's warning (making clear that as a black woman, she should know), forcefully spoken by Lynda Gravatt to the close-knit group of Horace, Alexandra and Birdie, those most sympathetic to its message: 'there are people who eat the earth, and eat all the people on it like in the Bible with the locusts. Then there are people who stand around and watch them eat it'.[25] This message forms the play's backbone, and the supposed 'good-guys' are initially as destructive as the rest.

Van Hove had Alexandra watch her parents fight, and she and Horace calmly watched as Regina got abused by her brother, Ben (played with pent-up fury by Marton Csokas); Leo watches as his aunt and uncle fight; Birdie watches as her son abuses Alexandra; and the powerless servants, Cal (Greig Sargeant) and Addie, constantly watch the continuously selfish behaviour of their employers. Oscar goes out hunting every day, throwing away his catch, but warns Cal, who tries to point out that many of the locals are close to starving, 'if I catch a nigger in this town going shooting, you know what's going to happen'.[26] The maintenance of 'nigger' in the mouths of these characters, despite the eradication of the play's period and geography, startled, and served to emphasize the awfulness of their characters.

When Act Two closes with Horace's accusations against the Hubbards, and Regina's cold declaration 'I hope you die' (199), as Addie draws Alexandra away to protect her from her parents, van Hove plays Randy Newman's 1972 'God's Song', in which God explains to Seth: 'Man means nothing he means less to me / Than the lowliest cactus flower / Or the humblest Yucca tree'. The song imagines God laughing at the squalid lives of humanity, satirizing the very concept of a compassionate God: 'I recoil in horror from the foulness of thee / From the squalor and the filth and the misery / How we laugh up here in heaven at the prayers you offer me / That's why I love mankind'.[27] Newman's real targets, however, are those who listen to the song and their own indifference to suffering, which allows us to better understand van Hove's choice.

The song, like the play, is a critique of all of those who stand and watch rather than help. While some, such as Birdie and Cal, remain powerless to intercede, others, such as Alexandra, Horace and Addie, will learn to do better. The play operates in the same way as Newman's song, in that it makes its audience equally culpable as the characters they witness, as few have done anything to intervene in the types of selfish and greedy behaviour depicted on stage that is all too evident in their own world. The evident unease of the audience appeared in their awkward laughter at seemingly inappropriate moments, such as the Hubbards' realization of their own greed, Regina and Horace's fights, Horace warning Ben about Regina, and even over Regina's evident manipulations, including the question of whether or not Horace will live. The whole design suggested van Hove's desire to elicit a Brechtian response to the production: rather than any emotional catharsis in the watcher, he hoped for rational outrage against such behaviour and the need to get involved and change it.

The biblical context of the Song of Solomon quotation refers to the sinners and heretics of the world who teach false beliefs, seducing others away from better behaviour. This is certainly something of which the Hubbards are guilty, which, as van Hove explained, started with their father, Marcus, to whom Hellman introduced audiences in *Another Part of the Forest* (1946). Marcus is a negative role model of ruthless, exploitative acquisitiveness. His amorality rubs off on all of his children, leading to his own son, Ben, usurping his power and money. As we know from Regina, 'Papa died and left the money to Ben and Oscar' (211), despite an unnatural fondness Marcus displayed for his daughter. While in some productions this line may be tinged with nostalgic regret, here Regina screamed the line in evident frustration at having been denied the family inheritance.

Elizabeth Marvel, who won Obie awards for her previous collaborations with van Hove – as Blanche DuBois in *A Streetcar Named Desire* (1998) and as Hedda Gabler (*Hedda Gabler* 2004) – brought that same borderline insane intensity to Regina Hubbard. Though patently vicious, van Hove wants us to see why Regina has become this way, portraying her more as victim than victimizer, though with a foot in both camps. As he explains, 'Regina is a predator, like her brothers she goes for the kill, ruthless and egocentric'; but also, 'Regina fights the fight of her life and for a reason; she has an excuse.' In reviews, David Cote saw that Regina was 'just as bullied and exploited as the black servants' and that van Hove's production conveyed 'themes of rape and subjugation'.[28] Michael Feingold agreed, pointing out that having been deprived of choice all her life, 'destructive actions seem to stem partly from [Regina's] desperate situation, partly from a long process of being victimized as a woman, and partly from inner drives less easily fathomed'.[29]

Van Hove explained further:

Women have no social status in this family, in this society. As I said, this is Regina's only excuse and it doesn't make her a better person, as we will see very soon. Regina uses the same methods as her brothers. She is obsessed by her ultimate dream, to cut herself lose from her family and finally be free to do what she wants and not have to follow and obey rules imposed on her by men. Her whole life she felt like a prisoner craving freedom. This is the moment to break out of that prison.[30]

Marvel showed us a Regina surrounded by men who view her as a woman, and thereby lesser, insisting that she accept such a role. As Ben asserts, 'it's unwise for a good-looking woman to frown . . . Softness and a smile do more to the heart of men . . . For how many years have I told you a good-looking woman gets more by being soft and appealing?'[31] 'But Regina', van Hove declared, 'thinks she can beat the men at their own game'.[32] To some degree she does, as she is ultimately given power over her brothers, and van Hove pictures her as having 'exorcised the demon in her. Finally, she can have a life of her own. After Horace's death she manipulates her brothers into their defeat, like a perfect Machiavellian'.[33] The fight, however, is far from over, as Ben will wait for his next opportunity, and Regina's victory may only be temporary.

Ben Brantley reviewed Marvel's portrayal as a 'presexual, premoral 2-year-old, a squalling, grabby little girl with eyes way bigger than her fashion-plate stomach'.[34] While partly justified, this slightly misses the mark. Regina is over-filled with desire, and her morality can certainly be questioned, but there was nothing pre-sexual or 'little' about Marvel's performance. Indeed, her Regina was fully sexualized, even suggesting that her brothers hold the same unnatural fondness for her that her father had felt, albeit finely balanced against their sibling aggression. Her husband, too, tried to dominate by laying her on the ground and lying on top. This symbolic rape defused the harshness of Regina's 'I have contempt for you',[35] as she crawled away from him, to rise and simulate arousal against the far wall, clutching at her clothing and sprawling on the velvet. Marshall was drawn to her, and she flirtingly placed a hand on his heart. As a woman, Regina is restricted from the business world her brothers and husband easily inhabit, and we see how this eats away at her. It is not that she has no feelings for others, or sexual desire; quite the contrary, and her frustration manifests itself in screams and violence. Ben will try this same tactic of laying her on the ground to try and dominate in Act Three, when persuading her to forget about the bonds, but Regina again resists, breaking free and yelling her demands.

Regina is capable of affection towards her daughter; while she might yell at her, even trying to strangle her near the end, she also hugs her closely. And while Alexandra is less volatile than her mother, she does not seem as wary as she is often portrayed and returns the affection; indeed she does not turn until her father's death, at which point she becomes a virtual icicle towards everyone, ultimately spitting in her mother's face. As van Hove explains:

> The *deus ex machina* of the play is Alexandra. At the moment of Regina's victory over her brothers, Alexandra enters at the top of the stairs, silent and almost eerie. She has become the liberated, free, fully autonomous individual Regina was craving to be all her life.

He concludes:

> Alexandra brings a new perspective to this dark world of barbarism. She is able to break the cycle of violence, abuse, oppression and killing. She is the real hope Lillian Hellman's play offers us . . .. Alexandra has made the choice not to stand around and watch while people eat the earth. She is ready for the fight. A fight for a better world.[36]

However, the play does not end with Alexandra, but Regina. We watched Alexandra walk away on the video screen, and music played as the light focused on Regina sitting alone on the stairs, and then faded to black, leaving her trapped inside her tiny box. The performance ended with what might seem a surprising choice of music, John Lennon's 1972 'Woman is the Nigger of the World', from the same year as 'God's Song', a year marking the beginning of Richard Nixon's problematic presidency and an era of increasingly questionable morality and mistrust.

Don Shewey enjoyed 'the sheer audacity of juxtaposing a corny, transgressive political slogan from the 1970s with Marvel's portrayal of a thoroughly modern woman. Victim, victor, or both?',[37] which may have been the point; van Hove is not in the business of providing answers but in urging the audience to ask the right questions. 1972 may have been the year that marked the initial rise of those capitalists who blossomed in the later Reagan years, but it was also the year in which the equal rights amendment to guarantee equal rights to all citizens regardless of gender passed Congress. However, this amendment has not as yet been ratified in 2017, let alone 2010.

ANGELS IN AMERICA: *THE BARE, DUTCH VERSION*

Emile Schra

At the end of Part One of *Angels in America* the play reaches its climax as the AIDS patient Prior Walter is confronted with strange sounds in his New York apartment. The sounds reach a crescendo and become an insane noise, while blazing light fills the room, the walls start to shake and, finally, a magnificent angel with huge wings crashes through the ceiling. In the Toneelgroep Amsterdam (TGA) production directed by Ivo van Hove at the Brooklyn Academy of Music (BAM) in 2014 you will have looked in vain for the classical image of the angel with wings. In spite of feathers and plaster that fill the space with dust when the angel makes its appearance, we only see a doctor in a white coat cross the stage. To the music of David Bowie's 'The Motel' ('There is no hell. There is no shame') and on an almost dark stage, he starts dancing in circles with Prior Walter.

The central theme of Tony Kushner's Pulitzer Prize-winning two-part play, which bears the subtitle *A Gay Fantasia on National Themes*, is the American AIDS epidemic in the 1980s during the years of the Reagan government. First performed in 1991, *Angels in America* was an instant succes: innovative, epic, poetic, it has remained a very popular play ever since, staged in its many different interpretations in and outside the US. There are three main storylines in the play that become more closely connected as the action progresses. The main characters – Prior and Louis, Harper and Joe and Roy Cohn – are all at important turning-points in their lives and all of them lose their certainties. *Angels in America* is built on a broad spectrum of emotions and themes, tackled with humour and cynicism: despair, fear, guilt, friendship, tenderness, sorrow, loss of friendship, loneliness, discriminaton, struggle with prejudices and hypocrisy are just a few elements that Kushner weaves through the dialogue. Often the main action is interrupted by apparitions, hallucinations and dreamlike scenes in which the people that appear on stage only seem to exist in the imagination of a certain character. In Part Two the real and the imaginative worlds alternate much more frequently and the main characters are taken away in a vortex of nightmares, delusions and fantasies.

The constant change of locations, scenes and storylines in *Angels in America* can be a challenge for theatre directors. Kushner himself strongly believed that his play needed a sort of realism when staged, so that the additional layers of magic and surrealism could work effectively.[38] But in van Hove's direction the stage is almost empty. The cast of eight Dutch actors have a huge stage at their disposal, on all three sides framed by white fluorescent tubes on the floor. There is no set, unless you consider the back wall as one. Here we see projections, in slow motion, in close up, images that are mixed, but never take the audience's attention completely away from the onstage action. The projections, developed by the American video artist Tal Yarden, are more associative or atmospheric: slow-motion video images of a busy station hall with people criss-crossing each other, a hospital ward, the American flag waving in the wind, the World Trade Center towers (it is 1985), a child's feet dangling from a swing.

In this stripped-down version of Kushner's play, frontstage left there is a small cart with two turntables on it, two boxes and a few records of David Bowie's music from the 1980s. Fragments from songs or instrumental numbers, sometimes hardly perceivable, sometimes very loud, and often about changes, support dramatic moments or create an atmosphere. No further chairs, tables, beds or other props are used, except for a mobile IV-drip in Part Two. The telephone call at the start of the play is simply acted out by the familiar gesture of holding thumb and finger of one hand to the side of the face.

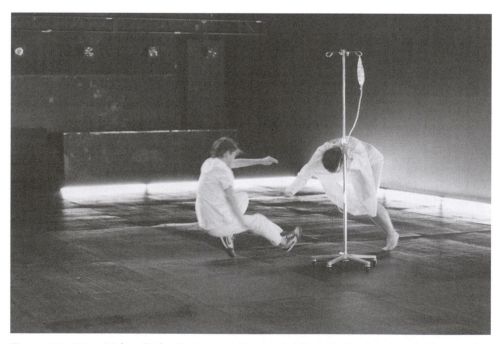

Figure 16 *Prior Walter (Eelco Smits) and the Angel (Alwin Pulinckx),* Angels in America, *Brooklyn Academy of Music (2014).*

Dramaturg Peter van Kraaij adapted Kushner's play by shortening it to five hours' playing time. Staging *Angels* again twenty-five years after it was written, van Hove decided that his staging could not be limited to the AIDS epidemic. If he wanted to do the play again, he would also have to deal with other developments of the past decades. With this shift in approach – to focus less exclusively on what had in the 1980s been a more or less terminal disease – the play's other interests about conflicts and events that are also about change became more prominent. The play offers important insights into the difficulties of change but also about its liberating aspects, about transformation as a positive concept. According to van Kraaij, van Hove created a very hopeful performance, a performance which shows that change entails sacrifices, conflicts, doubts and pain, but that it finally leads to fresh understanding and new relationships. As van Kraaij described: 'In our staging we still talk about the community that is confronted with AIDS, but at the same time it is a story about failing and starting all over again.' Van Kraaij was referring to Susan Sontag's *AIDS and its Metaphors* (1989), a follow-up to her *Illness as Metaphor* (1978).[39] The artistic team of *Angels in America* used Sontag's questions in the book as a source of inspiration. What is the meaning of AIDS in a broader, more philosophical context? What bigger ideas does the disease arouse about transformation, decline, suffering and death, about the finity of life? But van Kraaij also suggests that they saw fundamental changes as a motor for rebirth: 'For a long period of time Ivo van Hove made dark and pessimistic performances. But in this staging light enters into the darkness'.[40]

One of the play's storylines concerns the relationship between Harper and Joe. Joe's realization that he is more attracted to men undermines their marriage. His wife Harper has agoraphobia. She is depressed and has suspicions that something is the matter with her husband but she doesn't know what. When he reveals his homosexual desire, that moment is the start of a huge process of transformation for both of them: Joe leaves, Harper stays. Louis and Prior form the second couple. In one of the first scenes, Prior confesses that he has AIDS. Here the disease is the bomb under their relationship. The one who leaves is Louis; the one who remains alone is Prior. The genius of Kushner is that he created dreamlike scenes in which the characters who are left behind get to meet. They tell deep truths, they console each other. On the other hand, those who ran away get to meet in the 'real life' scenes. The third storyline concerns Roy Cohn, a character based on the real, historical person (1927–86). The American attorney was, of course, the right-hand man of Senator McCarthy during the famous House Un-American Activities Committee (HUAC) investigations into communist activities in the US in the 1950s. In the play, Cohn is interlinked with Joe who works for him. Cohn is a rude and cynical guy who loves power, a potentate capable of anything. He has AIDS but tries to ignore it, even when his body is in total decay and he is hardly able to stand on his feet any longer. Van Kraaij described how the Toneelgroep production brought these various storylines together: 'we focused upon transformation, change, upon the different ways the characters search for modes to survive'.[41]

At the climax of *Part One – Millennium Approaches* an angel arrives to have a word with Prior (the scene with which my essay opens). Crashing through the roof of Prior's apartment, the angel says:

> Greetings, Prophet;
> The Great Work begins:
> The Messenger has arrived.[42]

In *Part Two: Perestroika*, Act One, Scene Two, there is a flashback to this earlier scene, the wrecked ceiling in Prior's bedroom and the angel 'in the air',[43] but this time the angel explains why God left, eventually telling Prior 'YOU HAVE DRIVEN HIM AWAY! YOU MUST STOP MOVING!'[44] At first Prior is 'terrified and very angry', but then, in a crucial speech, he refuses the angel's reactionary ideas:

> I'M TIRED! Tired to death of, of being done to, um, *infected*, fucked-over and
>   tortured by you, by this –
> Is this, is this, disease, is the virus in me, is that the,
> the epistle, is that the prophecy? Is this just ... *revenge*,
> because we, because you think we ruined ...
> No. No, I want you to go away, you go away or *I* will.[45]

Prior wants to embrace life as it is, even if it leads to his death. And that is van Hove's essential statement in his staging of *Angels in America*: a person cannot live without suffering from loss, without changes, fractures, scars. But, in the end, life is worth living. According to van Kraaij, this element is becoming more and more important in van Hove's work, as his interests have developed away from too much darkness in texts that centre around breakdown and stagnation. Van Kraaij suggests that 'today he tends to focus more upon ideas that change the world in a positive way, that bring something new to the foreground. This is something I have become aware of since his staging of *Angels In America* in 2007'.[46]

In the epilogue of Kushner's play the 'survivors' meet 'four years later' and look back and discuss the events of their past. In van Hove's approach, this ending would have been too sentimental, too dated and too 'finished', and it is therefore hardly surprising that the ending was drastically cut. In the TGA performance, the epilogue is excised and replaced by fragments of an earlier monologue by Harper about the souls of the deceased who linger on earth. Then there is a final scene between Louis and Prior: they each confess that they are still in love with one another but, according to Prior, it will be impossible for Louis to ever return to him again and he leaves the stage. A little later Louis leaves. The stage is empty. And in the final moments of van Hove's version of *Angels of America*, we see on the huge back wall a video projection of a dark ocean by night and hear the sound of waves.

Projection and lighting play a crucial role in van Hove and Jan Versweyveld's approach to theatre and the production of *Angels in America* was certainly light-driven. Versweyveld suggested that light use and light changes structured the whole performance and helped to link its many scenes: 'I really love using those two rows of four black boxes above the acting area. Hanging on thin wires from the ceiling they each contain two fluorescent lights.'[47] And indeed, the performance, despite its almost five-hour duration, had a very high tempo facilitated by quick and smooth scene changes. A change of light was sufficient to let the audience know that a new scene was starting. Acting was very accurately adjusted to these seamless switches of action. Ten seconds before the end of a scene the actors for the next one entered, sometimes already in conversation, a technique which drives action forward.

The big challenge for van Hove and Versweyveld has been to make this very complex play with its ingenious structure as simple as possible for the audience. At the start of the design process they discussed several set ideas. They wanted to create a space in which the omnipresent theme of transitions between life and death would be possible. They arrived at the idea of one big hospital ward. Versweyveld started to design that space as a kind of uterus that welcomes you back, invites a kind of rebirth, a new start. He planned this space in skin colour and also involved a sort of navel string in the form of a spiral staircase that would disappear in the theatre's roof. But then he came up with the idea of using a full ward with a staircase, hospital beds and offices on wheels. At one moment in the designing process Versveyweld threw all those ideas aside and started rethinking from scratch. They wanted a space where transition was ultimately possible. And what served this objective better than an empty space? Versweyveld notes: 'Everything is possible there. Our video designer Tal Yarden got involved because we also wanted to evoke the more subjective and emotional side of the United States, together with David Bowie's music. Our aim was not to use video images to indicate that you are in a hospital, in an apartment or at court. No, we wanted to create a framework in a more associative way and one that refers to a country in crisis with itself.'[48]

For Versweyveld designing an empty space for *Angels in America* ('An empty space is never completely empty!'[49]) has been one of the bigger challenges in his career. Generally, the effect of the 'bare bone approach' can be twofold: it awakens the audience's imagination and it helps them to focus on text and actor. Like theatre pioneer Peter Brook discovered long ago, the use of an empty space facilitates mutual contact and exchange between actors and spectators. Moreover, in van Hove's staging of *Angels in America*, the use of a bare stage was not only able to create impact in relation to the theme of transition between life and death, but it also gave a strong impression of the human condition, of the soul of modern mankind. Ben Brantley, writing in *The New York Times*, effectively described spectatorial response to characters struggling or suffering, together or alone, on the vast and empty stage: 'You imagine how lonely it must feel to be up there. That naked space is also a mirror, accurate and unforgiving, of the densely populated city that stretches beyond this outpost of the Brooklyn Academy of Music. I mean New York, or any of those densely crowded places where it's easy to think that the person next to you in the subway or the elevator, or even in bed, might as well be on the other side of the world.'[50]

The response of the New York audience in 2014 came as a complete surprise for the Dutch ensemble. To date, they had only performed *Angels in America* in Europe, but in BAM's Harvey Theater they realized how it was really the audience's story, 'their' world and 'their' characters that the company was performing. When the rabbi enters at the start of the performance, shambling over the bare stage and impersonated by the actress Marieke Heebink, and the audience is wished a good afternoon and welcomed to a funeral, in the Netherlands you could sometimes hear a small giggle. In New York, however, the rabbi was met by thunderous laughter, prompted by Kushner's text (spoken in Dutch, surtitled in English) but also by the way the actress performed her role. The character of the rabbi proved to be more anchored in American than in European culture and resonated more deeply. The actors of TGA discovered that they were back at 'the source', back where it all began.

The Dutch cast had been nervous about their American visit, as actor Hans Kesting, who played the role of Roy Cohn, explained. But it was a tremendous success. Kesting noted: 'Of course you first have to get acclimatized as a spectator to the "van Hove approach"; certainly in America things are generally done quite differently. It is first of all a matter of becoming familiar with the idea that things can also be done differently.' Kesting believes the performance must have been an eye-opener especially for that part of the American audience who had seen other productions. Could you also do it this way?! Kesting remembers very vividly the moment in 2007 when van Hove and

Versweyveld entered the rehearsal space with the idea for their minimal set: 'Their explanation for the use of a bare stage made complete sense. All characters are in transition, are in search, had not found their destination yet. That's why the idea of an empty space was so marvellous. A magnificent *trouvaille* that offered a lot of freedom to us and to the audience to project their own images on the characters'.[51]

For Kesting, his work on the role of the homophobic lawyer Roy Cohn was challenging and intensive. He did not do any serious character studies, but googled, looked at images and read a bit. And he saw a short black-and-white film fragment on YouTube, featuring Joe McCarthy during the HUAC hearings in the 1950s. Next to him he saw Roy Cohn, who was still very young then. But to attempt to imitate this image would have been complete nonsense: Kesting is not a small, bald Jewish male but a Dutchman, who is almost two metres high and 100 kilos in weight. Kushner said of Kesting's interpretation: 'It was awe inspiring, it completely blew me away. . . . America is full of actors desperate to feel something on stage. The playwright's words merely provide them with the sounds to match those emotions. I need actors who devote excessive attention to the detail of the script. And I get that here. . . . I love Hans Kesting's recklessness, his ruthless passion and his quick tempo. His physical acting is better than any Cohn I've ever seen before'.[52]

In an artist talk at BAM in October 2014, van Hove spoke of how he had seen *Angels in America* fifteen years earlier and that, since then, it had never completely disappeared from his mind. Why did he decide to stage the play? He doesn't know. But he said it was like a love affair – it started with a feeling, with intuition: 'It's a process. It is like wine. It takes time'.[53] The reason why van Hove found Kushner's play so attractive was that 'it is very American and at the same time universal'. Many people would recognize the characters on stage who are stuck in impossible or loveless relationships: 'It is about getting out of your own frames, frames of society, frames you are unhappy in. . . . That was important for me to stage: people who got stuck and suddenly got in touch with another life or person and then transform slowly. And develop into a new life'. But for van Hove there was one other crucial element in *Angels in America* that he discovered while directing it, that is, the quality of ambivalence: 'The person that you hated most in the play, Roy Cohn, you really feel for in the last half hour of the production. For me that was really important. At the end of the day it is also a human being dying from AIDS'.[54]

A VIEW FROM SALEM: IVO VAN HOVE'S THE CRUCIBLE

Joshua E. Polster

In 1692 Salem, Massachusetts, a group of girls, among them Betty Parris and Abigail Williams, claimed to be possessed by the Devil and then accused several local women of witchery. Fear of witchcraft quickly grew to hysteria and paralysed the judicial faculties of the townspeople and those in authority. Rumours of witchcraft turned into suspicions, which then turned – in the minds of the townspeople – into facts. Prompted by greed, jealousy, vengeance, and, in some cases, a sincere belief in witchery, neighbour accused neighbour of allegiance to the Devil. Witchcraft trials were soon established to verify the charges, and those who refused to confess, atone for their sins and name other conspirators were executed by public hanging. By the end of the hysteria, fourteen women and six men – including the elderly grandmother Rebecca Nurse and farmer John Proctor – were put to death for witchcraft.[55]

In modern-day Salem, past the busy commercial extravaganza of shops, tours and museums that heavily promote and sell remembrances of the 1692 witch trials, there is Burying Point, a quiet and calm cemetery on Charter Street. It is the oldest burying ground in the city and the final resting place of Justice John Hathorne, one of the infamous judges of the Witchcraft Court and the great-great-grandfather of author Nathanial Hawthorne.

Hawthorne was notoriously haunted by his ancestor's actions during the witch trials, as well as by the judge's unrepentant position in the years that followed. The author, as a result, changed the spelling of his surname to distance himself from his family history and, he believed, family curse. In the introduction to *The Scarlet Letter*, one of Hawthorne's many works that deal with overbearing Puritan rulers, he repudiated 'the persecuting spirit' of his great-great-grandfather that 'made himself so conspicuous in the martyrdom of the witches, that their blood may fairly be said to have left a stain upon him. So deep a stain, indeed, that his old dry bones, in the Charter Street burial-ground, must still retain it, if they have not crumbled utterly to dust'.[56]

Adjoining the north-eastern section of this burial ground, and a stone's throw from Hathorne's grave, is the Witch Trials Memorial, where twenty granite benches cantilever from a low stone wall to solemnly memorialize the fourteen women and six men whom

Hathorne helped to sentence to death for witchcraft. It is a stark reminder – beyond the exuberant modern commercialism – of the great sufferings and actual lives lost during the witch trials. Each of the benches is boldly inscribed with the names of the accused, as well as the means and dates of their execution:

Bridget Bishop
Hanged
June 10, 1692

Rebecca Nurse
Hanged
July 19, 1692

Giles Corey
Pressed To Death
September 19, 1692

At the memorial's entryway, there are inscribed stone slabs that harrowingly recall the victims' unheeded protests, which were taken directly from court records:

For my life now lies in your hands
On my dying day, I am no witch
God knows I am innocent
Oh Lord help me
I am wholly innocent of such wickedness
If I would confess I should save my life
I do plead not guilty

The proximity of this sombre memorial to Judge Hathorne's grave, as well as to the many surrounding graves of Salem residents who lived during the witch trials, gives a damning verdict to those who promoted or did little to prevent this atrocity, and serves as a timeless warning against unrestrained religious and political tyranny.

Arthur Miller's *The Crucible* (1953), as well, harshly sentences Judge Hathorne and the many people who allowed these cruelties to occur. It disparages those who promote fear for power and personal gain, and advocates taking a stand against ignorance, hysteria and tyranny in order to preserve civil liberties. For the 1953 première production, *The Crucible* served as an analogy and critique of the Cold War, the period that reignited the Red Scare and the actions of the House Un-American Activities Committee (HUAC), which was established in 1938 to investigate subversive

Communists and Fascists. Miller, who went before HUAC and was convicted of contempt of Congress for refusing to reveal names of alleged Communist writers, wrote that one can 'tell what the political situation in a country is' when *The Crucible* is performed and 'is suddenly a hit'.[57]

Indeed, for over sixty years, productions of Arthur Miller's *The Crucible* have provided an essential space for dissident voices, representations and means of action for people throughout the world fighting against tyranny. In director Ivo van Hove's first-rate 2016 Broadway revival of *The Crucible* at the Walter Kerr Theatre, he, as well, highlighted many of these important thematic components in Miller's work. *The Crucible* arrived, once again, at a crucial point in history when, in the post-9/11 climate and current US election cycles, theocratic demagoguery and persecutions threatened the very foundation of democracy. 'When you listen to the Republican debates', the director pointed out, 'and when you hear how people blame, scapegoat and call one another liars, you realize that this story resonates with what's going on right now'.[58] Ben Brantley also saw how the production spoke to various times and places in human history, as well as to its contemporary context: 'When an officer of the court comes to arrest [John Proctor's wife] Elizabeth, they have the incredulity of people caught unawares by a tide of history that they simply can't believe could happen in the world they know. Nazi Germany comes to mind. Certain pundits might even think of the United States today'.[59] In an interview for *American Theatre*, van Hove expressed how Miller's work moves beyond the particulars of its initial setting: 'What Arthur Miller is very good at is taking a specific society, like Red Hook or Salem, and turning it into a society that becomes emblematic, a metaphor for the whole world'.[60]

Van Hove's Broadway revival, led by an astonishing international cast including Ben Whishaw, Sophie Okonedo, Saoirse Ronan and Ciaran Hinds, created another oppressive, dangerous and extremely anxious world comprised of fear of the unknown and the other. This dark world was constructed with the muscular, minimalist avant-garde aesthetic that has become the hallmark of the director. Van Hove was also well aided by his highly talented creative team. The sombre light and set designs of Jan Versweyveld, seemingly influenced by the imagery of paranormal horror films, altered and isolated the location of the play to a stark, dreary and quite eerie modern schoolroom (see Plate 7). The clothing designs of Wojciech Dziedzic were intentionally drab, utilitarian and constrictive, and the choreography of Steven Hoggett had the group of accusing schoolgirls gather and disperse like bats in modes of protection and predator. Animal trainer William Berloni had a pure-bred Tamaskan dog play a scavenging wolf that slowly prowled onstage and turned its cold preying eyes on the audience (it brought

Figure 17 *From left, Betty Parris (Elizabeth Teeter), Susanna Walcott (Ashlei Sharpe Chestnut), Abigail Williams (Saoirse Ronan, foreground), Mercy Lewis (Erin Wilhelmi) and John Proctor (Ben Whishaw),* The Crucible, *Walter Kerr Theatre, New York (2016).*

the audience to a stunned silence). There were also the chilling sustained violin notes and moody original score of Philip Glass, which included three hymns and a funeral dirge.

The music of Glass was partly inspired by his research on late-seventeenth-century Massachusetts music. Besides this, the creative team behind van Hove's production stripped many of the period designs of *The Crucible* in order for the play to have greater contemporary relevance. It had, as said by Chris Jones in the *Chicago Tribune*, 'a tinge of retro – but only a tinge, for it also conveys pre-apocalyptic modernity . . . this production feels more attuned to our world of school shooters and suicide bombers than blowhard anticommunists'.[61] In Philip Glass's comments on the production, he noted, 'The way society organizes itself and humiliates people and murders a few, is very true of America right now. It's true of America but I imagine it could be true of anywhere'.[62] Ben Whishaw, who gave a superb performance of a fiery but morally and spiritually vulnerable John Proctor, also observed the contemporary relevance:

When the bombings and attacks happened in Belgium earlier in the year, it seemed to be very much impossible to not feel that it was speaking to that event in terms of the kind of religious fundamentalism that was at work there. But then, at the same time, in the Brexit that's just happened in the UK, it seems to speak very much to that as well – about community and about fear and hysteria ... Obviously, a lot of people are feeling that it is very prescient with the political situation here [in the United States] and particularly what Donald Trump has been up to over the last while ... So it's one of those plays that's absolutely specific and, in its specificity, manages to speak about so many things.[63]

This has often been the case with productions of *The Crucible* – time constantly shifts through the continuum, as the play comments simultaneously on the past, present and foreboding future. Van Hove, though, did not just revive *The Crucible* for a history lesson, a contemporary parable or as a forewarning of unrestrained demagoguery (such as what many, at the time of this writing, expect of the Trump presidency); he also brought his audiences back to historic Salem for a retrial. It was a retrial not just for the accused protagonist John Proctor, who was executed for witchcraft, but also for the judicial bodies Judge Hathorne and Deputy Governor Danforth (played with great authority by Teagle F. Bougere and Ciaran Hinds), as well as all those who believed in the witchery and necessity of the tribunals. Unlike Nathanial Hawthorne's introductory note to *The Scarlet Letter* or the numerous past productions of *The Crucible*, van Hove's production suggested that the Devil, indeed, was alive in Salem and, as a result, at least some of Salem's characters had been judged too harshly and others, perhaps, not judged harshly enough. This, among others, was the innovative and important concept that the director brought to the dramatic work.

Van Hove's interpretation moved well beyond a melodramatic portrayal of good versus evil to provide a more complex view of humanity caught in the grip of hysteria, a hysteria that, at least to some extent, was valid. In Brantley's review, he discussed how 'we are made to see what the terrified residents of Salem *think they see*, in visions formed from a collective, paranoid fever dream' (my italics).[64] Brantley clearly interpreted the play through the eyes of a disbeliever. In the world of van Hove's production, though, certain characters were undeniably bewitched, as clearly seen in several added scenes where black magic was present. For instance, among the group of girls who went into the forest to dance with the Devil, at least Betty Paris (performed by Elizabeth Teeter, who gave a stirring portrayal of a terrified and terrifying schoolgirl) was truly possessed. An early moment in the production had Betty, assumedly comatose, rise into the air from her bed when no other character was present. The audience saw this startling and horrific event as it actually occurred in dramatic time and place – and not from any character's perspective since, again, no one else was there. Moreover, the scene was not stylistically presented as an expressionist depiction of Betty's subconscious.

This early and brief moment was all it took to help shift audience perspectives on Salem and its people. As Jesse Green observed in *New York Magazine*, 'In van Hove's vision of Miller's world, the distinctions between human and inhuman, between animate and inanimate, are always collapsing . . . it seems to be saying to us: look again'.[65] If the rising of Betty Paris – an isolated moment with an individual character – was not enough proof, the production intensified the presence of black magic with scenes of several characters who simultaneously witnessed 'spectral evidence'. Further into the performance, for example, powerful winds blasted open a wall of windows, scattering paper, debris and people. At the same time, a chalkboard, scrawled with the biblical commandment 'thou shalt not kill', animated and contorted the letters to emphasize the word 'kill' (via spectacular video projections by Tal Yarden). The commanding winds appeared to force open not just classroom windows, but the eyes of any disbeliever to the presence of actual witchery. It extended beyond the fourth wall, as well, as stage curtains during these macabre moments fell and rose as if given a life of their own.

With these occurrences of deviltry, an interesting shift happened in how one perceived Miller's characters. Rebecca Nurse, portrayed with great compassion and strength by Brenda Wehle, no longer appeared entirely convincing when she warned that 'there is prodigious danger in the seeking of loose spirit . . . let us rather blame ourselves'.[66] John Proctor seemed naive when he altogether denied the presence of witchery: 'I cannot believe they come among us now'.[67] Moreover, Deputy Governor Danforth no longer came off as altogether foolish when he stated, 'This is a sharp time, now, a precise time – we live no longer in the dusky afternoon when evil mixed itself with good and befuddled the world. Now, by God's grace, the shining sun is up'.[68]

The Devil, certainly, was not in all of them (there were clear fakers among the accusers), but, indeed, in particular characters. Van Hove's production, therefore, asked: shouldn't something be done? This perspective has been largely absent in past productions of *The Crucible*. The Belgian director, therefore, provided an exciting provocative new look at a classic play, as well as a more intricate view of those – in the past and present – who are alert to actual dangerous forces and are compelled to combat them. It illuminated complex considerations – throughout the time of humanity – about the importance of recognizing real threats, understanding the extent of the threats, and dealing appropriately with such threats. The production still powerfully scrutinized the rampant ignorance, hysteria and cruelties of the witch hunt, but not the necessity of the hunt in its entirety.

In a personal interview with Ben Whishaw, the actor discussed how this is 'a thoroughly accurate reading of Ivo's production,'[69] and one of van Hove's methods was to 'move the audience from detachment' towards a new level of intimacy with the production. Indeed, van Hove has frequently discussed, about his work in general, how he likes to bring audiences a fresh appreciation of classics by ambushing them with the unexpected, and shaking them out of tired readings and reactions. 'A director', explained van Hove, 'always has to reinvent a text for his age ... Reinventing the meaning of the text for today – that's the thing'.[70] For *The Crucible*, he set out to do this by debunking the more traditional and secular view of Miller's Salem village and infiltrating it with the supernatural.

Of course, the Devil does not work alone, and the many crimes that the characters commit in the play still need to be recognized and responded to with justice – the Devil cannot be given full blame. The story that Miller and van Hove seemingly wanted to tell was not of a town victimized by the sole menace of the Devil or, again, a melodramatic or binary depiction of good and evil, but of people that collaborated with evil when the Devil came to town. As Philip Glass observed, Salem was a place that had 'evil within goodness, and goodness within evil'.[71] The flawed persons in this drama are not reliable characters whom an audience can necessarily trust to interpret events.

There are those like accusers and opportunists Abigail Williams and Thomas Putnam (superbly performed by Saoirse Ronan and Thomas Jay Ryan as skillful manipulators and menaces) who fabricate facts and take advantage of crises for personal gain. This, of course, occurs in many calamities; see, for instance, the Bush administration, the Iraqi War and Halliburton profits – a connection illuminated in the 2002 Broadway revival of *The Crucible*, directed by Richard Eyre. For van Hove's production, though, he made it clear that, in addition to human evil, there truly was a real threat of supernatural intervention that could not be ignored. This approach brought greater complexity to characters like John Proctor and Rebecca Nurse, who completely disregarded any presence of witchcraft, as well as those like Judge Hathorne and Deputy Governor Danforth, who actually had a difficult task to determine who among them was truly possessed. 'There is this whole fight', van Hove observed, 'between the word of the law and the right human decisions to make'.[72]

New York Magazine noted that 'literalists may not like the intrusions of magic' in Mr van Hove's production, and that 'some audience members complain[ed] that these effects muddied Miller's argument by suggesting that witchcraft really occurred'.[73] The director's approach, though, did not weaken *The Crucible*'s themes or even its analogous ties to HUAC; it greatly strengthened them. There was, certainly, Soviet espionage operant in the United States, as self-confessed spies Whittaker Chambers, Louis Budenz and Elizabeth Bentley made apparent (the extensiveness of that spy network, though, never matched the imagination of the US people). Furthermore, there was a real threat and need to combat the dangerous rise of Communism, as seen when the Soviet Union tested its first atomic bomb, when the Communist Party took control in China or when Communist North Korea invaded South Korea, bringing the United States into the Korean War.

When *The Crucible* first premièred, there were many people who believed that Communism was a real and present threat to the nation, and that cooperating with HUAC was a necessary responsibility of each citizen, even at the expense of civil liberties. For instance, Molly Kazan's 1957 play *The Egghead*, a direct theatrical response to *The Crucible*, discusses the dangers of soft liberalism allowing real dangers to preside and thrive. If the danger is real, then, according to those who endorsed HUAC, it would be completely foolish to disregard the danger and not take action to locate and eradicate the danger. (This is a similar argument heard today by those responding to the real menace of foreign and homegrown terrorism.)

Van Hove highlighted this concept in his production, which made it thrilling. He brought his audiences to the conceptual world of historic Salem, a world where witches were understood to be real and a menace to confront, an approach that agreed with the late playwright:

> Anyone standing up in the Salem of 1692 who denied that witches existed would have faced immediate arrest, the hardest interrogation, and quite possibly the rope. Every authority – the church in New England, the kings of England and Europe, legal scholars like Lord Coke – not only confirmed the existence but never questioned the necessity of executing them when discovered. And of course, there was the authority of the Bible itself [Exodus 22.18]: 'Though shalt not suffer a witch to live'.[74]

If theatre audiences entirely deny the presence of witchery in historic Salem as well as in *The Crucible*, then it can greatly deplete the power of the play and create misperceptions of character and character actions. What if the Devil was actually in Salem? What if some of the townspeople were communing with the Devil? For the latter, at least, Miller did not question it:[75]

> I have no doubt that people *were* communing with, and even worshiping, the Devil in Salem, and if the whole truth could be known in this case, as it is in others, we should discover a regular and conventionalized propitiation of the dark spirit. One

certain evidence of this is the confession of Tituba, the slave of Reverend Parris, and another is the behavior of the children who were known to have indulged in sorceries with her. There are accounts of similar *klatches* in Europe, where the daughters of the towns would assemble at night and, sometimes with fetishes, sometimes with a selected young man, give themselves to love, with some bastardly results. The Church, sharp-eyed as it must be when gods long dead are brought to life, condemned these orgies as witchcraft and interpreted them, rightly, as a resurgence of the Dionysiac forces it had crushed long before.[76]

For van Hove, among the hubris, fear, greed and vengeance, there was a real menace of deviltry in Salem and real judicial work that needed to be done – it, again, was the quality of the judicial work that was under interrogation in this production and not the necessity of the work altogether. In this way, the director challenged encrusted interpretations and scholarship on *The Crucible*. Similar to the Witch Trials Memorial, van Hove's production moved past the commercialism and tired readings of the 1692 trials – on Broadway as well as in modern Salem – to get to the heart of humanity. This production, though, moved closer to better understanding all of the persons involved, and not just those that were sacrificed to the calamity. As Brantley recognized, 'It insists that we identify with not only the victims of persecution but also with those who would judge them'.[77] Moreover, the production insists that we should also identify with those who – beyond the ignorance, ploys and hysteria – know and struggle with how best to respond when the Devil truly does drop by.

Section Four

Opera across Europe

IVO VAN HOVE AND OPERA:
A CRITICAL OVERVIEW

François Jongen

At the end of the twentieth and the beginning of the twenty-first century, several Belgian (and, above all, Flemish) directors achieved a certain international notoriety in the world of opera: namely Gilbert Deflo (b. 1952), Moshe Leiser (b. 1956) and Guy Joosten (b. 1963). Although less regularly a contributor, with about fifteen opera productions between 1999 and 2017 (barely one a year on average), Ivo van Hove's career as an opera director is part of this period. Notwithstanding different aesthetic styles, varyingly radical approaches and unequal successes with audiences, each of these directors privileges the theatrical dimension of opera and flirts, in a more or less relevant way, with an eloquent revisionist approach to Northern European opera that the Americans call 'Eurotrash' and which Europeans (other than Germans) call *Regietheater* (directors' theatre). None of these Belgian opera directors, however, goes so far as to fall into the excesses and provocations that sometimes characterize this genre.

Except for Leiser (who has built his career entirely within his own network, and who works systematically in tandem with the Frenchman, Patrice Caurier), it is important to note that these directors built their first operas in their native Belgium. And for two of them, Deflo and van Hove, their work in this genre has relied on the careers of other Flemings who were accomplished opera directors: Gerard Mortier, of course (1943–2014, successful director of the Théâtre de la Monnaie in Brussels from 1981 to 1991, the Salzburg Festival from 1992 to 2001, the Ruhrtriënnale from 2002 to 2004, the Paris Opera from 2004 to 2009, and Teatro Real de Madrid from 2010 to 2013), but also Marc Clémeur (director of the Vlaamse Opera from 1989 to 2008 and then of the Opéra du Rhin from 2009 to 2017), Serge Dorny (Gerard Mortier's former collaborator at la Monnaie and director of the Lyon Opera since 2003) and Peter De Caluwe (1963, also a former collaborator of Gerard Mortier at la Monnaie, and director of la Monnaie since 2007 after having worked for a long time at the Amsterdam's Nederlandse Opera).

Van Hove was already more than forty years old when he directed opera for the first time with *Lulu*. This was in January 1999 at the Vlaamse Opera whose performances are traditionally held in Antwerp and Ghent, and Jan Versweyveld was already part of the team as a designer. Van Hove was not in unknown territory since he had already directed Wedekind's play, the inspiration for Berg's second opera, but the critic of the Brussels daily *Le Soir* did not seem totally convinced, writing:

> The somewhat frozen distancing could have been an interesting approach and it should be pointed out that Ivo van Hove succeeds well with the last act (especially the vertiginous cross-chase of the Parisian scene). But the first two acts seem to be carried out in a total absence of emotion, and on more than one occasion we have the impression that the theatrical play is rather imprecise, very often lacking in affective investment.[1]

In September 2002, van Hove made his debut at the Nederlandse Opera in Amsterdam with Leoš Janáček's *Vec Makropoulos*. Here again, his work did not seem entirely successful with the critics:

> Beyond characterization, the staging of van Hove seems to lack a strong idea that guides all the protagonists, a clear axis around which the whole action would be ordered. His work is certainly characterized by able direction of actors, but without its purpose being clear.[2]

In 2004, at the Opera in Amsterdam, it was van Hove's task to direct the creation of *Iolanta* by Tchaikovsky. Writing in *Opera International*, Rudi van den Bulck was rather sceptical about the coherence of the project, but it was not the director that he critiques:

> Half-conceptual, half-abstract, Jan Versweyveld's scenic design falls completely flat and even triggers some snickers. Laughs, again, salute the rather beautiful costumes of Dirk van Saene, modern clothes and antique swords. Too bad, since van Hove's management does not go against the music: often inspired, it contrasts unfortunately with sets and costumes.[3]

With Richard Wagner's tetralogy entrusted to him by Marc Clémeur at the Vlaamse Opera, van Hove undoubtedly accelerated his lyrical journey, staging the four episodes of the famous Wagnerian cycle, one per season, starting in 2006. Even if the productions of complete cycles of the tetralogy have multiplied since the end of the twentieth century, *Der Ring* is always a project that marks a climax for an opera director, and a typical opera house can only afford to undertake it once every thirty or forty years. For the occasion, van Hove teamed up with Hungarian conductor and pianist Ivan Törzs, then music director of the Flemish house, as well as his usual designer Versweyveld. The context for the project was not an easy one: the main theatre in Antwerp was closed for two years of major renovation work and the first shows were only staged in Ghent. At the same time, the government had announced a reduction in public subsidies and there was even talk about removing the orchestra from the Opera or, more exactly, merging it with the Philharmonic of Flanders. A demotivated orchestra has often proven the Achilles' heel of the cycle.

The project opened in June 2006 with *Das Rheingold*. This time, the clarity and coherence of the concept were indisputable:

> Ivo van Hove plunges straight into today's world of computers, vast television screens and electronic gadgetry: the Rhinemaidens sit in an office at their PC screens bringing up various images which turn soft porn-ish to arouse the business-suited Alberich; the Gold lights up to reveal an all-powerful superchip, subsequently embedded in the Ring ... Despite some of these oddities – and a question mark against the viability of van Hove's basic concept for the later operas in the cycle – it works.[4]

The direction of the tetralogy marked a decisive turning point for the rest of van Hove's operatic journey to date, namely his transposition of opera to contemporary times (the exception being *Brokeback Mountain*, already set in recent times as the action takes place between 1963 and 1983). Of course, a critic's appreciation of the contemporaneity of an interpretation also depends on his own references: for some, this production of *Der Ring*, which in 2006 the management of the Vlaamse Opera described as the 'Ring of the twenty-first century and new technologies', is likely to appear dated very soon. And one of the characteristics of this contemporary world that van Hove imposes on the stage is to be familiar, perhaps too well known to audiences, diminishing the production's impact:

> If one perceives the meaning of the concept, it does not convince, for all of that: this way of bringing everything back to our reality makes us lose all opportunity to dream, and the work is deprived of its universal dimension.[5]

In the productions that followed, van Hove continued to deploy technology and to modernize, but it was undeniable that he was strengthening his skills in the development of characterization and in the direction of actors. In February 2007, a critic in *Opéra Magazine* suggested that, while the staging of *Das Rheingold* provoked mixed responses, *Die Walküre* was much more convincing since it better adhered to the director's concept.[6] Besides, references to the contemporary world no longer existed only in the stage design and properties, but also in the extreme violence that saturated the production.

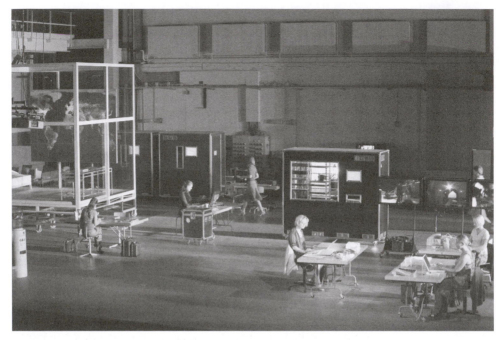

Figure 18 *The setting of* Das Rheingold, *Flemish Opera, Ghent (2006).*

Figure 19 *Siegfried (Lance Ryan) and Mime (Peter Bronder),* Siegfried, *Flemish Opera, Antwerp (2007).*

Plate 1 *Hedda Gabler (Ruth Wilson) and Berte (Éva Magyar)*, Hedda Gabler, *National Theatre, London (2016).*

Plate 2 *Henry VI (Eelco Smits), Kings of War, Stadsschouwburg, Amsterdam (2015).*

Plate 3 *From left, Cassio (Reinout Scholten van Aschat), Emilia (Janni Goslinga), Othello (Hans Kesting), Desdemona (Karina Smulders) and Jago (Roeland Fernhout), Othello, Stadsschouwburg, Amsterdam (2012).*

Plate 4 *From left, Petruchio (Hans Kesting), Grumio (Fred Goessens), Katharina (Halina Reijn) and, in the background, Bianca (Hélène Devos) and Lucentio (Eelco Smits), The Taming of the Shrew, Stadsschouwburg, Amsterdam (2012).*

Plate 5 *From left, Lovborg (Chukwudi Iwuji) and Hedda Gabler (Ruth Wilson), and, in the background, Berte (Éva Magyar), Hedda Gabler, National Theatre, London (2016).*

Plate 6 *Alfieri (Michael Gould), and, in the background, from left, Officer (Pádraig Lynch), Rodolpho (Luke Norris), Catherine (Phoebe Fox), Marco (Emun Elliott), Eddie (Mark Strong) and Nicola Walker (Beatrice), A View from the Bridge, Young Vic, London (2014).*

Plate 7 *Mary Warren (Tavi Gevinson), Betty Parris (Elizabeth Teeter), Mercy Lewis (Erin Wilhelmi), Abigail Williams (Saoirse Ronan), and, in the background, Giles Corey (Jim Norton),* The Crucible, *Walter Kerr Theatre, New York (2016).*

Plate 8 *From left, Leo (Nick Westrate), Oscar Hubbard (Thomas Jay Ryan), Cal (Greig Sargeant) and Regina Giddens (Elizabeth Marvel),* The Little Foxes, *New York Theatre Workshop (2010).*

Plate 9 *Lance Ryan (Siegfried) and Jayne Casselman (Brünhilde)*, Götterdämmerung *(2008)*.

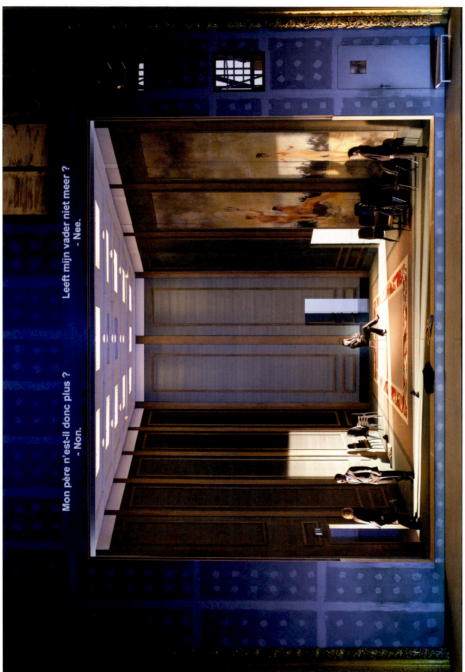

Plate 10 *The setting of Idomeneo (2010).*

Plate 11 *The setting of Macbeth (2012).*

Plate 12 *Ennis Del Mar (Daniel Okulitch) and Jack Twist (Tom Randle), Brokeback Mountain, Teatro Real, Madrid (2014).*

Plate 13 *Gino (Jude Law) and Hanna (Halina Reijn), Obsession, Barbican Centre, London (2017).*

Plate 14 *Marianne (Janni Goslinga), Scenes from a Marriage, Barbican Centre, London (2013).*

Plate 15 *Martin von Essenbeck (Christophe Montenez), The Damned, Avignon Festival (2016).*

Plate 16 *The setting of* The Fountainhead, *Stadsschouwburg, Amsterdam (2014).*

Presented in November 2007, *Siegfried* proved to be the most successful of the four dramas:

A *Ring* for the 21st century, not afraid to violate the letter of the text (no sword but a radioactive substance that Siegfried implants like a chip in his hand, no hammer on the forge but the clicking of the keyboard of a computer, no forest but a sort of electrical discharge), but which, in its own ways, succeeds in delivering a contemporary reading less distant than it appears from the spirit of the work. *Siegfried* is the most coherent and convincing of all three opuses so far: Siegfried's ignorance of the outside world (and especially of fear and femininity) is embodied in this great, yet mentally slow adolescent with a rapper's looks.[7]

And even critics who were tired of van Hove's modernizing approach emphasized his ability to handle direct confrontations:

Presumably the point of the chaotic decor is to suggest that the old 'world order' is now disintegrating, but this sort of demythologizing is a dreary business and, of course, very little of the music (let alone the stage directions) supports such a dismal view of what Wagner clearly saw as the most hopefully joyous part of his great cycle. The two scenes where the production makes most sense are the confrontations at the start of the third act between the Wanderer and Erda and then the Wanderer and Siegfried, and indeed, these were the most impressive *quarts d'heure* of the evening, both dramatically and vocally.[8]

In June 2008, *Götterdämmerung* proved to be less convincing, as if fatigue or a lack of inspiration had set in (see Plate 9). It was also that we were still waiting for the last episode of the tetralogy to illuminate the previous ones, while van Hove kept failing to give the final key to the avalanche of images shown until then:

Besides the inconsistencies (no Hagen spear to swear or kill Siegfried, no *tarnhelm* to give Siegfried the appearance of Gunther when he tore the ring out of Brünnhilde), and out of the incontestable enjoyable side that exists in transposing the myths of the Tetralogy into situations from today's life, this aesthetic of ugliness, confusion and everyday life seems a little vain. At the end of this fourth episode of the Wagnerian Tetralogy directed by Ivo van Hove, one does not feel that one has learned anything new about the characters of this fabulous epic. There are, as in previous episodes, one or another successful scene (here, that of the plot in Act II) but, more often, a feeling of annoyance, even boredom.[9]

In March 2010, van Hove made his debut at la Monnaie (Brussels) with Mozart's *Idomeneo*, with Versweyveld once again in charge of the design. Again, the opera was updated to a contemporary context. In an interview for the production press release, van Hove explained:

In 'Idomeneo,' the ancient world is only a pseudo-utopia, on which the ideas of the Enlightenment can be projected. In his 'Roman Tragedies,' Shakespeare used the framework of the Roman Empire to speak of his time. In the eighteenth century, Mozart used an ancient narrative to speak of his time. The view of the world of the Greeks, as it emerges from the ancient tragedies, is a thousand leagues from Mozart's developments in this opera. However, Mozart uses this framework to criticize the religious situation of his time. It is this aspect, drowned in most interpretations, that we wished to raise by showing the constant threat of terrorism. What is interesting in this opera is that it shows the friction between two blocks of power.

In this re-reading where Idomeneo resembles former US President Bill Clinton, the three acts are renamed 'The Coming of a New King', 'The Fall of the Present' and 'The Birth of a New World' (see Plate 10). The vision is radical and once again we can ask whether it is really necessary to transpose every detail of the action of an ancient drama to the present day in order to convince the public of its relevance. But, as a critic in *Opera* wrote:

Most of these ideas fit well enough with the action of Mozart's great opera, with disbelief suspended, except, almost inevitably, at the *deus ex machina* moment of the denouement announced by the off-stage Voice.[10]

Van Hove's preference for updating was confirmed again in the Nederlandse Opera's opening production of their 2012–13 season. But this time the Flemish director had been entrusted with the very rarely performed *Der Schatzgräber* (*The Treasure Hunter*) by Franz Schrecker. This production revealed that van Hove's tendency to modernize is probably better suited to pieces well known to the public (precisely because they already know the story and can therefore make better sense of a distanced point of view) than to works that audiences have never seen before:

Ivo van Hove ignored the medieval setting to transfer the action to the present (in rather poor sets by Jan Versweyveld), creating an uninspired and banal context for the drama. The Inn of Els's father seemed to be located in some American backwater, frequented by white trash, and Els herself was presented as a cheap whore. The royal palace resembled an old people's home; the beauty of the score suggests something very different. Occasionally van Hove tried to evoke some atmosphere through video projections (by Tal Yarden), slightly reminiscent of David Lynch, Terrence Malick and Lars von Trier. But these often bordered on kitsch, and more than once completely dwarfed the singers.[11]

It was at the invitation of Dorny, director of the Opéra de Lyon, that van Hove undertook his first opera staging in France. In October 2012, he took on Verdi for the first time, with a representation of *Macbeth* whose images refer to his Tetralogy:

> According to the Flemish director Ivo van Hove, who has also staged Shakespeare plays in the spoken theatre, *Macbeth* constitutes a reflection on power. But today power doesn't belong to the politicians anymore, he claims: in Europe, it belongs to the worlds of finance and business. So, in his new production . . ., the witches become public-relations gurus who are so powerful that Macbeth accepts their prophecies and wants them to become reality . . . The action of the opera didn't take place in a Scottish castle but, in Jan Versweyveld's set, was transposed to a spacious room in a skyscraper in the heart of a financial centre, with the walls covered with computer monitors . . . This concept had some good points, but it also had many incongruities and left a lot of questions unanswered.[12]

His operatic debut in Berlin followed the next year, in February 2013 at the Komische Oper, a hall known for its theatrical audacity and distinguished by the great lineage of directors from East Germany, from Walter Felsenstein to Harry Kupfer. Van Hove returned this time to Tchaikovsky with *Mazeppa*, and the scenic choices, if not surprising, were convincing:

> Belgian director Ivo van Hove chose to set the military tale in a modern-day country, unnamed but politically troubled. The sparse, monochrome fixed set conveyed a faded and scruffy barrack room with random tables, chairs and steps. Although there was a roof, the use of sodium and mercury lights suggested that at times we might have been in the street, or deep in an underground bunker. To add further menace, there was a small, man-sized cage on the floor and a larger industrial meshed entrance to an unseen room. At times a partition was rolled across to allow vivid images of modern warfare to be projected on it. Costumes were modern-day dress for the People, and bottle-green uniforms for the Military. Racks of machine guns decorated the set.[13]

For his second production at la Monnaie in Brussels (October 2013), van Hove was again entrusted with an *opera seria* (comedy is definitely not his universe), Mozart's *La Clemenza di Tito*. Even more than in his previous opera productions, the use of video proved integral to van Hove's vision for it:

> The Monnaie's new, modern-dress production of Mozart's *La clemenza di Tito* ... is a fascinating affair. The director Ivo van Hove projects virtually nonstop live video of the action onto a large screen, placed dead centre of the stage and high enough not to interfere. The resulting concentration on the characters, their reactions and, from time to time, their surroundings is riveting.[14]

Not surprisingly, in January 2014 in Madrid, it wasn't van Hove's staging of the world première of *Brokeback Mountain* that was at the forefront of media interest. Its composer Charles Wuorinen is even less known in Europe than in the United States, but the novel by E. Annie Proulx has already been brought to the cinema by Ang Lee and *Brokeback* had been a success in both print and screen versions. And critical attention was focused on the theme of homosexuality, a subject rarely directly approached by opera, and on the production's context: Gerard Mortier, who had commissioned the production and who had almost been fired a few months earlier from his role as director at Teatro Real before finally being kept as an 'advisor', was terminally ill. The opera was composed in a rather retrospective musical aesthetic (an atonalism close to the second Viennese school of Arnold Schoenberg and his pupils), but van Hove's directorial work was applauded: 'Apart from a few ellipses, there are many scenes of the novel and the film ingeniously transposed on the Teatro Real's stage by Ivo van Hove.'[15]

In June 2017, van Hove returned to Amsterdam for his fourth production there. The last show in their season and, traditionally, the most prominent because it is the one that is entrusted to the prestigious Concertgebouw orchestra.[16] It was also the first opera by Richard Strauss to be directed by van Hove: his *Salome* was, as we might have guessed, transposed to the present time, and the critic for the *Financial Times* was wildly enthusiastic:

> Why take a severed head when you can have the whole prophet? Johannan's decapitation for Amsterdam's new Salome is incomplete; the dying prisoner is served whole, in a gigantic silver bowl, marinating in a soup of his own blood. That leaves Herodes' stepdaughter plenty to play with, and play she does. It is unashamedly orgiastic. The gore-splattered excess of Ivo van Hove's finale is all the more formidable for the restraint that characterizes the rest of his production. ... Van Hove's

production pays careful attention to the fine details of Strauss's text, beginning with the setting – a political conference somewhere in the Middle East in which religious debates play an important role. This is a military, male-dominated affair where niceties like human rights do not feature. It translates seamlessly to today.[17]

Van Hove is scheduled to direct opera again in June 2018: it will be Modest Mussorgsky's *Boris Godunov* at the Opéra Bastille in Paris. Can we bet that it will be about modern Russia, as we know it today?

Translation by Samantha Carron

MORE THAN WALL STREET IN MACBETH

Frédéric Maurin

In contemporary productions of the classics, power can easily be given different faces, shapes and meanings. Opera, even more than theatre, has provided Ivo van Hove with a number of works in which to analyse the mechanisms and changing forms of power by updating its components and stakes. In *Der Ring des Nibelungen* by Wagner (2006–8), he equated the Rhine gold with the quest for worldwide control of information and changed the magic sword *Notung* into a RFID (radio-frequency identification) chip. In *Idomeneo* by Mozart (2010), he broke up power into its military, political and religious dimensions. And when he tackled *Macbeth* by Verdi (2012), he took it for granted that the significance of power had shifted from its political to its financial dimensions. Drawing loosely on writer-director J. C. Chandor's film *Margin Call* (2011) and its narrative of traders struggling to keep afloat in the aftermath of the 2008 stock-market crisis, van Hove set the opera in the world of Wall Street teeming with today's rulers, Stock Exchange tycoons bent on making profit and driven by a lust for dominance.

In the context of this premise, the transformations proceeded apace: Macbeth (sung by Evez Abdulla) became a Wall Street mogul stopping at nothing to crush the competition, and the witches were dressed in well-tailored suits like spin-doctors ready to give him advice as much as predictions. Macbeth moved from the grey open space of a rating agency, surrounded by LCD monitors flickering with quotation graphs and equity curves, to his sleek penthouse apartment overlooking New York. Accordingly, the large images projected on the three walls of the stage alternated between green binary codes and dizzying views of the city at night (see Plate 11). All characters were duly equipped with smartphones and Lady Macbeth used her iPad to read the letter in which her husband tells her of the prophecies. Chance even had it that, for the initial performances at least, the actor playing the silent part of King Duncan (Gérard Desmoulins) bore a striking resemblance to American billionaire investor Warren Buffett. Access to the 'throne' unleashed scenes of contemporary urban violence. After Duncan was treacherously murdered in his room, Banquo was attacked by a gang of thugs in an underground parking lot. Although both murders are committed off-stage in the play and in the opera, they were projected as negative black-and-white films, fully visible to the audience and even to the guests of the banquet in the second case. Visual technology served as a surveillance fact-checking tool. With images of the characters meeting their deaths like ectoplasms, it also created a ghosting effect, visualizing the line Shakespeare gives Macbeth, 'Life's but a walking shadow' (5.5.23).

Figure 20 *A stage view at the end of* Macbeth, *Opéra National de Lyon (2012).*

Definitely absent were Scottish mists, medieval supernatural beliefs and the Romantic imagination. The uncanny gave way to realism, or perhaps hyperrealism, to represent both the greed for, and the terror of, big money. Given this dramaturgical reading, it logically followed that the oppressed people ('*Patria oppressa*') should be our contemporary activists in jeans and sneakers, a colourful crowd denouncing global capitalism, rather than some patriotic predicament, and marching towards Wall Street like a contemporary version of Birnam Wood advancing towards Dunsinane in disguise. Filmed by Tal Yarden, archival footage showed authentic demonstrations and Zuccotti Park (which served as a campground for the Occupy Wall Street opponents in autumn 2011). The Park itself was emulated on stage by the chorus and some extras holding signs reading 'Democracy for sale', 'Poets for peace' or Martin Luther King's iconic words, 'I have a dream'. An excerpt from a speech delivered by Slavoj Žižek at Liberty Plaza on 9 October 2011 was translated into French and shouted during an interruption of the music: 'They tell you we are dreamers. . . . We are not dreamers. We are awakening from a dream which is turning into a nightmare'. Macduff appeared as the leader capable of overthrowing the tyranny of unbridled capitalism, the saviour offering alternative ways of living, and Malcolm soon joined forces with him. The production ended with the triumph of anti-global ideology, although the nationalistic air '*Vittoria*' did not quite suggest what might come out of this victory for the world in this new expanded context. Dystopia had been defeated, but answers were left in abeyance; it was not clear how utopian dreams (which utopian dreams) might come true in the context of the new order freed from the power of money.

On the face of it, van Hove's updating of Verdi's opera became almost self-evident in its relation to the immediate context of our time, and most critics were quick to draw attention to it – sometimes discussing this change of time period exclusively. However, such an analogy was not unprecedented in *Regietheater*: Krzysztof Warlikowski had had Macbeth performed as a veteran suffering from post-traumatic stress disorder (2010), Michael Haneke had pitched the well-to-do against the wretched in the office tower which provided the setting of *Don Giovanni* (2006), and countless other examples have been staged in the wake of Peter Sellars' ground-breaking Mozart-Da Ponte trilogy, with *Così Fan Tutte* set in a diner (1986), *Don Giovanni* in Spanish Harlem (1987) and *The Marriage of Figaro* in Trump Tower (1988).

Besides, the ending of van Hove's *Macbeth* suggested another interpretation. Macbeth was not actually killed, but left haggard and distraught, sitting on a bench with a blanket over his shoulders and a can of soup in his hand, like a social outcast caught in his own illusions. It was as if the entire story had taken place in his mind and the production had played out his fantasies and fears, his dreams and nightmares. This would explain why he stood by Lady Macbeth (Iano Tamar) even when the character is not supposed to be onstage: for instance, during her first cavatina ('*Vieni! t'affretta!*') and, above all, during the sleepwalking scene as he helplessly watched her grope and fall. The candle that could be seen burning downstage from the beginning of the production was both hers and his: it continued burning after she laid it down and died – or, in other words, it did not completely go 'out' for him, as Macbeth begs in Shakespeare's play.

More than in Verdi's opera, van Hove enhanced the couple's relationship, her driving force and his loss, as a counterpoint of intimacy with the outside world of ruthless money politics. The director once said that he staged the gruesome sleepwalking scene as yet another 'scene from a marriage', quoting the title of Ingmar Bergman's film that he had adapted earlier for the theatre.[18] Indeed the destruction of the couple superseded Macbeth's own destruction and left him disconsolately defeated before Macduff, Malcolm and the Occupy Wall Street movement 'dethroned' him moments later. And it even seemed the notoriously childless couple had a daughter, playfully riding a broomstick and ironically leading Duncan to his room like a little witch.

As is often the case, the enemy was within as much as without. A cleaning lady, both unobtrusive and intriguing, hovered silently amidst the witches/spin-doctors, witnessed the goings-on and eavesdropped on the protagonists. In the end, it was she who let the people in to claim revenge. Couldn't she embody Hecate whose part Verdi cancelled altogether, yet whose responsibility for Macbeth's downfall van Hove restored? Consequently, couldn't the seemingly compliant businesswomen appear to have turned against Macbeth of their own accord and carried out their prophecies by themselves? A mere change of costume was enough. In retrospect, one could not help but recall that in Act One some witches had their faces marred with lipstick and a couple of others had surreptitiously worn 'Anonymous' masks – discreet harbingers of the production's outcome. The opera thus came full circle, yet not to a conclusion. No doubt it addressed the issue of power in financial terms and took a fierce anti-liberal stance, but behind this façade there were other ambiguities and intricacies lurking for the audience to consider.

LA CLEMENZA DI TITO *AND THE CRISIS OF DEMOCRACY*

Marcin Bogucki

The first season of the American television show *House of Cards* premièred at the beginning of 2013.[19] This political drama created by Beau Willimon was based on the BBC's mini-series of the same title, which was itself an adaptation of the novel by Michael Dobbs. The American version focused, obviously, on the local context: US politics. The main character is the cynical, cruel but – alas – likeable Frank Underwood, a politician who has only one goal: the presidency. A few months after the première of *House of Cards*, Ivo van Hove staged *La Clemenza di Tito* at the Théâtre Royal de la Monnaie in Brussels. Mozart's opera is also a political drama, but an ancient one. The closest friends of the title Roman emperor lead a conspiracy to topple the ruler. Eventually the rebellion is supressed; however, would-be assassins are not convicted but are shown the mercy of the emperor. Both works were trying to analyse the contemporary crisis of political leadership, each of them giving a different diagnosis of the existing situation.

House of Cards has been an award-winning and remarkably popular Netflix show. Despite its verisimilitude, this production is a fantasy about politics. Agnieszka Holland, director of some series episodes, confirms this thesis:

> This is not a realistic story, although it pays great attention to details. It is nearly operatic, quasi-Shakespearean work, exaggerated but, at the same time, deeply truthful – it denounces real politicians because it shows their most embarrassing dreams. It is not a chance that politicians around the world are admirers of the show (fortunately not only them, also millions of subscribers and double the amount of people illegally downloading it) – they dream about the cold-bloodedness and freedom of agency that Frank Underwood gains.[20]

House of Cards is indeed fascinating because of its moral ambiguity; despite all their misdemeanours, viewers root for the main characters and their actions.

Caterino Mazzolà and Wolfgang Amadeus Mozart portray the world of politics quite differently. Mazzolà's libretto is based on an earlier text by Pietro Metastasio, written in 1734 but rewritten many times and used throughout the long eighteenth century. The court poet wrote his work to celebrate the nameday of Charles VI, the Holy Roman Emperor, and to fit with the ideological programme of the Habsburg monarchy. Although the fictive world of the opera is dominated by love and political intrigues, there is a clear division between good and bad characters, and the conflict itself is quite mechanical and predictable – the title reveals everything. Mozart's opera can also be seen as part of the Habsburg propaganda: it was prepared to celebrate the coronation of Holy Roman Emperor Leopold II as king of Bohemia in 1791. Changes made by Mazzolà were designed to appeal to modern taste: the libretto was reduced to two acts, part of the text was deleted (for example, Act Two from the original was changed into an ensemble that ends the first part), and the number of arias was reduced to eleven.[21] *La Clemenza di Tito* was not well received at its première in 1791 at the Estates Theatre in Prague, but later it became celebrated and not only in Prague. The opera was staged frequently until the late 1820s as a work that reflects on the past and former types of ruling practice. It returned to the stage at the end of the 1960s, in the wake of totalitarianism and in an era of turbulent political change.[22]

House of Cards is an important context for van Hove's production of the opera. In the programme to the Warsaw performance (the show was a co-production of La Monnaie and Teatr Wielki [Polish National Opera]), the director admitted that there were some similarities between his production of the opera and the television show.[23] However the resemblance was not in the lead role, but rather in van Hove's artistic concept for the work: to peep into the backstage of politics and private lives of people in power, our modern rulers. Van Hove was not interested in the work's original context, but instead he treated the plot as if it were a contemporary one. This was, I think, the main weakness of his staging. On the one hand, we can easily find arguments in support of a modern reading. Metatasio used antiquity as a pretext – the story is only partially based on the historical sources. Except for Titus, the rest of the characters are fictional.[24] On the other hand, van Hove was not interested in the world of the Enlightenment and eighteenth-century speculations on power. Instead he very mechanically transferred the discussions about an absolute monarchy that wants to prove its power in unstable times (it is, after all, 1791!) onto contemporary (post-)democratic regimes.

Van Hove's production was set in a luxurious hotel room, devised by set and lighting designer Jan Versweyveld. The room was glamorous but at the same time intimate and the use of video made the stage resemble a laboratory and, at the same time, a particular interior and abstract space of political intrigues. Cameras, most of them hidden, followed the characters all the time; the action was filmed live from different angles, frequently from above with a smooth movement and projected onto nine screens located above the stage. Tal Yarden's video work gave the impression of a well-constructed and edited television news report. The stage furniture referenced a 1960s aesthetic and a similar nostalgia informed the costumes designed by An D'Huys: chic modern suits and gowns in dark, strong colours matching the dark brown that dominated the interior, taken not from a wardrobe of a politician (even the most stylish one) but from fashion magazines.

The opera was staged without any cuts, including all the *secco* recitatives that were written by one of Mozart's pupils. Compared to other works by Mozart, they are more opulent and therefore are often cut, but van Hove's interpretation enabled the singers to build psychologically nuanced portraits. The problem was the contrast between the lively pulse of these recitatives and the suspension of time in arias and ensembles where the dramaturgy slowed down, unveiling not real characters but puppets. In modern stagings of the opera, Titus has been often portrayed as a tyrant, bending the law according to his own caprice, but van Hove's Titus (Charles Workman) was a different kind of emperor. He was a victim of his own naivety, triumphing unexpectedly thanks only to his willpower. His inner drama was presented during the overture, which is, musically, a summary of the opera.[25] We saw Titus at his desk, deep in thought, while on the other side of the stage a tense pantomime took place between the main pair of intriguers: his bride-to-be Vittelia (Ewa Vesin) and her friend Sesto (Anna Bonitatibus), madly in love with Vittelia. Near the end of the overture, the whole division of assistants came on stage, creating chaos in a perfectly organized world, by unmaking the bed at the centre of the stage and flipping over chairs and lamps. It was a clear sign that not only personal factors are crucial for the opera's conflict, but that the political system itself had also created tension. Van Hove tried to make the plot more complicated (not simply a case of private feelings), but weakened it at the same time – he did not answer the question about the main cause of contemporary political tensions and how we can spot the flaws within our political system.

As a stage director, van Hove is a master of precision: he pays attention to details but at the same time thinks about a larger frame, moving between concrete social environment and metaphor. Stage props (glasses of whisky, tablets, smartphones) construct a realistic world, yet the space itself changes constantly and functions as an abstract representation of political strife. At first we found ourselves in this messy room, cleaned up only before the triumphant march that announces the arrival of Titus. The space opened up after the three rows of curtains that bordered the room from three sides were drawn back, revealing stands with chairs at the back of the stage that would be used in the second act by the senators, witnesses of the Emperor's

Figure 21 *The setting of* La Clemenza di Tito, *with Tito (Charles Workman) centre stage, Théâtre Royal de la Monnaie in Brussels (2013).*

triumph. From this place of private intrigues, we were moved into a more complicated world in which the boundary between public and private disappeared. Neutral, delicate light dominated the first act of the opera, but changed dramatically at the end of the first part: the fire of the Capitoline Hill, part of the coup, was represented as an intense orange glow. The stage in the second act was bathed in an artificial, strong blue light resembling night time. In the final act, the triumphant Titus was illuminated centre stage, but the rest remained in darkness. Van Hove intimates that the hero achieved individual victory but he did not change the world around him, for sure.

Van Hove wanted to prove that *La Clemenza di Tito* could be an up-to-date meditation on the theme of political leadership. However, by erasing the historical context of the work and not paying attention to its propagandist purpose, I think he created a not very convincing morality play – a lesson in how the modern politician should behave. Fantasies about politics in *House of Cards* are lively because they are based on the recognizable mechanisms of American politics. By contrast, *La Clemenza di Tito*, despite the appearance of a concrete situation, remained empty, an Enlightenment treatise detached from modern times. The main flaw in the opera is the presence of unambiguous characters – even when they are psychologically deepened and the acting of the singers is convincing, they are only puppets created to legitimize the title idea. In *House of Cards*, no kind of transcendence occurs as Frank Underwood implicates the viewers by frequently addressing his comments *a parte*. Similarly, in *La Clemenza di Tito*, with the last chords of the orchestra, the camera, filming from above, zooms into the face of Titus (see Figure 19). He stares back, piercingly and challenging. Once again he proves his mettle and confronts the audience to assure them of the ultimate correctness of his decision.

Oddly enough, in the context of Web 2.0 and WikiLeaks, van Hove's stage world seems to be ruled by television, not the Internet, and appears naive, bypassing the brutal core of modern politics. He proposes a simple solution to the crisis of democracy – moral restoration. *House of Cards* works differently: it tries to stoke anxiety in the viewers, as Agnieszka Holland sums up: 'I think we are ruled by a generation of narcissists, all those post-war generations (mostly men by the way), who were brought up to be egoistic babies who chiefly care about their own profits and pleasure and they treat politics more as a game than service. I do not know what it would take to change this. But I am afraid that it will be something really dramatic.'[26] The more cynical fantasy of modern politics shown in *House of Cards* seems closer to today's reality than van Hove's optimistic perspective. Unlike his production, the television series questions rather than tries to convince us that the eponymous 'clemenza' exists.

CRUELLY BEAUTIFUL: IVO VAN HOVE'S MAZEPPA

Johanna Wall

On 24 April 2013 *Mazeppa*, an opera by Pyotr Ilytch Tchaikovsky that premièred in Moscow in 1884 and only recently, yet all the more powerfully, entered European opera repertoire again, celebrated its opening night at the Komische Oper Berlin, one of three major opera houses in the German capital. Founded in 1947 by Austrian-born actor Walter Felsenstein in the former eastern part of the city, the Komische Oper (its name refers less to its repertoire than to the Paris-based Opéra Comique) can look back on more than seventy years of being a place where scenography and acting are worked on with the same mindfulness as is brought to the music of an opera. When it comes to music theatre, the Komische Oper is said to be the 'mothership' of modern *Regietheater* (directors' theatre), as *Intendant* and *Chefregisseur* (artistic director) Barrie Kosky put its reputation in a nutshell on the occasion of the seventieth anniversary of the reconstruction of the house in 2017.

When Australian director and 2012 Laurence Olivier Award-laureate Kosky became artistic director at the Komische Oper, he invited, in the same year, Ivo van Hove to stage *Mazeppa* for the first time in Berlin (excepting a guest performance, in 1969, by the National Opera of Belgrade). Van Hove was already widely known in Germany for his theatrical work with Toneelgroep Amsterdam and proved to be the perfect match for Tchaikovsky's masterpiece. As a dramaturg and permanent employee of Komische Oper Berlin, I had the privilege of supporting this production through the rehearsal process.

The libretto of *Mazeppa* is based on the narrative poem *Poltava* by the Russian national poet Alexander Sergeyevich Pushkin, who also provided the literary sources for Tchaikovsky's popular operas *The Queen of Spades* and *Eugene Onegin*. While the latter works treat more personal issues, *Mazeppa* is highly political and focuses on one of the most important battles of the Great Northern War (1700–21) during which Peter the First established an empire that later became the foundation of today's Russia. The protagonist of the opera is the historically documented Cossack warlord, Ivan Mazeppa (*c.* 1644–1709), who first fought on the side of the tsar but later turned against him in a bold yet futile attempt to gain independence for the Ukrainians from Russia. Even today Mazeppa is despised in Russia as a traitor while glorified by Ukrainians as a national hero.

In Tchaikovsky's musical version the historical facts are blended with one of many popular romantic anecdotes about the legendary Mazeppa. The story goes that the young boy was brought up at the Polish king's court but, having been caught in an improper affair, he was tied to a horse and driven out into the wilderness. He survived, was made chief of the wild Cossack bunch, and is said to have passionately fallen in love with a much younger woman, Maria Kotschubej. However, her father, a rich squire and friend of Mazeppa, not only disapproved of the relationship but also disagreed with Mazeppa in fighting against the Russian emperor. In the version by Pushkin and Tchaikovsky, Kotschubej reveals Mazeppa's plans to the tsar but he is ignored and surrendered instead to Mazeppa, who is in turn falsely assumed to be a loyal follower of the Russian ruler. Shortly thereafter, the merciless Ukrainian hitman executes Kotschubej before his daughter Maria. At the end of Tchaikovsky's version, Mazeppa, having lost the battle of Poltava and being pursued by the emperor's troops, stumbles into Maria's former admirer Andrej, who hates Mazeppa profoundly. Andrej attacks Mazeppa but he is shot and killed by the old warlord. When Maria turns up, Mazeppa attempts to run away with her, but soon gives up when he realizes that she has obviously lost her mind. Trying to save his own life, he leaves her behind, even though he knows that the hostile hordes of the tsar will reach her any minute. The opera ends with Maria singing a simple lullaby to her dying childhood friend Andrej.

Asked what was the perfect subject for an opera, Tchaikovsky wrote to his brother Modest in 1878: 'Neither tsars, nor marches, nor any other typical subject of the grand opera suits my musical style. It's only love, love, love.'[27] According to this claim, one might be tempted to think of Tchaikovsky as a romantic dreamer; however, the composer's view on love was as bleak as it was fatalistic, a view mirrored in van Hove's statements on the same subject. In an interview he mused on the question of the true nature of love: 'Is love really a power that unifies us? I don't think so. Much more I think,

Figure 22 *Maria (Asmik Grigorian), Mazeppa, Komische Oper, Berlin (2013).*

it is a power that sunders us.'[28] In his typically cool and aesthetically finely calculated staging, van Hove, moreover, never avoided addressing the abhorrent content of Tchaikovsky's masterpiece. In fact it is precisely in the unexpected and shocking moments of realization that the beautiful music we hear is, in fact, the soundtrack to torture that it comes to mind how close Tchaikovsky's and van Hove's perceptions not only of love, but of art, might be.

In the course of the preparations for the production, van Hove was quite preoccupied with the composer's biography. For all of his life Tchaikovsky was torn between his private desires and his wish to fit in a society that was neither able nor willing to accept homosexuality. Van Hove's interest in this idea of love as 'impossible love' or 'love that is not accepted by one's social environment'[29] was a defining theme in his approach to *Mazeppa*. The entanglement of private and political matters – in the case of Mazeppa, especially society's refusal to accept individuals who stand out from the masses – was an aspect of the story that particularly captured van Hove's interest. And Tchaikovsky did not only work this perspective into the central scenes: he also inserted a hilariously wild dance by a seemingly drunk soldier who claims his right to enjoy life in the midst of the execution of Mazeppa's former confidant and would-be father-in-law, Kotschubej. It was a slight but important direction that van Hove gave the singer of this small part during rehearsals: 'The singer should not pretend to be drunk! On the contrary, it's just the others who call him a drunkard, as drunkenness is the only socially acceptable explanation for this embarrassing behavior.'

Scarce and precise stage directions like this one were typical of van Hove's way of working with the singer-actors in the course of the production. Always keeping in mind his carefully prepared and overarching visually-based interpretation, van Hove took his time during the rehearsals to find out about otherwise undiscovered underlying motivations for even the smallest role in the piece. In close collaboration with stage designer Jan Versweyveld and video artist Tal Yarden, every arrangement of soloists and chorus was set on the rehearsal stages so that only minimum adjustments had to be done once the project entered the main auditorium for the final rehearsals. Apart from concentration on psychological character development, the use of pre-produced video footage was an essential element of his production.

Van Hove's very focused working method, as well as the results he achieves, could be simply put: reduced to the max. His approach encompasses all elements of the production, from his time-conscious collaboration with the assistant directors (whom he relied on widely for their co-arranging of the large collectives during the chorus sequences) to the lean style of the German, English, French and Turkish surtitles that were stripped of any redundant adjective or of any word that didn't add something one couldn't already perceive from stage or pit.

Similarly, stage designer Jan Versweyveld went for a one-room solution. All the actions took place in a desolate, wide hall, stripped of any ornament or folkloristic decor and was only slightly adapted to the requirements of the different situations of individual scenes during the course of the opera. Everything in this room served a certain purpose, whether a column where the rifles for war and execution were kept or simple stairs that provided the only place to sit except for a heavy wooden desk, the symbol of the protagonist's overwhelming power. The reduced, yet realistic, stage 'room' was counterpointed by a huge video screen that could be moved smoothly across the stage. Video images were projected onto the sliding screens mainly during instrumental sections such as the overture or the 'Battle of Poltava' interlude at the beginning of Act Three. For the overture, video artist Tal Yarden created a collage of images of natural disasters, from catastrophes to environmental pollution. During the 'Battle of Poltava' interlude (a tone poem within the frame of the opera), images taken from current war reporting were combined with those of soldiers in everyday situations and were projected in tandem with the musical structure and rhythm. The torture and killing scene of the rich Kotschubej was commented on by images of torture and humiliation in war zones: soldiers walking over rows of wincing bodies and an allegedly real-time decapitation. Yarden decided to use this very explicit material, having only modified and distorted it by blurring and altering its original colouring. The realistic depictions of human brutality were counterpointed by dynamic and associative video clips of running horses that could be read as an allusion to the many famous pictures of the young Mazeppa being tied to his horse (for example, the 1820 painting by French artist Théodore Géricault). The simplicity of the set and the overwhelming and shocking videos stood in harsh contrast with each other, creating an air of daunting awe and melancholic vanity one can associate with the state of total human war (whether private or public) that forms the core of Tchaikovsky's thoroughly fatalistic opera *Mazeppa*.

Van Hove's production of *Mazeppa* turned out to be one of the most controversial staged at the Komische Oper Berlin over the last five years. Critics' views of the *mise en scène* ranged from 'showy and unnecessary'[30] to 'bold [and] terrifyingly intense.'[31] The critics' opinion was split, as was the audience's. Whereas some people in the regular audience were irritated by the minimalistic acting, interestingly enough it was especially the younger generation of spectators (those in their twenties and thirties) who objected to it, albeit for a different reason. During public discussions of the opera, some of the younger ticket buyers made it very clear what offended them most: the stumbling block was the use of the above-mentioned 'snuff video', even though those sequences were only one aspect of Yarden's work, an art installation in its own right. Though legally obtained, as Yarden pointed out frequently, these depictions of allegedly real humiliations and abuses of people in war zones were rated as morally highly controversial, especially in media-conscious circles. Discussions focused of how far the showing of brutality and torment is a crime in itself – or at least ethically inappropriate in so far as it violates the privacy of the victim who probably hadn't been asked beforehand if his/her suffering should be displayed publicly. Should brutality as it exists be shown? Yarden's video work might be seen as a recent iteration of the long-standing debate about freedom of artistic expression and whether art should take upon itself the responsibility to mirror the world in all its facets, without avoiding its dark sides. This unsolved question Tchaikovsky and Pushkin answered in their own times and van Hove and his artistic colleagues did so too in 2013. Notwithstanding the controversy, van Hove's interpretation of Pushkin's and Tchaikovsky's *Mazeppa* was one that shunned compromise, doing justice to a disturbing and brutal story while realizing the sad beauty of the music of a composer whose complexities are rarely fully explored.

BROKEBACK MOUNTAIN: 'WHY CAN'T I SAY WHAT I WANT TO SAY?'

José Máximo Leza

The pleasures and satisfactions deriving from artistic experiences, like those in other spheres of life, largely depend on our expectations. And in these expectations we find a combination of what is familiar and safe with the risk of what is yet to be discovered, a delicate balance that precludes both boredom with the trivial and the difficulty of the incomprehensible. The first circumstances that condition our individual and collective expectations are the conventions and codes that govern different artistic genres. The novel, the theatre, the cinema or the opera have formulated their own rules, which means that transferring a work from one genre to another necessitates significant changes in their structures and languages.

The opera *Brokeback Mountain*, with the libretto by E. Annie Proulx, music by composer Charles Wuorinen and stage direction by Ivo van Hove, had its première in Madrid in 2014. The work is based on Proulx's own short story, published in 1997 and adapted for cinema by Ang Lee in 2005. The film version enjoyed worldwide recognition, great praise and numerous awards. The projected opera, conceived over the period 2008–12, was the brainchild of Gerard Mortier when he was still director of the New York City Opera, and accompanied him to the Teatro Real in Madrid when he became Artistic Director there (2010–13). Thus, in fewer than twenty years, the public has had access to three different iterations of a plot whose originality derives from the portrayal of the intense but troubled relationship between two ranch hands of humble origin, Ennis Del Mar and Jack Twist, and set in rural Wyoming from 1963 to 1983. Their doubts and insecurities, especially in the case of Ennis, and the oppressive society surrounding them, form the basis for this drama.

The creation and staging of the opera *Brokeback Mountain* faced a series of unavoidable artistic challenges. Some of these had to do with operatic conventions, but others arose from the images left in the minds of potential audiences by Ang Lee's film, and, to a lesser extent, by Proulx's short story. The traditional language of the western, regularly revised for the cinema, although unaccustomed to the explicit presence of a homoerotic element at the forefront of the action, constituted an added difficulty, as well as an extra motivation, for the project's creators. Therefore, any critical approach to this opera must take into account the creative itinerary that leads from the short story to the opera, considering the theatre (in the restrictive sense of the libretto) as an implicit link between the two, and having its background in the cinema.

In contrast to the usual process of adaptation, both Proulx's libretto and Lee's screenplay had to be expanded from the spare initial story from which the author had eliminated all superfluous detail. Many of the ellipses and nuances implicit in the story are made explicit in the stage text. The characters of Alma and Lureen, the protagonists' wives, acquire a greater dimension in the libretto, and their dialogue, largely quarrels and arguments with their respective husbands, gives a crude and direct vision of their background: traditional family ties and their precarious employment and financial situation in the face of the unending demands of their children, conditions which continue after Ennis's divorce. Van Hove portrays these oppressive domestic surroundings by the simultaneous presentation of Ennis's and Jack's homes, by means of cluttered interiors with no partitions, reminiscent of the disorder of a furniture

Figure 23 *From left, Alma (Heather Buck), Ennis Del Mar (Daniel Okulitch) and Jack Twist (Tom Randle),* Brokeback Mountain, *Teatro Real, Madrid (2014).*

showroom. In both cases, the marital bed is located in an insignificant background position, whereas in the foreground we see the most alienating elements, such as Jack's father-in-law's farm machinery shop in which Lureen works and the wide range of electrical appliances that highlight Alma's asphyxiating domestic routine.

The addition of some entirely new scenes can be considered more closely linked to purely operatic conventions. This is the case in the ironic apparition of the ghost of Jack's father-in law, forewarning of Jack's fatal end, in an allusion to the Commendatore in Mozart's *Don Giovanni* and backed by a choir of spirits in the style of Greek drama. Van Hove presents the group as dark silhouettes of anonymous cowboys who express the impossibility of society tolerating the situation of two men living together in deepest Wyoming. The association of the characters with their voice types also follows operatic tradition: the lyricism of the tenor voice for Jack, the conquering lover; the more introspective baritone for Ennis, who is reluctant to show his sexual identity; the threatening characters of the trail boss, Aguirre, and Lureen's father conveyed in a bass voice, or the soprano and mezzo soprano voices of the respective wives. In spoken theatre, the word and the realistic way in which it is delivered are essential tools to transmit to the audience the authenticity of the characters. However, in opera, the music acts as an essential mediator in the communication of feelings: this means that the choice of a certain expressive style is immediately understood by the audience.

It is in this regard that *Brokeback Mountain* has given rise to the greatest criticism on the part of the national and international critics in attendance at its world première. The core of the drama – the difficulties and the tragic end of the love between the two ranch hands – is no more than a contemporary version of the many impossible loves that have sustained the opera throughout its history. Above and beyond the expression of the constraints of this impossibility, the emotional and sentimental effects on the protagonists are not easily ignored. This is where the text demands a certain amount of lyricism and the music requires an element of communicability in order to do justice to this dramatic core. However, Wuorinen's score follows the aesthetic model of post-dodecaphonism and atonality, making few concessions to consonance (showing recognizable influences of Arnold Schoenberg and Alban Berg). His was a musical style and grammar whose complex polyphony and generous use of percussion are more appropriate for the portrayal of the oppressive elements surrounding the characters than for their lyrical outpourings. Thus, the taciturn and introverted Ennis, a man of few words in the story, expresses himself at the beginning of the opera using a half-sung, half-spoken *Sprechstimme*. His emotional awakening becomes more explicit as the score progresses, first in some short duets with Jack, and finally in the monologue after his lover's death. It is here that the brief moments of relative lyricism can be heard, and where the limits of the rigid musical language in the expression of the feelings involved in a loving relationship are most evident.

The beginning of the work is more coherent, however, where the music begins with a droning pedal tone in the orchestra, using the low C to represent the mountain (between the B natural and the C sharp associated with the two protagonists), and where the comparison with the opening of Wagner's (formidable) *Ring Cycle* is inevitable. In *Brokeback Mountain*, the mountain is presented as a wild and dangerous place, a hostile setting for a hard job, as Aguirre's menacing shadow warns us in the first scene. As occurs in other operatic productions he has staged, van Hove has opted for the use of video footage as a vital part of his project. Here images of the mountains of Wyoming (filmed by Tal Yarden) acquire, through the music, a dramatic dimension that is very different from the more amiable one shown in Lee's film (see Plate 12). And there is nothing in the music that reminds the audience of an Arcadian dimension of nature, even when, as the opera progresses, the mountains become the only real space of freedom for the lovers.

Paradoxically, the international musical language used, taking the historic European avant-garde as its reference, instead of bringing the contemporary audience closer, causes an aesthetic rift with the essence of the drama, whose undeniable romantic elements have been more effectively translated through other musical languages throughout the history of the opera. And at the same time, there are no musical references, even in suggestions or recognizable reminiscences, that remind us of the surrounding rugged Western landscape whose characteristics engender the most transgressive and currently relevant elements of the drama. The colours of pop or country music or the songs mentioned by Proulx in her story are not present in Wuorinen's palette, and neither are those of the traditional American musical.

In van Hove's project, all the coherence of the beauty of the mountains on film, the omnipresence of tents, cowboy hats and shirts or even the serene stylization reminiscent of Edward Hopper's paintings do not succeed in lessening the feeling of alienation and aesthetic dissonance with what the orchestra and singers are trying to transmit to us. And then Ennis's question, when he confesses his fears and inability to reconcile his feelings and his life, 'Why can't I say what I want to say?', could be answered by himself in the final scene, illuminating our perception and expectations regarding this opera of cowboys in love: 'I never said what you wanted me to say.'

FANTASY AND REALITY IN SALOME

Frédéric Maurin

Presented at the 2017 Holland Festival, *Salome*, the opera by Richard Strauss, fits into the larger picture of Ivo van Hove's work – a series of productions, both theatrical and operatic, that focus on larger-than-life female characters who are at once strong and vulnerable, unflinching and fallible, pure and sinful. These women are 'outsiders', as the director likes to call them, who overthrow an established order and, more often than not, cause the downfall of a dysfunctional family. As Salome heralds Elektra in the composer's oeuvre, she is related, in van Hove's career, to such figures as Antigone or

Hedda Gabler, with Blanche DuBois in *A Streetcar Named Desire*, Regina Giddens in *The Little Foxes* or Mary Tyrone in *Long Day's Journey into Night*. She belongs, too, with the Lulu of Alban Berg's opera, the paragon of the murderer *femme fatale* turned murdered prostitute; Emilia Marty in *The Makropulos Case* by Leoš Janáček, the lonely diva weary of immortality; and Brünnhilde in Wagner's *Der Ring des Nibelungen*, the deceived lover whose immolation brings to an end her father's dream of omnipotence.

According to van Hove,[32] the opera does not so much harp on about Salome's evil nature let loose and her supposed embodiment of female wantonness and perversity as it narrates her coming of age through the ordeal of unrequited lust. At the outset, the protagonist is a virgin teenager, innocent and somewhat melancholy, living in luxury at the court of King Herod of Judea, her uncle/stepfather. She has won the heart of Narraboth, a young, timid Syrian whom she hardly notices and whose suicide she completely ignores, and is lasciviously coveted by Herod himself. Gradually, she becomes aware of her beauty, her body and the power of her charms. Her curiosity about John the Baptist (Jochanaan[33]), who is held prisoner in a cistern and keeps insulting her adulterous mother, turns into fascination. Yet she fails to catch his eye, however 'terrible' she admits he looks, and is unable to awaken his desire. The opera thus charts the way in which Salome comes into her own by discovering the world of men and taking revenge on the one who spurns her, expressing her utmost frustration in a paroxysmic outbreak leading to death.

In this emotionally drunken and physically draining production, the dramatic crescendo did not, however, take place in the void of some legend adapted to decadent tastes. On the contrary, van Hove was careful enough to invert the clichéd *fin-de-siècle* Orientalism into a criticism of today's Western civilization. Drawing inspiration from Avishai Margalit and Ian Buruma's text, *Occidentalism: The West in the Eyes of Its Enemies*,[34] he assumed that just as the Romans decided on the fate of the world in ancient times, neglecting the rise of Christianity and silencing those who predicted the coming of a Saviour and the advent of a new world vision, Westerners today ignore those who fight against materialism and liberal capitalism. As van Hove updated the historical context and honed in on religious disputes between the Jews, the Nazarenes and sceptics or polytheists like Herod, Jochanaan became a romantic alternative in the callous, violent environment of the Roman province of Judea where Salome lives.

From the outset, even before the overture, a gathering of political, religious and military leaders was taking place in the background and could be glimpsed through an opening in the backdrop. In an opulent reception room overlooking a city at night, replete with palm trees and leather armchairs, Herod's busy guests and staff hurried self-importantly, paced back and forth, and fiddled with their smartphones. Whereas in *Antigone* van Hove used a circle hollowed out to let the sun run its course and graphically coincide with the development of the tragedy, this opening in *Salome* gradually shrank during the theological debates and closed up like a camera's shutter during the Dance of the Seven Veils, blocking off the 'real' world of politics and focusing on the private sphere and the inner drama, no matter how many witnesses were in attendance.

For the most part, however, the space designed by Jan Versweyveld delineated a large semi-circular playing area with the Prophet's cistern at the centre: it felt like 'a black hole' from which no light could escape, a barren counterpoint to the intensity of the music, an abstract arena where the characters, stepping forward from the real-world background, could express their inner thoughts and hidden fantasies. In an echo of Lars von Trier's *Melancholia*, a moon travelled diagonally on the backdrop and waxed for the first two scenes, then turned red during the first encounter between Jochanaan and Salome, and was later eclipsed by a black circle surrounded with a white halo, encroaching upon the whole stage as if to signal the end of the world – or at least the end of *a* world. The moon, as a female principle, served both as the mirror of the characters' subjective perceptions and desires (which seldom meet in this drama of impossible looks and averted glances) and as a metaphor for Salome herself. Indeed, it is alternately compared with 'a woman rising from a tomb' (the Page, anticipating Salome's fate), 'a princess who has little white doves for feet' (Narraboth, unwillingly hinting at the Dance), 'a little silver flower, ... cold and chaste, [who] has a virgin's beauty' (Salome, describing herself as she enters, before portraying Jochanaan as 'chaste as the moon is' too), or later with 'a mad woman ... seeking everywhere for lovers, ... naked, ... drunken' (Herod). And moonlike did Salome appear. Sung by Malin Byström (making her debut in the title role), Salome was dressed in an off-white gown and went bare-foot after she took her shoes off, cutting a distraught figure not unlike Hedda Gabler in van Hove's production. But the development of the moon and its eclipse also materialized Jochanaan's prediction in advance: 'the sun shall become black like sackcloth of hair, and the moon shall become like blood.' As a whole, the production achieved a perilous balance between utter faithfulness to Strauss's opera – both to the libretto and to the music, which the director dared compare to 'hard rock, sometimes even metal'[35] – and abstract interpretation, between lyricism and dissonance, between the fleshy and the formalistic.

So close to the libretto was the staging that when Salome asked for Jochanaan's head she was served his whole 'unbeheaded' body in a large silver bowl – a dying body still searing and slithery with blood. But this image, which caused much dismay among

Figure 24 *From left, Herod's Page (Hanna Hipp), Narraboth (Evgeny Nikitin), Jochanaan (Peter Sonn) and Salome (Malin Byström),* Salome, *the Dutch National Opera, Amsterdam (2017).*

critics as it clashed with both pictorial and operatic traditions, was dictated by Strauss's work itself. Van Hove made a point of following Salome's words literally as she impatiently awaits the revenge that is her reward: 'He is afraid, this slave. He has let his sword fall. He dares not kill him [Jochanaan]'. On the other hand, subjectivity came so much to the foreground that in their first encounter Jochanaan (sung by tattoo-covered Evgeny Nikitin) held Salome from behind, embraced her softly and drew her head on his shoulder as she fantasized he would: it was an explicitly erotic embrace that turned their duel into a duet and fulfilled her wish for a kiss instead of demonstrating his curse. Tenderness later gave way to fierceness, especially in the testing Dance of the Seven Veils, choreographed by Wim Vandekeybus to 'the wild rhythm' of the music. It was performed with graceful seduction by Salome, gradually took over the whole court and guests in a collective handkerchief ritual perhaps derived from a Jewish tradition, and accelerated as smoke pervaded the stage and a blindfolded Salome reached a trance-like state recalling Marina Abramović's performance piece *Freeing the Body* (1976). But the Dance was also simultaneously projected, a pre-recorded black-and-white video made by Tal Yarden. In it, Herod could happily see himself dance with Salome, as opposed to the possible impotence that van Hove wished to stress and the sexual fetish that had him pick up Salome's shoes and smell them before ordering her to 'dance for him'. In the meantime, Salome could engage in an alternately amorous and pugnacious *pas de deux* with Jochanaan, both of them stripping naked in close physical intimacy.[36] Thus the Dance shifted points of view and performed the main characters' hidden desires. It became a substitute for impossible intercourses: only in fantasy could the unions between Salome and Herod, Salome and Jochanaan, Salome and the community of men, be carried out.

Reality, however, came to supersede imagination. The last scene was not so much an orgy – albeit of gore – as the ultimate orgasm in death. The Prophet who Salome had craved could not but yield to her voracious kiss and seemingly vampiric, necrophilic or even cannibalistic embrace. But her coming of age became self-destructive and she herself died a *Liebestod* after singing 'the mystery of love is greater than the mystery of death'. She was sacrificed on the altar of boundless passion and 'killed' by order of Herod; yet the soldiers lifted her up instead of 'crushing' her, so that she was last seen with her arms stretched out, an exhausted martyr of her own delusion, a crucified figure setting right Jochanaan's Christian prophecy. During the course of the production, feelings ran from sensuous desire to sexual consumption, but in the end were repressed by the 'real' world and its harsh rules. After Salome had kissed Jochanaan's dying body to her heart's content, the crack in the backdrop opened up again in a flash, revealing a landscape of ruins somehow reminiscent of the rubble in van Hove's production of *Siegfried*. Although it suggested that Salome had wrought havoc in Herod's universe and the pre-Christian world order, she was nevertheless vanquished.

Free unquenchable libidinal impulses were quelled by the objective world of power and framed within an aesthetic concept on the part of the artistic team. Just as geometrical triangles helped visualize the recurrence of the number three in the opera (the waltz beats, Herod's rejected offers of an emerald, peacocks and jewels in exchange for Salome's Dance), the overall black, white and red colour scheme – primarily seen in the ominous backdrop, Salome's gown and the neon lights, the moon and Jochanaan's bloody carcass – not only magnified the colours of the Prophet's fetishized body parts – his black hair, white skin and red mouth – but also intensified the production's physical strain with pure plastic emotion.

Section Five

Creation, Adaptation, Direction

DIRECTING ACROSS GENRE:
FILM, FICTION, MUSIC, THEATRE

Susan Bennett

Ivo van Hove has deservedly earned the designation of polymath. His attention to and skill with canonical texts from the Ancient Greeks to Shakespeare and through to mainstays of the American theatre are by now well recognized and frequently honoured across the English-speaking world and beyond. In Europe, he has tackled the classics of opera repertory as well as experimental musical works such as Leoš Janáček's song cycle *The Diary of One Who Disappeared*. But the breadth and richness of van Hove's cultural knowledge and creative engagement is perhaps most vividly on display in the extraordinary variety of his exploration and adaptation across twentieth- and twenty-first-century works with their origins not just in the theatre, but in film, the musical and the novel.

The early productions in van Hove's career were staged by several of Antwerp's important experimental theatre companies including Akt, Theater-Vertikaal – the two merged in 1985 as Akt-Vertikaal – and De Tijd (in English, The Tide – itself a merger of another company, White Crow, with Akt-Vertikaal[1]). The history of this work in Belgium reveals a predilection for modern texts including Harold Pinter's *The Servant* (staged in 1982–3), Marguerite Duras's *Agatha* (1983–4) and *India Song* (1984–5), Botho Strauss's *Morocco* (1983–4) and Heiner Müller's *Russian Opening* (1985–6). From 1990 to 2000, as director of Het Zuidelijk Toneel [The Southern Theatre] (based in Tilburg in the Netherlands), he continued his interest in directing Modernist drama with productions such as Jean Genet's *Splendid's* (1994–5) and Albert Camus's *Caligula* (1995–6). But, by the late 1980s, van Hove had already started to build the oeuvre of productions of canonical works that have become his best-recognized directorial signature: *Macbeth* at De Tijd (1987–8), Eugene O'Neill's *Mourning Becomes Electra* (1988–9), Sophocles' *Ajax/Antigone* (1990–1), *Hamlet* (1992–3) and Tennessee Williams's *A Streetcar Named Desire* (1994–5), all at Het Zuidelijk Toneel. And, only a decade later, van Hove was managing the Holland Festival,[2] directing plays that were co-produced by the Festival and Het Zuidelijk Toneel, fostering a working relationship with the New York Public Theatre (O'Neill's *More Stately Mansions* [1996] was his first project there; it earned him an Obie award), and undertaking ventures in performance genres new to him: opera (starting with Alban Berg's *Lulu* in 1999 for The Flemish Opera) and the musical. This new foray into the musical brought about a production of Jonathan Larson's *Rent*, the hugely successful, Tony award-winning New York Theatre Workshop show that ran for twelve years on Broadway and which was also seen nationally and internationally in touring and resident productions. While Michael Grief's original direction had typically been used by other productions, van Hove, not surprisingly, charted his own path and introduced a radically different 'take' for his Dutch-language version: 'In the original production . . . the character of Mimi almost dies but is miraculously resurrected. In van Hove's pitiless version, Mimi dies, with her last moments represented on video.'[3] His production toured to fifty theatres across the Netherlands and Belgium.

About his directorial work, van Hove has said 'Reinventing the meaning of the text for today – that's the thing'[4] and, by the end of the 1990s through to the first years of the new century, he was increasingly committed to expanding the kinds of texts that might receive this approach. As well as canonical dramas from across the Western world, operas and the musical, van Hove also turned to film sources that might be adapted into new stage productions. His first film-into-theatre project was another co-production between the Holland Festival and Het Zuidelijk Toneel (1996–7), a reinvention of John Cassavetes' Oscar-nominated *Faces* – a black-and-white film that had first premièred in Toronto (1968) with a running time of 183 minutes. In an interview, van Hove admitted to laughing when *Faces* was suggested to him: 'Almost impossible – but then I read the script and it was written just like a play, eleven long scenes.'[5] On his move into the adaptation of film, he continues: 'I found in these scripts themes and characters and extreme situations that I couldn't find in other plays.'[6] *Faces* was produced again in 2005, this time a co-production between Theater der Welt, Schauspielhaus Hamburg and Staatstheater Stuttgart, followed by an adaptation of Cassavetes' 1977 *Opening Night* (a co-production between Toneelgroep Amsterdam [TGA] and NTGent in 2005–6). He has continued with projects that are inspired by, or adaptations of films by, many of the most highly regarded European *auteur* directors: Ingmar Bergman, Luchino Visconti, Michelangelo Antonioni and Pier Paolo Pasolini. In 2017–18 van Hove directed a sell-out stage version of Lee Hall's 1976 film *Network* at London's National Theatre with Bryan Cranston in the Peter Finch role of Howard Beale, the 'mad as hell' TV newscaster.

The challenges of adapting film for the stage – and there are surely many: scale, control of point of view, smoothness and rapidity of shifts in setting among them – are mitigated in van Hove's work in two particular ways. First, there is ample evidence from his theatrical collaborations with partner and designer Jan Versweyveld that they understand and, indeed, love film. Ranging from scene-setting backdrops (such as the vistas of New York City and Berlin in *Lazarus* or the mountain peaks of Wyoming in *Brokeback Mountain* – see Plate 12) to oversized close-ups of actors projected onto giant screens (frequently seen in *Roman Tragedies* and *Kings of War*), the incorporation of original video work is commonly and confidently a part of their theatrical toolkit. Second, van Hove has emphasized time and again that he and Versweyveld do not construct their adaptations from repeated or even single viewings of their subject film; rather, a film's screenplay serves as just another text for their extended scrutiny before committing to realize a version for the stage. The benefit, van Hove explains, is that the transformed screenplay is 'like a world première' and, in an oft-repeated and very quotable comparison, he suggests 'It's as if *Hamlet* comes through the mail and you have to stage it for the very first time.'[7] While an analogy between the screenplays he chooses and *Hamlet* might work on the basis of the pedigrees behind their creation, it surely falls apart on the proposition of the 'first time' – even if the films themselves are but distant memories for the director, it is more than likely that sections of his audiences for these adaptations know well the creative history behind his text or, out of curiosity, have taken the time to review the subject film ahead of seeing the van Hove performance.

While van Hove's work with film is known chiefly through its deployment within a theatrical creation or via his conversions of screenplays into stage drama, he has also directed a television series, *Thuisfront* (*Homefront*, 1997) and a full-length feature film, *Amsterdam* (2009). The film's screenplay was written by Jeroen Planting, a Dutch actor with a number of technical film credits, and produced by Martin Lagestee (Lagestee Film BV) and Marijke van der Molen (Palentino Pictures). *Amsterdam* received a limited theatrical release in the Netherlands and is available in DVD and digital formats with English subtitles. Described as 'an ensemble film',[8] it tells the interlinked stories of a wildly diverse group of people – a Dutch family caught up in a world of violent theft, a working-class German family on their first-ever trip outside their homeland, a wealthy American couple celebrating their fifth wedding anniversary with a lavish vacation in the city, a gay French couple also on vacation, two illegal immigrants from Morocco and a tough but empathetic police detective. Shot on location in Amsterdam and Morocco and cast almost exclusively with Dutch actors, only two cast members are likely familiar to North American audiences: Marisa Tomei (Best Supporting Actress Oscar winner for *My Cousin Vinny* among her many film and television credits) plays the shrill and demanding American wife, and Omar Metwally (Dr Vic Ullah in *The Affair* and Agent Santiago in *Mr. Robot*) her philandering husband. Others in the cast are familiar from the TGA ensemble – Eelco Smits plays Omer, Hans Kesting the detective Martin. Even van Hove himself has a brief cameo as Willem, the 'boss' the thieves report to, as does his TGA associate director, Wouter van Ransbeek, who appears as a hotel receptionist!

A taut 85 minutes, *Amsterdam* is perhaps most interesting as a puzzle for the viewer as to what kind of film it is. The narrative takes place over five days, although the film opens with a short sequence from Day 3 that signals the film might be about a kidnapping gone wrong. It is that, but it is also a socio-economic commentary, an interrogation of human sexuality, a black comedy, a political critique, a family drama and a paean to the city van Hove has long made home. No one filmic genre predominates across the five-day action and while the ending provides forms of closure, at least for some of the characters, *Amsterdam* registers more as a playful exercise in weaving together this dazzling variety of genres into an overarching plot. If van Hove's genre mixing was not entirely successful (the film moved quickly to DVD), *Amsterdam* does illustrate his deep knowledge of filmic convention and explores how different genres might open new ways to respond to stock character types. What prevails is the pleasure the film takes in its seamless referentiality, its treatment of so many familiar types of popular film. In many ways, *Amsterdam* stands as an example opposite to the originality of van Hove's stage work, given its love for the filmic commonplace, but this single excursion into making a feature film indubitably displays the director's considerable knowledge of standard Hollywood fare – a counterpoint to, but also a resource for, his process of film-to-stage adaptation.

This section tackles the variety of genres out of which van Hove makes his contemporary work. Julie Sanders looks at his adaptation of Luchino Visconti's 1943 film *Ossessione* (*Obsession*), staged at the Barbican Theatre in 2017. She carefully elaborates how the screenplay of Visconti's movie is transformed into a sparse stage drama and considers, too, a history of adaptation and appropriation that produces, in van Hove's iteration, particularly textured theatrical effects. P. A. Skantze imagines a performance archaeology that might uncover and unravel the tensions in van Hove's film-to-stage adaptations, focusing on his reworking of Bergman's *Scenes from a Marriage*. She attends to the layers of space and sound that his productions activate and how they shape audience response(s).

Turning to what is certainly one of van Hove's more surprising selections for adaptation, Denis Flannery compares Ayn Rand's 1943 novel *The Fountainhead* and van Hove's stage version. Flannery points out not just the success of this particular production, but how it has triggered a surge in novel-to-stage adaptations. While Skantze's discussion

Figure 25 *Thomas Jerome Newton (Michael C. Hall) and Girl (Sophia Anne Caruso),* Lazarus, *New York Theatre Workshop (2015).*

of van Hove's productions concentrates on the elements of space and sound, Flannery looks specifically at the work of lighting in Jan Versweyveld's staging designs and how contrasts of light and shade translate Rand's novel for the contemporary stage. The success of his production of *The Fountainhead* appears to have provoked van Hove's further interest in stage adaptations of novels: at TGA he has directed versions of three novels by Louis Couperus (1863–1923, a pre-eminent writer in the Dutch literary canon), *The Hidden Force* (*De Stille Kracht*, 2015–16), *The Things That Pass* (*De Dingen die Voorbijgaan*, 2016–17) and *Small Souls* (*Kleine Zielen*, 2017–18).

Van Hove has often spoken of how he and Versweyveld spend as much as two years reading and thinking about a text before deciding on a production and starting rehearsals.[9] The last two contributions in this section look at his creative output in contexts that required different – certainly faster – working methods. Van Hove and TGA were commissioned, as part of their residency at London's Barbican Theatre, to design and curate the 2016–17 Barbican Box project – an annual community-engagement initiative that encourages arts learning and creation with teachers and students from secondary schools and further education colleges in East London. Rachael Nicholas examines the composition of the box that van Hove and TGA prepared for the participating students as well as the methodologies with which they were charged to explore, create and perform. My own contribution looks at van Hove's involvement in the David Bowie and Enda Walsh collaboration, *Lazarus*. Van Hove joined the production team without the opportunity to follow his preferred trajectory of a two-year period for script development since Bowie and Walsh had already completed a first draft. Thus, for the long-awaited sequel to the 1976 film *The Man Who Fell to Earth*, the work of adaptation into stage musical was already well in hand when he became the *Lazarus* director. Nonetheless, van Hove emphasizes that he was an 'artistic collaborator' in the project and not a 'for hire' appointment as director.[10] I examine how both the untimely death of Bowie during the play's original New York run and a subsequent restaging in London in a much larger capacity venue recalibrated van Hove's directorial 'vision of universal solitude and dislocation'[11] and produced an unanticipated adaptation to the particular circumstances of its later production and reception.

SYNECDOCHE, ADAPTATION AND THE STAGED SCREENPLAY: VAN HOVE'S OBSESSION(S)

Julie Sanders

There is no stage curtain. A pared-back scene confronts us, provocative in its spareness. A woman seems to be at work in a small space with a counter surrounding (encasing, enclosing, entrapping?) her; this space is suggestive of a kitchen – a piece of meat lies provocatively on the otherwise empty counter – or perhaps a bar. The latter image sparks strong associations with Edward Hopper's painting *Nighthawks*, a picture redolent of Hopper's broader palette of desolate individuals in landscapes of bars, diners and gas stations, the spatial coordinates of early twentieth-century Modernism. This woman is clearly visible to the audience but she does not directly acknowledge or explain herself, or her actions, to us.

An oversized accordion hangs from the ceiling, performing – seemingly of its own accord or by some clever offstage mechanism – a form of folk music, not entirely locatable and yet evocative of a moment (and a place?) not quite our own; an uncased combustion engine suspended nearby prompts all kinds of similar immediate yet confused and clouded associations – with cars, certainly, and by extension with the open road and notions of mobility – but the full signification of those links is still not immediately clear. A male actor, soon seen working beneath the engine, as it lowers itself ever closer to the wooden stage floor, implies through his embodied presence that we are in a mechanic's workshop or a garage of some sort. As an object the engine seems to loom over him, to carry threat. These stage artefacts (set, props) are loaded with (uncertain) meaning.

Similarly, on an otherwise sparse and almost empty stage there stands a working water tub. The tub carries with it connotations of labour, especially when onstage characters such as the man working on the car or the drifter who arrives suddenly, disruptively, onto the stage and into the action, use it to wash hands, or soothe hot foreheads – and even later to bathe, to wash off oil, sweat, blood; this is a seeming workspace yet also one with blurred domestic connotations. In turn the tub also becomes a signifier of the setting (the *mise-en-scène*) – an atmosphere of dirt and heat, the wider social and cultural environment in which these objects and these people are (temporarily at least) located. We will, without question, return to these issues, this idea of place and of purpose.

The production is Ivo van Hove's *Obsession*. We are at the Barbican Theatre, in London, in April 2017. The production is a highly layered experience which brings a series of symbolic and interpretative frames to bear in its meaning making. Van Hove's production, featuring English actor Jude Law as well as cast members drawn from his more familiar Toneelgroep Amsterdam ensemble (all performing here in English), is a stage adaptation of the *screenplay* of the Italian director Luchino Visconti's 1943 film *Ossessione*. And this point about screenplay or film script is important to stress from the outset: this is no straightforward screen to stage adaptation that seeks to maximize the audience potential for a popular film by remaking it shot by shot for the stage. Van Hove will talk in interviews about remaking films into 'conceptual artwork'.[12] And yet … it would be equally disingenuous to suggest that there is no relationship at all between the film and van Hove's production. The director is keen to stress in almost all interviews associated with the production that he did *not* go back to the film before rehearsals began (this is a point that, intriguingly, recurs in his interviews on other productions with a specifically cinematic provenance[13]) and while the predominantly 'empty stage' *mise-en-scène* described above would seem to strip the production of any vestigial trace of a film that is often credited with being the precursor of Italian neorealism, there remain important interrelationships, ones which perhaps enrich and inform the watching experience for those spectators who carry a knowledge of the film in their cultural backpack.[14]

But Visconti's own controversial film (it was banned on two occasions by the Italian fascist government in the 1940s[15]) had significant precursor texts and artworks – not least James M. Cain's taut work of popular crime fiction *The Postman Always Rings Twice* published in 1934 and set in Depression-era rural California. This text has itself undergone several multimodal adaptations, some even prior to Visconti's film. It was adapted by Cain himself for performance on the New York stage, and then received a French film treatment, directed by Pierre Chenal and with the title *Le Dernier Tournant* [*The Last Turning*] (1939). Cain's novel, with its quintessentially US opening location in a diner, a setting directly appropriated by the 1946 US film version directed by Tay Garnett and starring Lana Turner and John Garfield, has its own kinships with the social and aesthetic world depicted by Edward Hopper's paintings of the same era. The conjuring in my mind of that visual association by van Hove's production in its opening moments – the set and lighting conceived as so often in his productions by his chief collaborator, Jan Versweyveld – may, then, be far from accidental. This *Obsession* is a version of the Visconti script but one informed by experiences of and, perhaps, partial, even submerged, memories of, an accretive history of adaptation and creative reinterpretation.[16]

Visconti's version of the narrative is filtered and mediated by all these other obsessive re-makings, including the most recent English-language film version directed and scripted by David Mamet – another practitioner adept at negotiating the space between theatre and cinema – and starring Jack Nicholson and Jessica Lange (1981). That film was also set in a Californian rural diner. This teleology is an important part of the complex inheritance of van Hove's adaptation; his version is no simple linear movement from singular film to stage production and the ambiguities described above enable its associational operations to work in an often highly personalized way, and with varying impact, for the spectator depending on the wider intertextual and intertheatrical knowledge they bring to the experience. And yet, the specific adaptational relationship with the Visconti film is still deep and significant for van Hove. This is the fourth of the Italian director's films that he has (re)interpreted for the stage. In each case he has spoken about going back to the original script rather than the film per se. *Rocco e i suoi Fratelli* [*Rocco and his Brothers*] (dir. Visconti, 1960) is a story about migration from southern to northern Italy that found obvious contemporary parallels in its Toneelgroep staging in 2007–8; *Ludwig*, adapted for the Munich Kammerspiele in 2010, also found contemporary political purchase with its theme of arts and the state; and, perhaps, the most successful staging of all, *The Damned* for the Festival d'Avignon in 2016, won two Molières, the highest accolade in French theatre, but also spoke with real urgency to contemporary Western politics. Visconti's *La caduta degli dei* [*The Fall of the Gods*] was a 1969 Italian-German co-production. Its plot focussed on the Essenbeck family, wealthy German industrialists who, when the film (and play) opens, are collaborating with the Nazi regime. The story opens in Berlin on 27 February 1933 when the Reichstag is on fire. There are huge historical touchpoints for this story, then, but also additional contemporary resonance with the rise of the alt-right both in the US and on the European mainland in recent years. Recent ISIS-led terrorist events, such as the Bataclan shootings in Paris, were still raw in the French psyche when van Hove undertook his Avignon festival performance in the epic space of the Palais des Papes.[17]

So there is a recognizable methodology legible in van Hove's curriculum vitae of 'Visconti plus', a version of Visconti's seminal films, filtered through other related versionings, and actively adapted for new contemporary sociopolitical contexts and circumstances as well as for the particular technologies of the stage. And this can all be traced in his *Obsession*, although the epic scale of a production like *The Damned* and its very specific festival commission context were tangibly different both in its realization and effect to the small-cast intensity of the Barbican production. *Obsession* was performed by six actors and ran for a little under two hours without interval and was intended to give the audience an unsettling experience in a number of ways, not least through its visceral and uncompromising sense of its protagonists' sexuality and of related acts of violence.

The physicality of the production was achieved through a number of specific techniques and tactics. The previously mentioned water tub became a focal point on the stage for attention to the physical body (and to bodily needs, from washing to sex). The persistent references in the dialogue to the heat also led to significant removal of items of clothing at key points in the action – one particularly uncomfortable moment of proximity saw the husband Joseph (the Bregana of the Visconti film) insisting his wife Hanna help to towel him down in full view of Gino; later the same space would witness the adulterous lovers washing off the evidence of their crime (the murder of Joseph) in a sequence that depicted them almost like the archetypal Macbeths, mired in their own sexually driven ambitions. Halina Reijn's performance as Hanna was visceral, self-aware, as she touched and manipulated her own body into acts of coercion and submission in equal measure.

This physicality was also emphasized by the particular ways in which the cinematic medium was deployed on the stage. Projected onto the high walls at the sides and back of the stage we had various encounters with Gino and Hanna as lovers through intense and oversized close-ups. As spectators, we became embroiled in their relationship in very specific and potentially compromising ways through this use of close-up – it also collapsed the distance between spectator and the stage in ways that van Hove has capitalized on previously in, for example, his Shakespeare productions with their use of live filmed action.[18] The televisual as well as the cinematic is brought into the heart of theatrical practice and 'liveness' here in challenging ways.[19]

Towards the close of *Obsession* film projections on the back stage worked at the other end of the spectrum to bring a sense of epic landscape into a production that otherwise emphasized claustrophobia and entrapment. Gino stood against a huge epic-scale seascape – suggestive of the sweeping coastal sequences of the film – extensive panning shots which were themselves ruminations on liberty and escape (and the impossibility of the same in a story governed by fate). Elsewhere Gino's drifter's need to escape the confines of paid work and social expectation has been figured by the actor's running on treadmills built into the stage floor. These sequences (admittedly much maligned in the reviews) both ensured a sense of genuine physicality (actors literally made to work up a sweat and get out of breath) and of hopelessness: the treadmill was going exactly nowhere and bringing Gino back to where he started (see Plate 13). It was a dangerous version of fatalism, verging as it did on the edge of comic motif, but it was a tactic not entirely out of step with the messages of the adaptation.[20]

Whether the Barbican Theatre was the right scale of venue for a production so intent on creating unsettling intimacies and yet also keen to open out to widescreen emotional and psychological landscapes and vistas is a genuine but unanswerable query. The subsequent performances in European venues may well elicit a different critical and indeed audience response. Certainly, van Hove self-consciously eschewed the neorealist elements of his film source – largely gone is Visconti's intensely drawn Po Delta setting, and the forensic detail with which he examines the proletariat lives of the film's protagonists from the opening sequence of panning shots that bring the drifter Gino on the back of a truck to the trattoria run by Bregana and his wife Giovanna to the end sequences on the marshland coastline and on its hazardous roads. Van Hove has in interviews spoken consistently about wanting to create not an 'Italian' play as such but rather one of mythic proportions, dealing with passion, with Eros and Thanatos, the life instinct and the death instinct. In the London production programme notes, and other related interviews, the director makes repeated reference to his simultaneous reading of

Peter Conrad's highly wrought book on opera, *A Song of Love and Death*, while developing *Obsession*. He notes that he was drawn to its sense that the 'courting of danger is the energy of theatrical performance'.[21] Van Hove drew particular attention to the following quotation from Conrad, which he described as becoming a kind of motto throughout the development process for the play: 'Opera is a song of love and death, of conditions which bypass rational understanding'.[22]

As discussed in detail elsewhere in this volume, directing opera has had a serious shaping effect on van Hove's aesthetic, but it also provides a very direct link to Visconti's oeuvre. Visconti oscillated between work in theatre, opera and film throughout his career and each medium visibly and audibly informed the other in terms of practice and possibility. There is, for example, a strong operatic undertow to the fatalistic narrative of *Ossessione*. Henry Bacon makes the point that 'Right at the beginning' of the film, 'as the truck stops in front of the trattoria, the aria "*Di provenza il mar, il soul*" from Verdi's *La Traviata* is heard'.[23] In the Verdi, '*Di provenza il mar, il suol chi dal cor ti cancello?*' ['Who erased the sea, the land of Provence from your heart?'] is a song of ill-fated love and separation and we can immediately register the links to the yearning landscapes and actual and emotional environments of *Ossessione*.[24] This in turn finds its place in van Hove's aesthetic through the knowingly Romantic, and even consciously melodramatic, projected seascapes (these sequences were loudly underscored with music). He has also directly signalled his retention of the aria in his production: 'I have removed the film references to Italy, to the Italian atmosphere – only one very famous aria from *La Traviata* remains – so I could analyse the story of what real passion is'.[25] As ever this assertion is both insightful and playfully disingenuous. In the Visconti, opera is a plot driver in the form of the singing contest which Bregana wins and the drunken celebrations of which are a stimulus for the murder plot. A variety of song snatches are heard as part of the competition sequence, not least those of Verdi – *La Traviata* and also *Rigoletto* – but also, tellingly, those of Georges Bizet – *Carmen* and *Les Pêcheurs des Perles* ('The Pearl Fishers'). Van Hove has removed all Italian references other than the Verdi but there remains the vestigial trace of opera both in the singing competition and the onstage live performance of Joseph, but also in snatches of *Carmen*, among other things, which provide the musical pulse throughout.

Music in van Hove's productions is always a key signifier – from the interjections of Neil Young's 'Heart of Gold' in his stage version of the John Cassavetes screenplay *Opening Night* (2015–16), a production that also made extensive use of the interplay between cinema and theatre through the utilization of onstage screens and live cameras;[26] Philip Glass sounded in the classroom update of Arthur Miller's *The Crucible* (Walter Kerr

Theatre, NY, 2016); Joni Mitchell's 'Blue' punctuating scenes and introducing reflective pause in his recent excoriating version of *Hedda Gabler* (National Theatre, London, 2016); through to the underscoring of Gabriel Fauré's *Requiem* in his groundbreaking interpretation of Miller's *A View from the Bridge* (Young Vic, then Wyndham's Theatre, London, 2014–15). Van Hove has not made explicit the connection in any interview I have been able to trace but it is interesting that one of the best-known contemporary stage dance/musical adaptations of *Carmen* currently in the repertoire is Matthew Bourne's *Car Man*, itself scaffolded on Bizet's score but in actual fact a loose adaptation of Cain's *The Postman Always Rings Twice* rather than the Bizet opera. The sense this creates of the multiple technologies and texts informing the (re)mediations of *Obsession* is compelling.[27]

Van Hove, and by extension his work with Toneelgroep Amsterdam, has been understood in the mainstream UK theatre as someone determined to avoid the calcification of the classics in ways that have challenged the understanding of the canon in the repertoire. He is in part liberated in this mission by already working in translation. Nevertheless, the very difficulties which critics had with *Obsession*, and what they consistently highlighted as its clunky deployment of onstage symbolism and abstraction to rework a seminal example of neorealism, may also be the point of entry to what van Hove regards as the ultimate challenge of the medium in which he is working. He is also striving to avoid the calcification of medium-specificity, rejecting a delimiting expectation of what is or is not possible in the theatre. The sheer difficulty, practical and philosophical, of handling the two car crashes of *Obsession* embodied this fact: 'What is [a] car crash in the theatre?' he asks and asks us as spectators.[28] In this production the car crashes are realized through the freighted work of bodies (van Hove described the murder sequence as a combination of sex scene and struggle) and by means of the aforementioned combustion engine and through the use of huge amounts of black fluid to symbolize oil (to 'create the world') – which itself might be seen to represent blood – and which covered the actors and the stage. One incredibly moving moment following the first car crash sequence was when Joseph, now dead, returned as the actor to clean the stage of that same oil. There is a theatrical pragmatic at play here – the substance was slippery and posed an obvious risk to the other performers throughout the rest of the performance – but the physical act, the ultimate humiliation of the formerly dominant *machismo* of Joseph, was fully lit and became incorporated into the performance and part of the meaning making of this production in its own right.

The heavily notated use of fluids to coat and cover actors has kinships to other recent van Hove production decisions – stills for the Avignon performance of *The Damned* (see Plate 15) reveal a tarring and feathering of performers there; in *Hedda Gabler* Ruth Wilson

Figure 26 *From left, Hanna (Halina Reijn), the Inspector (Chukwudi Iwuji), Joseph (Gijs Scholten van Aschat, foreground) and Gino (Jude Law),* Obsession, *Barbican Centre, London (2017).*

in the lead part was shockingly and sadistically covered in tomato juice by her enemy Judge Brack (recast as threateningly young in Patrick Marber's rumination on the Ibsen original – see Figure 6). If as a production *Obsession* did not receive the glowing reviews and plaudits of many of those other productions, there nevertheless remains a consistency with van Hove's wider body of work, a logic to this adaptation, that repays attention.[29]

In the 'Author's Note' section to her epic novel based on the life of Marilyn Monroe, Joyce Carol Oates observed that her method in writing what she stresses is a work of fiction and not a biography was to make story from small details of Monroe's life:

> for all its length, synecdoche is the principle of appropriation. In place of numerous foster homes in which the child Norma Jeane lived, for instance, *Blonde* explores only one, and that fictitious; in place of numerous lovers, medical crises, abortions and suicide attempts and screen performances, *Blonde* explores only a selected, symbolic few.[30]

We might see an analogous principle of the 'selected' and 'symbolic' at work in *Obsession*; one where part for whole, the use of symbol and trace, of leitmotif and quotation, and synecdoche as the principle of appropriation, played themselves out in the less than two hours of performance, in the music and the use of props, in the screen projections and in the operatic and cinematic allusions, as well as in the rehearsal room with its determined opposition to 'back story' (a point revealed in interviews by Jude Law), and in the particular tense interplay between the conventions of film, opera and theatre in the meaning making of this production.

Philip Auslander has said that in an era of digital media and ubiquitous computing we need to understand liveness as hyper-mediated and take into account 'the multiple ways in which live performance now endeavours to replicate television, video, and film'.[31] Van Hove's aesthetic though is much more than simple replication. His use of close-up or live action, the presence on his stages of screened and mediatized matter, and the complex relationship between his theatrical creations and their adaptation of pre-existent artworks, is not a simple matter of remaking or even repurposing for a new medium. It is a philosophical question about what is possible in theatre. Japanese calligraphy works with a strong sense of the past and the legacy of previous creations within the triple concept of imitation, breaking and transcendence. The critical response to *Obsession* suggested that the moment of transcendence had not been found with this particular production and yet the breakings and significations that can be found and returned to again and again in those seemingly straightforward opening gestures, visual statements, of a bar, an accordion and a car engine might tell us much about van Hove's work in theatre, film and adaptation.

ARCHAEOLOGICAL ADVENTURES IN SPECTATING: OBSESSION *AND* SCENES FROM A MARRIAGE

P. A. Skantze

From the political mobility at the surface down to the slow movements of 'material civilisation', ever more levels of analysis have been established: each has its own peculiar discontinuities and patterns; and as one descends to the deepest levels, the rhythms become broader. Beneath the rapidly changing history of governments, wars, and famines, there emerge other, apparently unmoving histories: . . . the history of drought and of irrigation, the history of crop rotation, the history of the balance achieved by the human species between hunger and abundance.[32]

MICHEL FOUCAULT, *THE ARCHAEOLOGY OF KNOWLEDGE*

What might a spectator's trowel resemble? In the hot lights not of the sun on ancient lands but of the designer's lighting bleaching out the faces of the actors on a stage, do we dig deeper, sift, gently place found objects on the bed of sand next to us? Working backwards, honouring Michel Foucault's sense of the languor of 'material civilization' resting under the fast-moving political moment, I travel in this essay from *Obsession* (2017) towards *Scenes from A Marriage* (2013). Beginning near the surface of theatrical time 2017, the strata of productions that lie between *Obsession* and *Scenes from a Marriage* include *Hedda Gabler, The Crucible, Kings of War, A View from the Bridge, Antigone* and *Roman Tragedies*. I have been to many Ivo van Hove sites of archaeological disruption and knowledge-making theatrical encounters over these years. Watching the not very well received *Obsession* in the midst of writing this essay on *Scenes from a Marriage*, I simultaneously recognized and remembered the particularly 'skeletal' nature of van Hove's work created with his designer Jan Versweyveld. Past productions returned in memory as layers, fissures, caves laid bare amidst the political ruins and the stagecraft constructed to encourage a spectator's fieldwork.

Unless you believe theatre is urgently needed, why make it or go to see it? This question like this essay moves horizontally and vertically. In the aftermath of memory, I see again the first and largest skeletal remain, an enormous motor hoisted above the set for *Obsession* suspended like a dinosaur in a (Un)Natural History Museum. Aha, I thought, digging tentatively in with my participant tool of interpretative sifting, the Internal Combustion Engine: too big, eventually way too noisy. Not only an engine of retribution in the production, the hulk of automotive machinery signalled the murder of bodies on stage by leaving them covered with oil like pelicans after a BP spill. Aha, I thought, the vertical emptiness of the barren stage with a bar tucked in the corner evoked a wasteland over which that thing depended, on which we depend, the sign of our fidelity to compulsive travel at any cost.

So times are bad, yes? And even if we look away from short-sighted stupidity masquerading as political discussion (those swiftly moving idiocies distracting us from the foundations below) and try to focus on something important like the destruction of the climate, still everywhere there is not enough food and way too much fuel and/or its by-products. Thus that engine hovering over the disaffected ruin of a drifter and a woman or women or a man or men invited me to dig under the affectless acting, the slow and uninteresting speech towards a devastation underlying everything, painful in its truth.

For Michel Foucault, in the methodological meditation that is *The Archaeology of Knowledge*, archaeology often comes paired with the word 'description'. The grouping of Foucault, spectatorship and van Hove comes in part from the nature of van Hove's work and the nature of the work we might embark upon as spectators. I have suggested elsewhere that for the spectator description is 'a form of critical immanent attention', so a trowel might be for digging but it might also be for sculpting, the finding in relation to the recounting.[33] While layers and strata seem apt for the way van Hove works, attending with Foucault I understand how when watching we are invited to witness actions before us:

> in order to consider them in their discontinuity, without having to relate them, by one of those shifts that disconnect them and render them inessential, to a more fundamental opening or difference ... to seize their very irruption, at the place and at the moment at which it occurred ... to rediscover their occurrence as an event.[34]

Of the archaeological layers or, as Foucault might more aptly note, of the series of surface layers in van Hove's productions my explorations for *Obsession* and *Scenes from a Marriage* take me towards irruptions of space and strata of sound. All well-trained directors pay attention to space and sound, but I would suggest that when watching van Hove's work we are encouraged to consider shifts and irruptions in the production until the sand of the past, of earlier productions, of the recent political dust storms, create new formations. The spectator in this fieldwork discovers and invents because a certain freedom left to those around the ruins means that we can find what is not there, nothing on the list of what we are looking for might account for what we find. This visual spelunking has an aural counterpart, listening to what lies above, around and through.

Skeletal, then, this production of *Obsession*, but also archaeologically rich, encouraging us to see the fossil that is fossil fuel. Trace this history, from James M. Cain's 1934 novel *The Postman Always Rings Twice*, an instance of a variation on the genre that America perfected, the noir and its discontents, into the visually sumptuous, stutteringly flat world of a Visconti movie, *Ossessione* (1943), which premièred three years prior to the classic noir film named after the novel with John Garfield and Lana Turner. The layers include all the transnational love/hate affairs such crossing implies between Italy and the United States, between Cinecittà and Los Angeles. So we arrive at the desert landscape[35] of *Obsession* with its English script scraped away from the Italian dialogue of Visconti, hinting at the 'why talk when you can slap a woman and shoot a man' patter of traditional film noir, but stretching the time of such patter into a wasteland of 'what are we doing this for' anyway?

Across the transnational divide other tensions surface; as an ex-pat spectator of European theatre for years now, I have become more and more exasperated by the 'whiteness' of the iconic productions by van Hove and Thomas Ostermeier, to name just two of the major directors. The enormous portraits adorning the lobby of the Berlin Schaubühne, where I saw a production of *Richard III* in 2016, made explicit the nature of this entirely white ensemble. How can this be in 2017 in Berlin? How can this be in 2017 in Amsterdam? To its credit the National Theatre now consistently casts actors of colour, and when I saw van Hove's *Hedda Gabler,* it was a relief to finally see a van Hove production with Chukwudi Iwuji playing Lovborg. The word relief, however, signals the inequity of the 'one-offness' of casting actors of colour in secondary roles. Happily Iwuji appeared as well in *Obsession* but again playing small roles on the periphery of the action. Though Howard Overshown was cast in the Los Angeles production of *A View from the Bridge,* van Hove's work and the ethnic makeup of Toneelgroep Amsterdam itself convey a very clear sense of who gets trained to be on stage and thus, inevitably, who is the expected audience attending the theatre.

Expectations of who is in the audience usually err as well on the side of the heteronormative with those familiar scenes of male/female tension supposedly at the heart of dramatic conflict. Visconti digs under the surface to the homoerotic in all of US cinema – in fact, perhaps more precisely, to the fact that, in most art forms, men are (still) fascinated by themselves, seduced by each other. So Johnny (a character not in the original film) loves Gino and even Joseph, the eventually wronged husband, loves Gino and, of course, Hanna loves Gino. Gino remains hot, sexy and perplexed, wanted and somehow only active when responding to being wanted. A political question surfaces watching this drifter who reacts and runs: who are we all now, in the face of too much information and not enough concrete action to waylay disaster? The script, an adaptation from Visconti's movie created by Simon Stephens, falls out of the mouths of the actors like fitful subtitles, spoken not seen.

From the first I have been fascinated by van Hove's thirst for difficult, opaque, rarely performed texts as well as those canonical items that he turns weird. At this juncture, at this point in my experience of going on digs with his creative team and casts, I continue to find the power of theatrical language to meet, transfigure, re-order the words of a text fascinating. Why is theatre urgent? Because a theatre maker like van Hove and his extraordinary collaborators enter willingly into the paradoxical power of utter care and specific attention to detail in the live production, mixed with an indifference to reception absolutely vital to inviting a spectator to be an explorer. We pick up our tools because there is space between us and the stage, because what we are offered does not need us; we can choose to make in tandem with the production and its representations, but we can also watch the unfolding without deep digging. The artistic creation establishes the territory: like *Roman Tragedies*, it is left to you whether you come up on stage, physically and metaphorically. Here too Foucault's faux apologetic insistence on archaeological description in the service of knowledge has an apt companion in van Hove's enigmatic offerings. Van Hove himself in interview and by report of actors is enigmatic, but Ruth Wilson, among others, recounts the freedom of not being told what to do, of being placed in a space to discover.[36] For the spectator, the invitation to dig, to notice what tools blister the hand when used too much, to sit back on your heels in your seat and wipe your forehead and wait before making the next interpretive foray into the layers, offers a place from which to participate beyond judgement or reductive assumption.

Let's project our excavations up through layers of air, flipping the idea of digging on its ear, towards the sky rather than down through layers of the earth. Van Hove's work creates layers sonically as surely as it traces layers of the theatrical, artistic remains accumulated in original productions, film adaptations, and translations of texts. In *Obsession* the first sonic, nay Orphic clue, is the sound of a harmonica. Through the Italian/English space of performance a sound associated with the United States reaches my ears. Its wheeze evokes the eternal Southern American porch or Western American campfire with cowboys and the mouth harp creating a backdrop to poverty and hardship as well as company and release from a day's work. My tentative exploration of the complexities in that layer of air is rewarded when the tune coalesces into Woody Guthrie's 'This Land is Your Land'. A protest song with verses expunged by those who want to ignore its socialist message, this song is also an ironic one when played against the backdrop of a spoiled and bitter landscape. Think of how a generation coming of age in this twenty-first century might hear the lyrics, 'This Land is Your Land / This Land is my Land / From California / to the New York Island', when global warming suggests a cursed inheritance and a future of famine everywhere.

As all artists and scholars who write on the sonic connect sound to time, so the drawl of the harmonica makes a shimmer across the air of time passing, of the drifter's drifting marked by notes and melodic lines. Later in the production, a new layer, over? under?

the Guthrie song appears when Gino runs away while staying in the same place. Bruce Springsteen's harmonica, more determined, a film noir sound rather than one of Italian neorealist cinematic brooding, proceeds Springsteen's version of 'This Land is Your Land'. He sings in homage, he sings in anger, he sings for reclamation. And three more layers appear in the air of sonic space. Foucault's terms of irruption and discontinuity become useful tools as I explore the sonic qualities of an increasingly wavy border between singing and speaking in van Hove productions. Lately, particularly with *Hedda Gabler*, I have noticed a faintly audible, sometimes quasi-imperceptible move to the sung or at least the chanted spoken in the 'straight' dramas. I saw *Hedda Gabler* twice, and the lines to my ears had the sound of a libretto rather than a script. I started counting between the speaking of the lines, one, two, three, four, turn and answer, one, two, three, repeat. I listened for the stretch of recitative, the sudden explosion of an aria with the squeaky voiced Mrs Elvsted and the over-passionate Lovborg.

In *Obsession* there is opera playing as a teaser to the moment when Joseph suddenly sings, and sings powerfully, beautifully, oddly unselfconscious. It happens again when Hanna sings and the distance between speaking and singing shrinks. The theatricality at work in the thin membrane between the recitative of acting speech and the sudden – it always feels sudden even when you know it is coming – shift to singing suggests to the sonic explorer that van Hove's work over these years in 'straight' drama and in opera create aural faultlines where we hear the closeness between the two forms.

The calendar months fly off the page, the hand drops the paper as the sitter falls into a reverie of flashback: movies have marvellous synecdoche for turning back the clock. So imagine a theatrical version of the flashback, time dissolving in the Barbican Theatre until, on a night in 2013, the audience mills about waiting outside the stage doors, coloured wristbands a clue to who we accompany and where we begin. As a director and performance maker I am always surprised at how a very little disruption in the convention of entering and sitting can cause so much agitation among spectators. As a spectator I am wary of participant tricks constructed to make me 'feel more a part of the production' as if I cannot decide how to do that myself. But it is a fact of going to theatre that innovations do have a material and immediate effect on reception.

In what Foucault might term a moment of considering 'discontinuity' without feeling an immediate need to interpret, it was only after moving between three spaces that I understood each was divided by curtains that not only hung between the sections, but also made a small central room with plastic windows through which one could see the actors at rest. Now I remember how in the scene with the couple at their most advanced

Figure 27 *Marianne (Janni Goslinga) and Johan (Hugo Koolschijn),* Scenes from a Marriage, *Stadsschouwburg, Amsterdam (2013).*

age it became clear that we had been sitting on the Barbican stage, because in that scene we sat with the entire, empty auditorium of the theatre rising up behind us. Now working backwards archaeologically, I can see how the skeletal design, the anatomizing of a traditional theatre into an unrecognizable space served to charge the intimate curtained areas in the heat of each couple's intense dialogue.

My journey through the ruins of marriage happened to be chronological that night. By chance I began with the couple in their youth at dinner, their discussion continuing as they lay in 'bed' – the table transformed by a sheet and pillows – all future before them. Time passed by way of the next curtain and entered us into the middle age of the couple at work, of toys scattered about suggesting the absent children. Then through the curtain of time once more to the huge cavernous space of empty theatre seats in rows behind us as we witnessed the last scene of the first part between the couple in late middle age: a bed on stage, discontent everywhere. Archaeologically speaking, those empty rows, the cavern of the empty theatre comes back to me now as a perfect evocation of the afterlife waiting, of passing beyond relationship towards the swirling atoms of our next stage of being. Lovely to think of those motes floating in the air in the waiting, hushed theatre as atoms of past spectators joined, swerving as Lucretius tells us, towards ours. Like *Obsession*'s faux wooden treadmill embedded on the warm and beautifully golden wooden stage of the Barbican that Gino used to run away while staying in the same place, his face appearing on the screens before us, his back to us, so that internal space created by the curtains in the first half of *Scenes from a Marriage*: a cave, an aquarium, something through which we could see actors drinking water, sitting for minute, moving about, only to suddenly spring through the door and become the character.

At the interval, talk in the vestibule was of the impossibility of what might come next. Spatially what came next now mingles in my memory with the suspended internal combustion engine of *Obsession*. The audience summoned to return finds themselves in a cavernous space with chairs, set in sections of bleacher seating. Like all spectators faced with unreserved seating, we see only the space, the chairs and the sightlines. Slowly I notice some people looking up, and then I do too. Above us like a goddess of theatre past, all of the curtains, even the ones with the plastic windows through which we looked earlier are now tucked up high above the space, waiting to drop? Providing theatrical benediction? Those curtains, as if a materialization of my earlier evocation of geological layers in the air, hang above us. But the sonic strata have been profoundly etched in this production already, before the extraordinary sonic denouement that awaits the spectator in the second half of the show. While narrated stories of couples and their loves and couples and their difficulties fill stages, screens and movie houses, what the sound of those voices making these scenes from a marriage remind the spectator of is the pure erotic pleasure of paying attention, of having someone pay particular attention to us. The erotics of spectatorship, indeed of the archaeological dig, arise from attention: if bored, the spectator will remain unanimated; if curious, engaged, the heat begins to build. The erotics of mimesis do not only come from the simple representation of something like us on stage; instead the erotics exist in the in-between of recognition and interpretation, watching attention being lovingly paid we return the gesture as spectators and the double of mimesis becomes the pleasure of our own attention, of the sweetness of attention portrayed, of the distance of memory and the heat of re-enactment. That night watching *Scenes from a Marriage,* again we were invited to excavate, to hear the keen excitement of the new love, the tinge of sorrow in the recognition of imperfection, the fear of the dying, the dying of the love, the dying of the loved one.

In the first half of *Scenes from a Marriage*, as I moved chronologically from a young love to a not-so-young love, I listened. I heard the voices of the young couple, fiercely testing, tentatively sure of themselves; these voices, the power of their sonic score, depended upon the talent of the actors from Toneelgroep Amsterdam. And perhaps, too, the sound was heightened by the pleasure to my ears of the sound of a peculiarly European soundscape, without the faux tension in the actor's voice of the British theatrical penchant for naturalism and/or realism. And, oddly, because the voices and the actors in *Scenes from a Marriage* don't strive for the authentic feeling or a convincing impersonation of the character of 'wife' or 'husband', they come closer to something we receive as authentic instead of the desperation of the 'realistic' that can block the reception of the nuance of relationship.

In contrast to *Obsession*, the layers in the air in *Scenes from a Marriage* were suffused with energy. While sitting in the section where the young couple talked babies and careers, from time to time we heard the sounds of the coming storm in the middle years, of the crash and burn in the last stages of the marriage. While in the other sections, each time at some point we could hear what sounded like a bellowing, an unbelievably loud argument. Many of us in the audience flinched, even the actors before us looked puzzled, cocked their ears to hear the aural prediction of what lay ahead. When finally I came to the section with the older lovers, unconsciously I was waiting for the revelation of what caused such volume, and strangely it never came because when caught up in the scene, the bellowing did not sound loud to the ears. The nature of eavesdropping in this work complicated the position of the spectator as explorer – scale and proportion constantly shifted our interpretations (see Plate 14).

When we returned for the play's second half, when we took our seats on the bleachers in the stripped-down space with nothing but floor and the container the audience itself made around it, all three couples entered and began to talk. I invite you to read that sentence again. Our decorous grammar makes order even when order has been broken. You would think they enter and discuss, or they enter and soliloquize, but no, they enter and speak, everyone, at once. As if we have hit the richest vein ever in the sonic strata, the noise is at once wholly confusing and glorious. With Foucault's method and our sifting ears, we might indeed 'seize their very irruption, at the place and at the moment at which it occurred . . . to rediscover [the] occurrence as an event.'[37] A sonic event in which all three couples swirl about, a verb one must use because the swirl was corporeal and acoustic, making the scenes from their marriage all at the same time. We did not move, we were not solicited by the actors, we had no headphones, we had no instructions, but the immersion into this sonic world made for an immersive theatre that hinged on us. Because we had to choose and we could not choose, our attention darted from one couple to another, our ears heard frenetic discussion, a violent, shoving fight, a quiet intervention, our eyes saw a kind of dance floor where the couples moved around in time to the music of dialogue. Later, as I talked about this scene to others, describing the glorious nature of something like three arias in the air, something like a chorus but with solos, something like operatic speaking, my companion reminded me that they were speaking in Dutch – a sonic layer I had bypassed in my willingness to make the work with them. I had simply translated sound into sense, remembered understanding what they were saying. Clearly because the heat of the noise had offered me something other than meaning, or meaning pressed into a kind of spoken song.

In her article about *Scenes from a Marriage*, dramaturg Duška Radosavljević suggests van Hove's 'theatre makes a unique kind of contemplation possible for the audience.'[38] While I would argue our work combines contemplation, excavation and discovery, with Radosavljević I see such work as intrinsically bound up in exploring 'theatre as an art'. Why is theatre urgent? Because 'the notion of theatre as public good (as opposed to show-business) frees up the theatre-makers to anticipate that their audience will want to be engaged intellectually, politically, emotionally and experientially, rather than being obliged to deliver sentimentality, entertainment and customer satisfaction.'[39] And, in a moment in which sentimentality, entertainment and customer satisfaction have infiltrated every sphere, most pointedly the academic, the time to be digging is now.

THE INTENSIFICATION OF THE NOVEL: AYN RAND'S AND IVO VAN HOVE'S THE FOUNTAINHEAD

Denis Flannery

'An acted play', Henry James wrote in 1872, 'is a novel intensified; it realizes what the novel suggests.'[40] When James made this comment he wasn't talking about adaptation from novel to stage – which is my preoccupation in this essay – but about how theatre gives, in his words, 'a vision of the immediate not to be enjoyed in any other way.'[41] Going (even conceptually) from the novel to the stage meant, for James, going from the realm of the suggestive to the realm of the intensely evident and present.

Ayn Rand's *The Fountainhead* (1943) is, though, one of the least suggestive of novels. A film adaptation, directed by King Vidor, was released in 1949; its IMDB plot summary reads: 'An uncompromising visionary architect struggles to maintain his integrity and individualism despite personal, professional and economic pressures to conform to popular standards.'[42] This sentence pretty much gets the novel's essence. In 1968 Rand wrote a new Introduction to mark its twenty-fifth anniversary. What shines most from the book's pages is an appetite for a discussion, or a conclusion. *The Fountainhead* is a novel with an argument and a moral. Everything in it seems to build towards the fabrication of the one and the enforcement of the other. Rand wrote the book wishing to accomplish 'the portrayal of a moral idea', to present an '*ideal man*'.[43] A major lesson she learnt in the course of writing and publishing it was that 'one cannot give up the world to those one despises.'[44] The novel ends with a view, from below, of its architect hero atop the unfinished skyscraper that will be his career's crowning statement: 'There was only', we read, 'the ocean and the sky and the figure of Howard Roark'.[45] *The Fountainhead* oscillates between the kind of romanticism evident in the concluding sentence I have just quoted and a proliferative paranoia. Everyone's vices are allegorized and on display: all weak and/or unclean bodies in the book signify conscious malice and danger. Yet Rand's fictional world endlessly keeps secret its schemes for your destruction: it almost becomes your moral duty to ferret out such schemes and to destroy them.

The trailer for Toneelgroep Amsterdam's (TGA) 2014 production of *The Fountainhead*, directed by Ivo van Hove, ends with a fragment of the show's closing moments – a long speech, in Dutch, by Ramsey Nasr (Roark): 'Man's first duty is to be himself', Nasr says, 'No man can live for another.'[46] As he makes this final speech other members of the cast, standing behind him in silhouette, make haunting, beautiful sounds on theremins. What is involved in 'intensifying' something already so intense, in bringing a novel already so forcefully (even relentlessly) 'realized' to the stage? Among the range of meanings for the verb 'to intensify' given by the OED online we find 'to strengthen' and 'to deepen'. How do you strengthen something so unyieldingly sure of its own strength and so confidently ambitious in its reach for profundity? 'To me', van Hove wrote, '*The Fountainhead* is a war of ideas'.[47] Like a latter-day Edmund Spenser, Rand has these ideas fight, almost diagrammatically, through characters: the weakling, perversely altruistic, architecture critic Ellsworth (Elsie) Toohey (played, with most of the caricature stripped away, by Bart Slegers) versus Howard Roark, who is in turn opposed to Peter Keating (played by Aus Greidanus Jr), his conformist and career-obsessed contemporary, the perverse and rebellious Dominique Francon (Halina Reijn) versus the kind and compliant Catherine Halsey (Tamar van den Dop in 2014, more recently Hélène Devos).

'Intense' is a word that well describes the show's popularity and global acclaim. *The Fountainhead* has been an enormous hit, with repeated performances in Amsterdam where it has often sold out. It has also been performed in Avignon, Antwerp, Barcelona, Paris, Seoul, Taipei and New York. The production, with a script by Koen Tachelet, almost seemed to precipitate a flow of plays and productions based on novels by van Hove and his contemporaries. The year 2015 saw the première of *The Hidden Force (De Stille Kracht)*, based on the 1900 novel by Louis Couperus. The following year a second play based on a Couperus novel, *The Things That Pass (De Dingen Die Voorbijgaan)* opened. Other TGA directors have also been bringing novels to the stage. Guy Cassiers directed a new play based on Jonathan Littell's monumental holocaust novel *The Kindly Ones* in 2015 and, in February 2018, his production of *May We Be Forgiven (Vergeef Ons)*, based on the book by A. M. Homes, opened. Luk Percevaal directed, also in 2015, *The Year of Cancer (Het Jaar Van de Kreeft)* from the 1972 novel by Hugo Claus. For van Hove and TGA *The Fountainhead* has initiated something of a novelistic wave. Furthermore, one of the most bold and striking aspects of this Rand adaptation is its readiness to put debate on stage. Van Hove once claimed that one of theatre's functions is to ask questions without fears and without restraint.[48] His *Fountainhead* takes this mission quite literally. The play doesn't just provoke questions: it stages the asking of them in very literal ways. You watch actors have discussions about theatrically unpromising topics and it's made – miraculously – compelling. And influential. Thomas Ostermeier's recent production *Returning to Reims*, based on the 2009 memoir by Didier Eribon, bears, in its brilliant staging of memory and theory, more than a small trace of debt to van Hove's work with Rand's novel.

The TGA *Fountainhead* is, then, not only vivid and publicly successful. In the few years since its première it has already had an extensive influence. When asked in 2008 why he had never worked on a novel adaptation, even though he had covered material outside of theatre such as film screenplays, van Hove answered:

> Because I love the cinema, in particular Cassavetes or Marguerite Duras (who called *India Song* 'text-film-theatre'). I need to work on a text that interests me passionately and which I feel the need to get heard. I like open texts that allow for different forms of representation. So far I have not found a novel that corresponds to what I want. I have to fall in love with these texts. . . . I've no idea what type of things I'll be working on in five years' time.[49]

Just over five years after van Hove made this comment, TGA premièred their *Fountainhead*. 'It's an engaging, addictive novel', he said at the time, 'that was begging to be staged'.[50]

Marguerite Duras and Ayn Rand are not names that go together like love and marriage but, in its elephantine way, Rand's novel *can* be considered under the heading 'text-film-theatre.' Duras's poetically sparse narrative prose can often read like stage directions or the outline of a scene in a film. Dialogue can often be the dominant form in her fiction so that reading a novel like *L'Amante Anglaise* (1967) can feel like reading a screenplay. On the very first page of her 1968 Introduction, Rand invokes Victor Hugo and nineteenth-century realism. Like Dostoevsky, she sees novel writing as a philosophical project. If Duras consciously blurs the line between cinema and fiction, then filmic feelings and scenarios can just erupt in Rand's prose. There is often a cinematic sweep and sensibility to *The Fountainhead* as in her description of the news tycoon Gail Wynand and Dominique Francon taking in the New York skyline: 'On a night of late fall they stood together on the roof-garden parapet, looking at the city. The long shafts made of lighted windows were like streams breaking out of the black sky, flowing down in single drops to feed the great pools of fire below.'[51] It is precisely this kind of moment that is reproduced by van Hove and TGA in a way that one reviewer, Fabienne Darge, described as a 'New York in Cinemascope'.[52] Darge claimed that the production was 'brilliantly cinematic', describing its stage-space as one that enabled a 'masterly' use of video, whether to screen massive architectural drawing or to create the kind of cinematic vistas I have been outlining. There are different kinds and sizes of screen in the production that enable visual encounter from the scale of the drawing board to that of the billboard to the grandest cinematic sweep. Van Hove and Jan Versweyveld, the show's scenographer and lighting designer, were not only celebrating their source material's fervent appreciation of cinema; they were re-enacting their own love of the medium. However much its status as the adaptation of a novel may represent a departure from previous work, their *Fountainhead* represents, both in scale and technical-visual ambition, a return to the elaborate, cinema-fixated show they had made in 2008 with *The Antonioni Project*, based on Michelangelo Antonioni's films *L'Avventura* (1960), *La Notte* (1961) and *L'Eclisse* (1962). This was performed using a combination of live action, blue-screen backdrop, a film crew filming live on stage and screens of different scales and intensities. Both *The Antonioni Project* and TGA's adaptation of *The Fountainhead* celebrate the power and presence of the screen. The later show, however, does so with far more narrative fury and drive.

Because it's an intensely *written* novel – one that is full of writers, readers and competing forms of writing – *The Fountainhead*, for all its lumpen fondness for the prescriptive, compels its reader to move between different styles and different kinds of story – and so does van Hove's adaptation. The novel's second sentence reads: 'He

Figure 28 *Howard Roark (Ramsey Nasr),* The Fountainhead, *Stadsschouwburg, Amsterdam (2014).*

[Roark] stood naked at the edge of the cliff.'[53] In the production Nasr's Roark, having begun by picking up a massive iron bar and slamming it three times onto some metal industrial plating, walks, fully clothed (though with an open shirt), to a large table downstage centre, picks up a paperback copy of *The Fountainhead* and reads these words – though, in the *present* tense: 'He stands naked at the edge of the cliff.' Later, Reijn's Francon quotes the novel's third-person narration of her first violent sex scene with Roark (again changing the grammatical past into the present): 'She feels his ribs', she says of herself, 'he forces her mouth open.'

If the production's multiple screens display cityscapes, close-ups of human faces and at the show's climax, the massive dynamiting by Roark of his building project, Cortland Homes, they also display text. More than any other show by van Hove, *The Fountainhead* compels its audience to literally *read* text as an integral part of their participation. Many newspaper headlines, the titles of different sections of the show (Part Two is called 'Valhalla', for example), a place name – 'Oyster Bay' – written in Roark's hand, or snatches of text by Roark's would-be nemesis Toohey, are all presented on screen. So too are different forms of writing machinery: a massive printing press is wheeled forward in the show's second part and is put into action by Hans Kesting's Wynand. Pencils and sheets of paper proliferate; we see many onscreen typewriters. The intense presence of onscreen writing is made equivalent to the architectural drawing on which the novel and the show focus with such passion. Darge noted how the acts of drawing become a powerful dramaturgical element in the show; at times the drawings almost assume the force and agency of characters.[54] Sketches made by Roark are filmed by small overhead cameras and projected onto vast white screens. When Roark steps away from these drawings they keep proliferating onscreen, brilliantly embodying the novel's (and this production's) love of creative energy. This spectacular element of the show is an act of fidelity to the novel's own writerly celebration of drawing: 'He seized the sketch, his hand flashed forward and a pencil ripped across the drawing … The lines … rent the windows wide; they splintered the balcony and hurled a terrace over the sea.'[55]

Post-structural, feminist and queer theorists tend to give *The Fountainhead* a very wide berth. And you can see why. The steamy faux-Lawrentian tone in which Francon and Roark's early attraction is described would make the most committed of feminists take to the hills or just lie down in exhaustion: 'He stood looking at her', we read as Rand goes into her hottest bestseller mode, 'it was not a glance, but an act of ownership.'[56] Van Hove's stage version might encourage us to wonder what could happen when *The Fountainhead* meets theoretically conscious reading because, in many ways, that is what happens in his production. From Barbara Johnson, we know that we encounter writing when we meet with 'materiality, silence, space, and conflict'.[57] *The Fountainhead* is a book that abounds in materiality but is also distinguished by conflict between different kinds of writing. There are also divisions between what it espouses, on the one hand, and what, on the other, it values. Recently described by Jonathan Freedland as 'Gordon Gekko with A-levels', Rand is regularly criticized by the left for espousing or enabling doctrines of relentless individualism, far-right *laissez faire* economics, and the dismantling of social support.[58]

But, reading the book, I was surprised by the forms of intimacy I found and by the tenderness with which it describes them. Rand's 1968 Introduction makes her novel sound like a love-letter to her husband. Indeed, part of what made the book so engaging and addictive for van Hove is that it is the story of the 'relentless' love between Roark and Francon. 'They were simply four people who liked being there together', Rand writes, describing how Roark, the sculptor Mallory, Francon and Roark's devoted foreman Mike Donnigan gather on-site in the evenings at Roark's soon-to-be-maligned Temple to the Human Spirit.[59] When we get to a brief conversation between an idealistic young man and Roark as they sit in a Pennsylvania valley looking at a nearly completed summer resort of Roark's design, the text takes on board the value and energy of this briefest of encounters: 'He [Roark] did not know that he had given someone the courage to face a lifetime.'[60] A sense of intimacy with and tenderness towards the novel itself is also evident in readers' responses to it. The briefest of glances at Amazon reviews will tell you that people tend to *love* this book. One of the reasons they do is that there is, perhaps surprisingly, a lot of love in this book.

And this love is replicated in van Hove's production where the interaction between the characters has, firstly, this element of sometimes tender responsiveness and is, secondly, stripped of the paranoid, freakish kinds of caricature over which, especially in her depiction of Ellsworth Toohey, Rand expends so much labour. Ayn Rand and Nina Simone might not be names most people would link, but part of the show's rich sonic palette is a 1964 recording of Simone singing – to utterly moving effect – Billie Holiday's song 'Don't Explain' during a second, tender erotic encounter between Roark and Francon. Most of the music in the production, composed by Eric Sleichim, is instrumental and played by onstage musicians. While the first erotic encounter between Roark and Francon is sensationally described in the novel and brutally enacted onstage, their second encounter is more tender, balletic and (quite literally) vulnerable: both actors are naked for much of it. The strength and fragility of Simone's voice, the sparse tenderness of the song's arrangement and the historical affect all bring out a pained tenderness that is there in Rand's novel but often forgotten in debates around her. The song's concluding lines are 'My life's yours love / Don't explain.'[61] These words contrast vividly with words spoken by Roark and which were considered so important that they were printed large, in English, in the centre spread of *The Fountainhead*'s Dutch-language programme: 'I could die for you, but I couldn't and wouldn't live for you.'

I'd like to end, though, by returning to a final sense of the verb 'to intensify' provided by the OED: 'to produce stronger contrasts of light and shade.' How do you sharpen contrasts of light and shade in a text that makes its world so unrelentingly oppositional? *The Fountainhead* is not a novel without its awkwardnesses and infelicities, but something fascinating seems to happen when Rand writes about light. Let's return briefly to that passage I quoted earlier with Wynand and Francon looking at the New York skyline and the 'long shafts of lighted windows . . . like streams'. Different forms of light – sunlight, waterfalls, cityscapes, candlelight – saturate this novel. One of the great pleasures or intensities of seeing a show directed by van Hove in collaboration with his partner and usual set and lighting designer, Versweyveld, is how sharp, uncanny, brutal – and often just gorgeous – the lighting is: the white strip lighting in their *Angels in America*; the alternating between golden ambience and brutal white spots in *Roman Tragedies*; the sickly off-gold mirrored lighting that accompanies Hans Kesting's soliloquies as Richard III in *Kings of War*. Part of the attraction of Rand's novel for van

Hove and Versweyveld must have been its sensitivity to light and, I would imagine, the poetry of Rand's prose when it slows down to describe, and emulate, luminous force. Notes I made when I saw the production in Amsterdam in 2014 refer to 'white lights', to a 'gold slant' in the lighting, to 'smoky light' and, as Roark draws the Cortland plans, just to 'LIGHT!' (see Plate 16). Part of what is involved in 'intensification' is a sharpening of contrasts between light and shade. This is also, however problematically, a distinguishing feature of Rand's novel. Such light-work is a spectacular part of van Hove's direction as he faithfully turns *The Fountainhead* from a reading experience to a vision of the immediate.

BUILDING BLOCKS: IVO VAN HOVE AND THE BARBICAN BOX PROJECT

Rachael Nicholas

In September 2016 twenty-six boxes filled with objects were sent to secondary school and further education drama teachers across East London. The boxes gave little away about their contents from the outside; they were sleek and simple in design, carefully and meticulously constructed of four interlocking rectangular layers of thin, bare plywood, stacking up to around half a metre high. These were the Barbican Boxes for the 2016/17 season, designed collaboratively with Ivo van Hove, Jan Versweyveld and the learning team at Toneelgroep Amsterdam (TGA) as part of an annual theatre education programme produced by Creative Learning, Barbican/Guildhall School of Music & Drama. As Jenny Mollica (Head of Creative Learning) describes it: 'At the heart of Barbican Box is a proposition we extend to an invited theatre company that has an existing relationship to the Barbican: if you gave students a box of ingredients to inspire them to make their own original theatre, what would you put in it? This is the provocation we put to Ivo van Hove and Toneelgroep Amsterdam for our 2017 Barbican Box.'[62]

Led by their teachers and artist-mentors, groups of students aged 11–18 used the contents of these boxes to undertake a devising project over the course of six months, culminating in a showcase in the Barbican's Pit Theatre to an audience of peers, friends and family. The theatre strand of Barbican Box – similar schemes are also conducted in music and visual arts – has run every year since 2011 and provides opportunities for students from diverse backgrounds to engage with the work of a theatre director or company resident at the Barbican during that year's season, and to create and perform original work inspired by this engagement. For Lauren Monaghan-Pisano, Creative Learning Producer in the Barbican/Guildhall programme, it was a 'privilege to work with Ivo van Hove and Toneelgroep Amsterdam'; she continues:

> Barbican Box gives young people in East London schools, living amid high levels of deprivation, a chance to express their personal creative voices. Through participating in the project, and interacting with the inspirational work of world-class practitioners such as van Hove, they learn that they can have an impact on the world around them, that they can carve out a small bit of creative space that defines and amplifies their voice. It changes who they think they are and what they think it's possible to achieve, and gives weight to a theory I hold: we are all creative, we all have something to say, and if you give us an opportunity to say it, it might well be beautiful.[63]

Whilst previous boxes have been based around a single theme or narrative, the focus of TGA's box was their theatre-making methodology. Along with the boxes themselves, teachers were provided with a learning resource: a 29-page booklet designed to guide them through the different stages in TGA's devising process and to outline the items in the box alongside suggestions for tasks and activities. As Rosa Fontein and Ilon Lodewijks, artistic educators from TGA, explained in this learning resource, the box is designed to enable students to 'explore Ivo's work, not only through his process of theatre making ... but also through his diverse work around the world'.[64] The central concept for the box is the *Gesamtkunstwerk* ('total work of art'), a term made famous by composer Richard Wagner and referring to a work in which a number of media or forms are synthesized together to create one coherent piece. The learning resource describes the box itself as a metaphor for *Gesamtkunstwerk,* having been 'built out of a number of different elements, which fit perfectly together to form the single object'.[65]

As well, the objects within the box were designed to enable a process that leads towards the creation of a total work of art. The levels of the box were designed to be encountered from bottom to top, with the three top layers representing the three main phases that TGA go through when creating a new work: concept, pre-production and rehearsal.[66] These levels rested on the bottom level which contained objects designed to facilitate exercises that 'help build trust and team spirit', including blindfolds, balls and

Figure 29 *Barbican Box 2017, designed by Ivo van Hove and Jan Versweyveld, Barbican Centre, London (2016–17).*

elastic bands.[67] The structure of the box made manifest the idea that collaboration and practicing 'the fun of failure' are 'essential when making risk-taking theatre' and support the rest of the theatre-making process.[68] With trust firmly established in the team, the process moved to the creation of a concept, before exploring the stages of pre-production: dramaturgy, scenography, video, sound and costume. Students and teachers were then prompted to bring all of those elements together at the rehearsal stage where acting and direction were explored, leading, ultimately, to the creation, and performance, of their own *Gesamtkunstwerk*.

Concept

At the beginning of the process students were strongly encouraged to come up with a concept, 'a plan or an idea about how the text needs to be staged' which then guides the work done in pre-production and shapes the final piece.[69] To help generate this concept the second level of the box contained a sketchbook for every student, wooden blocks, and a dossier on van Hove and Versweyveld. As the learning resource explained, van Hove's starting point is always a text, and this file included extracts from *Macbeth*,

Antigone and *Angels in America.* Teachers were prompted to assist students to come up with their own concept by exploring how they responded to one of these extracts on a personal or political level.[70] This initial exploration of text formed the basis for more rigorous textual work in the dramaturgy section of the pre-production stage, where students were prompted to create their own adaptation of the passage.

Pre-Production

It is interesting, in light of David Hare's criticisms of European directors, that, in this box designed to replicate van Hove's process in miniature, the text is not only the starting point, but continues to play a prominent part throughout the building of the collaborative creative work.[71] In the 'pre-production' section of the process, teachers were encouraged to facilitate workshops to explore each of the performance elements, each of which was introduced in the learning resource by a key collaborator from TGA and followed by suggested activities to explore the medium. Although text was obviously central to the 'dramaturgy' section of pre-production, every entry ended by instructing students to return to their chosen text and concept, prompting them to reinterpret the text through that medium and to build it into their *Gesamtkunstwerk.*

Students were encouraged to explore their text *through* the different media, rather than treating design, sound, video and costume as supplementary elements to the text in performance. In the section on video, for example, students were asked to think about what kind of material would widen the frame of reference for their text, and to capture an image using a 'selfie-stick' to 'explore the atmosphere of the piece'.[72] Through this task students were prompted to investigate the specificities of various media, but also to consider how different modes of expression might work together to represent one idea. The sound section was particularly illustrative of this notion: sound designer Harry de Wit asked students to draw 'silence' or 'the sound of the city' before picking words or phrases from their texts to build soundscapes.[73]

Rehearsal

As part of the project's 'pre-production', teachers from every participating school were invited to a Continuing Professional Development (CPD) weekend, designed to introduce them to the box, its concept and process. Over two days artist educators from TGA led a series of exercises exploring the elements of the box and the process. They were supported by professional artist-mentors, drawn from the East London community and local theatre companies who were then assigned to schools to work with the students and teachers throughout the project.

I participated with the teachers on one weekend (20–21 January 2016). The focus was to encourage teachers to act as artistic directors of student performances, mirroring TGA's emphasis on the importance of the artistic director in bringing the production together in its final stages. The fourth level of the box represented 'Rehearsal' and incorporated both acting and direction. 'Directing' was represented in the box by a conductor's baton, working 'as a metaphor and as a practical tool' to investigate the role of the director in creating the *Gesamtkunstwerk*.[74] Suggested activities were designed to get students thinking about the act of direction, especially the impact of *mise-en-scène* on meaning, but, ultimately, the CPD event underscored the need for the teachers to function as the overall artistic directors.

The responsibility of the artistic director is linked to van Hove's approach to acting. TGA actor Eelco Smits explained in the learning resource that 'Ivo searches for the intensity of being real onstage, of not playing' and he described that in some situations this approach can be dangerous, with non-rehearsed, real fights happening on stage.[75] Student safety rules out this level of physical intensity, but there are also non-physical ways that students can be put at risk by an acting style that searches for the real. During the CPD event, in response to the line 'Antigone says no', we were asked to talk in groups about times in our own lives when we have said no and to turn these experiences into three physical images. The discussion following this exercise focused on the challenges of working on personal material with students, with some of the teachers sharing experiences of dealing with particularly difficult personal stories from their students and in some cases intervening, when they felt that the real was too distressing to be shared on stage.

Gesamtkunstwerk

The challenges of transposing a theory of acting that privileges 'the real' onto diverse groups of young students, some of whom live with the memory of trauma, demonstrates that whilst the box set out a process that would ideally mirror that of TGA's, the demands of the classroom became part of the *Gesamtkunstwerk* – shaping how students worked with the material and, eventually, the performances that they presented at the showcase.

Many of the performances I saw in the Barbican's Pit on 14 and 15 March 2017 used large ensemble casts, shaped and determined by class sizes and the need to involve everyone on stage. They embraced the concept of the *Gesamtkunstwerk,* making imaginative use of choreography, movement, lighting, video, sound and costume. Despite the emphasis on text in the process, just four of the eight performances I saw had a clear relationship to one or more of the extracts in the box. This may have been impacted by the fact that some of the teachers used participation to fulfil the devising requirement of their GCSE programmes and thus could not use a play script as a stimulus because of exam board requirements.[76] In the performances where there was no obvious link to the text extracts, two dealt with a range of contemporary social issues (from online grooming to the gender pay gap), and one explored, in a particularly moving performance, the story of Ruth Ellis, the last woman to have been executed for murder in the UK.

The different degrees to which the box was present in these performances was particularly striking, and was suggestive of the ways groups had adapted the process. For the Circus Arts group from Hackney Community College, the first level of the box with its emphasis on 'practicing the fun of failure' was enough to inspire a mime narrative in which the students were able to showcase their burgeoning circus skills. In 'Fear, Change and Sexuality' by a group of 13–14-year-olds from Buxton School in Leytonstone, the entire box and its contents were brought on in perfect condition, unravelled on stage during the performance, and then reassembled out of order and taken off stage in a mess at the end. Using the box on stage pushed against the idea of the box as *Gesamtkunstwerk,* in which the different elements 'fit perfectly together'.[77] Rather, the messiness of the box at the end felt like a visual metaphor for the process of devising, as well as for the Barbican Box process, in which administrative demands, the abilities and needs of the students, and exam requirements were balanced alongside the demands of TGA's process. By strewing its contents around the stage, this group refused to create the clean-cut 'total artwork' promised by the box, instead creating a sense of work-in-progress that reflected the change and uncertainty portrayed in their 'coming out' narrative.

The Barbican Box project illuminated van Hove's theatre-making ideal – a collaborative, text-driven method that strives towards *Gesamtkunstwerk.* What teachers and students actually did with the box demonstrated the challenges of that method, but also the freedom and possibilities inherent in this structure. In an interview about the project, van Hove stated that education 'is a very important part of . . . our responsibility as theatre makers'.[78] The uses to which the box was put also raised the question that, if, as van Hove states, education is an important part of the job of theatre makers, what are they responsible for teaching? Through learning about and replicating van

Hove's process with TGA, students also learned about collaboration, creativity and failure, skills that are likely valuable beyond the single production of their own *Gesamtkunstwerk.*

A TALE OF TWO CITIES: LAZARUS *IN NEW YORK AND LONDON*

Susan Bennett

The announcement in April 2015 of the world première of *Lazarus* as part of the upcoming season at the New York Theatre Workshop (NYTW)[79] drew immediate attention for its pedigree credentials: Enda Walsh, who wrote the book for the Tony-award-winning musical *Once* (a show based on John Carney's film of the same name and a NYTW production), and David Bowie, advertised in the press release as composing new songs and rearrangements of old ones specifically for this project. This news was just as keenly received by fans of Walter Tevis's 1963 novel *The Man Who Fell To Earth* (the inspiration for this new production[80]) and Nicholas Roeg's 1976 film adaptation in which Bowie had played the story's protagonist, Thomas Jerome Newton: would *Lazarus* reveal what had happened to the strange alien who had made himself enormously rich but who was nonetheless unhappily stranded on Earth? In this same press release, NYTW announced Ivo van Hove as the production's director.

The selection of van Hove for this project was perhaps not surprising, given his previous successes at NYTW: *Scenes from a Marriage* in the then current (2014–15) season, but also *The Little Foxes* (in the same season as Walsh's *Once*, 2010–11), *The Misanthrope* (2007–8) and *Hedda Gabler* (2004–5). As well, van Hove had received considerable North American attention for his Dutch-language, European-touring version of Jonathan Larson's *Rent*, the original production of which had opened at NYTW (1996). Indeed, after Walsh and Bowie had a first draft of the *Lazarus* script completed in the spring of 2014, their producer, Robert Fox, was instructed to find someone for their project who was not 'a regular, conventional director'; Fox apparently only had one name for them, 'Ivo'.[81] Each member of the *Lazarus* creative team – Bowie, Walsh, Fox and van Hove – brought to the production impressively diverse and multi-genre experience, a group particularly well suited to develop a stage musical that would deploy extensive video work, a live band and Michael C. Hall (an actor with extensive stage credits, but better known for his television work as serial killer Dexter Morgan) assuming the role for which Bowie had such a cult following. In the Introduction to the published text of *Lazarus*, Walsh describes his reaction to meeting Bowie in a script development meeting: 'I was hit with the realisation that I was sitting opposite this cultural icon – this man who had created so much and influenced so many. This bloody genius. David Fucking Bowie.'[82] For van Hove too, Bowie had long been inspirational: 'I have all his albums at home. "Young Americans" was the first record I ever bought. My first Broadway show was *The Elephant Man*. I made a special holiday to come to New York just to see that.'[83]

Lazarus, almost inevitably, has become one of the most widely recognized of van Hove's directorial career, opening (after previews) on 7 December 2015 in NYTW's 199-seat theatre on East 4th Street. The show's US$1 million production costs were quickly offset by virtue of tickets selling out faster than for any other show in NYTW's 36-year history (including *Rent*), enthusiasm that generated an extension to the planned run even before opening night.[84] The production received its European première almost a year later, on 8 November 2016, at a 994-seat pop-up venue, the King's Cross Theatre in London.

Lazarus bore all the hallmarks of a van Hove production – a sparse but potent scene and lighting design by Jan Versweyveld, extraordinary and poetic video work by Tal Yarden, dynamic acting performances (particularly from Hall in the lead role and from Sophie Anne Caruso as Girl/Marley), and the director's own ability to conjure breathtaking images from an intricate interweaving of all production elements. Much like its novel and film predecessors, *Lazarus* has an odd and often opaque plot but the use of music well known from the Bowie songbook (including 'The Man Who Sold the World', 'Changes', 'Life on Mars?' and 'Heroes') worked as a kind of interpretive spine on which the Bowie-Walsh text could hang. Van Hove has said that Bowie read *Lazarus* to him and then asked what he thought: 'It feels to me as if everything is happening within his [Newton's] skull, that we are in his mind'[85] and this prevailing sense of interiority, in van Hove's production, both defied and explored the impact of the New York City setting in which Newton now resides.

The musical opens with '*a sudden cacophony of televisual sounds*', a perennial signifier of contemporary life for van Hove – those sonic environments familiar to us

Figure 30 *Setting of* Lazarus, *the New York Theatre Workshop (2015).*

from airports, shopping malls and hotel lobbies and which the director made a constant presence in his *Roman Tragedies*. Then the lights come up on Newton who '*sits detached – staring into a screen – the television switching between channels*'.[86] Newton's history (for those who don't know or remember the film) was relayed, over time, through the character of 'Girl' (whose identity is never quite clear although, in the some of the very last lines, remembers her name as Marley); Girl reminds Newton of what he's survived and, at the same time, revives the possibility that he might leave, that a rocket can be built:

Newton   But how will that happen? What makes you know that?

Girl   Hope.

Newton   Hope?

Girl   Right.

A slight pause.

Newton   Then I'm held by that hope. Only that word – there's nothing else.[87]

Their conversation segues into a particularly melancholic rendition of 'Life on Mars?' (sung by Girl) where the final line – 'Is there life on Mars?' – is interrupted by sounds of the streets and by videography, both intruding the external world of New York City into Newton's apartment-as-prison:

Suddenly a loud burst of traffic sounds.

Newton *watches a light coming up on* **Elly** [Newton's assistant] *talking to* **Valentine** [a character who appears in Newton's apartment claiming to be his long-time friend and who may in fact be a serial killer], *as the walls fill with 2nd Avenue.*[88]

The sparseness of the set – a fridge stage left and a bed stage right with the musicians and projected cityscapes (usually New York but, on one occasion, Berlin) serving as backdrop – did nothing to mitigate Newton's and, indeed, the audience's sense of claustrophobia, an effect van Hove has worked equally effectively in the apartment setting of his productions of *Hedda Gabler* at NYTW in 2004 and at the National in London in 2016–17. Van Hove has also suggested that the *Lazarus* stage design resembled a skull, the one he thought of in his first response to the text.[89] In the intimate space of the East 4th Street theatre, *Lazarus* was a fourth-wall-removed chamber piece that drew the audience into the painful and suffocating world that Newton endured (largely through the anaesthetic properties of the gin and television with which he sustained himself). There was little sense throughout that Newton and the Girl's shared 'hope' might translate into happy resolution, but the ending brought Newton to the embrace of a 'new family' and the Girl's promise that 'we'll travel on', before they together sung 'Heroes'. At the conclusion of the song, the stage direction reads:

Marley [the Girl] *leaves.*

Newton *finds rest.*

Blackout.

The End.[90]

At the NYTW performance, I found the ending strange and unfinished, but nonetheless consoling, creating some provisional expression of community between stage and audience – what Jill Dolan has called a utopian performative, 'fleeting, briefly transcendent bits of profound human feeling and connection spring from alchemy between performers and spectators and their mutual confrontation with a historical present that lets them imagine a different, putatively better future'.[91] Like my experience of other van Hove productions, images and sounds from *Lazarus* lingered long afterwards, teasing out thoughts about the precarity of human life and happiness, even at this time of exponentially expanding technological connection between peoples.

Midway through the NYTW run, on 10 January 2016, David Bowie died – shock news that was posted first on Facebook and confirmed by his son via Twitter.[92] Bowie's last public appearance had been at the opening night of *Lazarus*. From 11 January to closing night, the East 4th Street theatre became one of several memorial sites where fans left their tributes. Critical and popular reception of *Lazarus* (as well as for the album *Blackstar* that Bowie had released only a few days earlier and which included the song 'Lazarus') would from that day always be framed by the sad and unexpected event of the artist's passing.

With Bowie's enormous and enduring popularity in the UK, it was always likely that *Lazarus* would receive a London production before too long, although the availability of Hall for a second theatrical run may well have been a scheduling challenge. After Bowie's death, it was inevitable. The production's opening in November 2016 at the King's Cross Theatre was, then, even more of an event than the NYTW première and undoubtedly reported on a much larger scale. The design for *Lazarus* was unchanged – there was simply a wider stage space on which to set the musical.[93] But the size of the auditorium with close to a thousand seats significantly changed the stage–spectator dynamic. The show now had a more conventionally fourth-wall-removed dynamic where spectators are primed to silently attend to lives going on beyond and apart from us.

Lazarus in London was also altered by a wealth of critical attention, both in advance of the opening and in reviews that were, to say the least, mixed. Only Paul Taylor in the *Independent* was unreservedly enthusiastic, describing the performance as 'rare and mesmeric' and attributing a 'flawless expressiveness' to van Hove's staging.[94] More typical were Dominic Cavendish's remarks: 'The curiosity value is high ... but artistically, I'm not so sure'[95] or Michael Billington's 'while the separate ingredients are fascinating to watch in Ivo van Hove's kaleidoscopic production, I rarely felt moved.'[96] All critics, however, reflected on the exceptional circumstances of these London performances. Ian Shuttleworth opened his review suggesting 'anything short of the physical resurrection of the late David Bowie would have been a disappointment, as regards this musical based around his songs.'[97] Cavendish called *Lazarus* a 'musical-theatre epitaph' that required from its audience 'a commemorative duty';[98] Billington noted that Bowie's 'death lends the show a patina of melancholy';[99] Taylor called it Bowie's 'parting gift to the world'.[100] Certainly, the uncanny resemblance of Michael C. Hall's voice to Bowie's, at least in some of the songs (and memorably so in the denouement's 'Heroes'), gave the London performance a haunting quality, sustained and underscored by the only significant change made to the production. At the end of the show, a large headshot of Bowie was projected onto the centre-stage screen – signalling *Lazarus* as a 'poignant remembrance', as Shuttleworth described it. After the curtain call, many spectators wandered down to the front of the house to take selfies and group shots in the company of this last trace of David Bowie, a Lazarus that even the most devoted fans could not raise from the dead.

Notes

Foreword

1　This phrase is taken from Harold Pinter's 2005 Nobel Lecture, 'Art, Truth and Politics'. Available online at https://www.nobelprize.org/nobel_prizes/literature/laureates/2005/pinter-lecture-e.html (accessed 15 January 2018).

Introduction

1　This is the title of Pamela Newton's 2015 piece for *American Theatre*, 11 November. Available online: http://www.americantheatre.org/2015/11/11/ivo-van-hove-is-having-a-moment/ (accessed 4 September 2017).

2　'Biography: Ivo van Hove', Toneelgroep Amsterdam. Available online: https://tga.nl/en/employees/ivo-van-hove (accessed 4 September 2017).

3　Marvin Carlson, *10,000 Nights: Highlights from 50 Years of Theatre-Going* (Ann Arbor, MI: University of Michigan Press, 2017), 231.

4　Roberto Herrscher, 'In the harsh landscape of Charles Wuorinen's *Brokeback Mountain,* there is not a moment of joy or a single singable melody', *Opera News*, April 2014, 52–3.

5　Among the many publications where van Hove's background has been described, Rebecca Mead's article for *The New Yorker* (from which the quotation is taken) is a standout. See 'Theatre Laid Bare: Ivo van Hove's Raw Productions Bring Out the Elemental Drama of Classic Works', 26 October 2015. Available online: http://www.newyorker.com/magazine/2015/10/26/theatre-laid-bare (accessed 4 September 2017).

6　Rebecca Mead, 'Theatre Laid Bare'.

7　'Ivo van Hove is Having a Moment', *American Theatre*, 11 November. Available online: http://www.americantheatre.org/2015/11/11/ivo-van-hove-is-having-a-moment/ (accessed 4 September 2017).

8　'Obsession, Barbican, London Review: Jude Law is Muscular and Brooding but Wooden', *Independent*, 26 April 2017. Available online: http://www.independent.co.uk/arts-entertainment/theatre-dance/reviews/obsession-review-barbican-jude-law-a7702756.html (accessed 5 September 2017).

9   See Johanna Wall's discussion of *Mazeppa* (149–53) and Sonia Massai's of *Othello* (22–4) – eds.

10 Rebecca Mead, 'Theatre Laid Bare'.

11 See Figure 13 on page 92 as well as Plate 15 – eds.

12 Patrice Chéreau (1944–2013) directed for theatre, film and opera and was best known for his four-year *Ring Cycle* at Bayreuth (1976–80) and his film of Hanif Kureishi's novel *Intimacy* (2001) starring Timothy Spall, Marianne Faithful and Mark Rylance.

13 Gerard Mortier, who died in March 2014, brought in van Hove to direct Charles Wuorinen's new opera *Brokeback Mountain* at Teatro Real in Madrid where Mortier was now in charge. *Brokeback Mountain* had its première in January 2014.

14 More details are available on the TGA website: https://tga.nl/en/about-ta (accessed 19 September 2017). Thanks also to Laurens De Vos who shared further information.

15 See TGA website: https://tga.nl/en/about-ta (accessed 19 September 2017); the website records the support of the Ministry of Education, Culture and Sciences and the City of Amsterdam. More information about Adelheld|Female Economy can be found on their website: http://www.femaleeconomy.nl/#about (accessed 19 September 2017).

Section One: Directing the Classics

1   Ben Brantley, 'A Natural Cassavetes Woman, Theatricalized, Magnified and Multiplied', *The New York Times*, 4 November 2008. Available online: http://www.nytimes.com/2008/12/04/arts/04iht-04opening.18405877.html (accessed 7 July 2017).

2   'Jan Versweyveld in conversation with Sonia Massai' (February 2017), 11   – eds.

3   Peter Brook, *The Empty Space* (London: MacGibbon and Kee, 1968), 97.

4   The première at the New York Theatre Workshop was followed by a revival in 2006 by Toneelgroep Amsterdam and in 2016 by the National Theatre, London; a UK tour of the National Theatre production started in autumn 2017.

5   *De Gelderlander*, 16 September 1991.

6   After its première in 2007, *Roman Tragedies* was presented at the Avignon Festival in 2008, at the Barbican Centre, London, in 2009, and has toured to major theatre venues worldwide since.

7   Wouter van Ransbeek, in his interview with Keren Zaiontz (89–98), addresses *Roman Tragedies* and *Kings of War* as productions touring to major international festivals and other venues – eds.

8   All Shakespearean quotations in this section are from Ann Thompson, David Scott Kastan and Richard Proudfoot (eds), *The Arden Shakespeare: Shakespeare Complete Works* (London: Bloomsbury, 2011).

9   This production toured to Taipei as part of the National Theater Concert Hall's biennial International Theater Festival in 2014.

10 Alfred Hickling, '*Roman Tragedies*: Adelaide Festival Review', *Guardian*, 2 March 2014. Available online: https://www.theguardian.com/stage/2014/mar/02/roman-tragedies-adelaide-festival-review (accessed 7 July 2017).

11 Matt Trueman, 'Theatre Space-Man: Ivo van Hove', *The Stage*, 30 January 2015. Available online: http://matttrueman.co.uk/2015/01/theatres-space-man-ivo-van-hove.html (accessed 7 July 2017).

12 Edward Gordon Craig, *On the Art of the Theatre* (Heinemann, 1911), 180.

13 Richard Wagner, 'Art and Revolution' (1849), in *The Art-Work of the Future and Other Works*, translated by W. Ashton Ellis (Lincoln [Neb.] and London: University of Nebraska Press, 1993), 35.

14 Amin Maalouf, *In the Name of Identity: Violence and the Need to Belong* (New York: Arcade Publishing, [1996] 2012), 100.

15 Maalouf, 153.

16 Maalouf, 37.

17 Maria Shevtsova and Christopher Innes (eds), *Directors/Directing: Conversations on Theatre* (Cambridge: Cambridge University Press, 2009), 73.

18 *Ivo van Hove and Patrick Marber on 'Hedda Gabler', with Kirsty Wark, NT Talks, Podcast 21*, podcast audio, MP3, 23:49, accessed 5 September 2017.

19 *Ruth Wilson on 'Hedda Gabler', NT Talks, Podcast 20*, podcast audio, MP3, 32:58, accessed 5 September 2017.

20 Will Fisher, *Materializing Gender in Early Modern English Literature and Culture* (Cambridge: Cambridge University Press, 2006), 170.

21 Randy Gener, 'Ivo van Hove has a Passion for Extremes', *American Theatre*, 6 November 2009. Available online: http://www.americantheatre.org/2009/11/06/ivo-van-hove-has-a-passion-for-extremes/ (accessed 7 July 2017).

22 Maria M. Delgado, 'Journeys of Cultural Transference: Calixto Bieito's Multilingual Shakespeare', *Modern Language Review*, 101 (2006), 150.

23 *The Stage*, 30 January 2015.

24 'Ivo van Hove in conversation with Susan Bennett and Sonia Massai' (January 2017), 5–7 – eds.

25 Jeffrey Sweet, *What Playwrights Talk About When They Talk About Writing* (New Haven and London: Yale University Press, 2017).

26 Sweet, 69.

27 Sweet, 68.

28 Patrick Marber, *Henrik Ibsen, Hedda Gabler; A new version . . . from a literal translation by Karin and Ann Bamborough* (London: Faber and Faber, 2016), vii.

29 Marber, 44.

30 Marber, 59.

31 Marber, 45.

32 Marber, 95.

33 Michael Meyer, *Henrik Ibsen, Hedda Gabler* (London: Methuen 2001), 49.

34 Meyer, 101.

35 Christopher Hampton (trans.), *Henrik Ibsen: Hedda Gabler and A Doll's House* (London: Faber and Faber, 1989), 39.

36 Henrik Ibsen, *Notes on 'Hedda Gabler'* (1890), in Tony Cole, *Playwrights and Playwriting: The Meaning and Making of Modern Drama from Ibsen to Ionesco* (London: MacGibbon and Kee, 1960), 168.

37 Ibsen, 170.

38 Hampton, 17, 57.

39 Van Hove also provided 'Some thoughts on Hedda Gabler' for his 2015–16 production at the National Theatre. Available online: https://www.nationaltheatre.org.uk/blog/some-thoughts-hedda-gabler (accessed 11 December 2017).

40 Ben Brantley, '*A View from the Bridge* Bears Witness to the Pain of Fate', *The New York Times*, 12 November 2015. Available online: https://www.nytimes.com/2015/11/13/theater/review-a-view-from-the-bridge-bears-witness-to-the-pain-of-fate.html (accessed 1 August 2017).

41 Back in the 1990s, van Hove's production of a *Romeo and Juliet* adaptation leaned more towards choreographed stylization in the manner of Robert Wilson, whilst his *Richard II* included some medieval costumes and plastic chairs on a lily-strewn mound of mud.

42 *Kings of War* melds eras with a brass quartet 'galleried' in the MDF panelling, and a medieval crown in a glowing white 'discovery space' upstage.

43 Randy Gener, 'Ivo van Hove Has a Passion for Extremes', *American Theatre*, 6 November 2009. http://www.americantheatre.org/2009/11/06/ivo-van-hove-has-a-passion-for-extremes/ (accessed 16 May 2017), and Ben Brantley, 'A Natural Cassavetes Woman, Theatricalized, Magnified and Multiplied', *The New York Times*, 3 December 2008.

44 Van Hove discussed this with me in an interview conducted in April 2017.

45 Van Hove admits that matching translators to Shakespeare is hard, though there is not room in this essay to properly discuss those used or, indeed, the complex effects of Hafid Bouazza's translation combined with the white actor Hans Kesting playing Othello, not in blackface. About Kesting's Othello, see also p. 22–3 above – eds.

46 Brantley, '*A View from the Bridge*', *The New York Times*, 12 November 2015.

47 'Shakespeare's Take on *The Game of Thrones*', *The New York Times*, 4 November 2016. Available online: https://www.nytimes.com/2016/11/05/theater/review-shakespeares-take-on-the-game-of-thrones.html (accessed 6 July 2017).

48 Matt Trueman, 'Ivo van Hove Directs Shakespeare in *Kings of War*', *Variety*, 23 April 2016. Available online: http://variety.com/2016/legit/reviews/kings-of-war-review-1201759431/ (accessed 6 July 2017).

49 Trueman, *Variety*, 23 April 2016.

50 'Shakespeare400 [was] a consortium of leading cultural, creative and educational organizations, coordinated by King's College London, which [marked] the 400th anniversary of Shakespeare's death in 2016.' http://www.shakespeare400.org.

51 An essay devoted to van Hove's contribution to the Barbican Box project is included in Section Five 'Creation, Adaptation, Direction' (194–9) – eds.

52 Hannah Arendt, *The Human Condition* (Chicago: University of Chicago Press, 1958), 9.

53 Hannah Arendt, 'Truth and Politics', in *Between Past and Future: Eight Exercises in Political Thought* (New York: Viking Press, 1968), 259–60.

54 Agnes Heller, *The Time is Out of Joint: Shakespeare as Philosopher of History* (Lanham, Boulder, New York and Oxford: Rowman & Littlefield, 2002), 321.

55 Giorgio Agamben, *State of Exception* (Chicago: University of Chicago Press, 2005).

56 Giorgio Agamben, *Homo Sacer: Sovereign Power and Bare Life* (Stanford: Stanford University Press, 1998), 175.

57 Zygmunt Bauman, *Liquid Love: On the Frailty of Human Bonds* (Cambridge: Polity Press, 2003), xii.

58 Kwame Anthony Appiah, *In My Father's House: Africa in the Philosophy of Culture* (London: Methuen, 1992), 155.

59 Jozef De Vos, 'The Sweep of History: Ivo Van Hove's *Roman Tragedies*', *Cahiers Élisabéthains: A Journal of English Renaissance Studies*: 75.1 (2009), 56.

60 Cybercafés made available computers connected to the Internet to their customers, before Wi-Fi technology became widely available.

61 Martha C. Nussbaum, *Political Emotions: Why Love Matters for Justice* (Cambridge, Mass.: The Belknap Press of Harvard University Press, 2013).

62 'If you are not interested in the chorus as a director, better take your hands off a Greek tragedy. Better not do it'; Ivo van Hove, quoted in Charlotte Higgins, 'Death Becomes Her: How Juliette Binoche and Ivo van Hove Remade Antigone', *Guardian,* 18 February 2015. Available online: https://www.theguardian.com/stage/2015/feb/18/juliette-binoche-ivo-van-hove-antigone (accessed 1 June 2017).

63 'Ivo van Hove, in conversation with Susan Bennett and Sonia Massai' (January 2017), 5–7 – eds.

64 Duska Radosavljević, 'Layers of Complication', *Exeunt*, 10 March 2015. Available online: http://exeuntmagazine.com/features/layers-of-complication/ (accessed 1 June 2017).

65 'Programme Note', 2015 (Producers: Barbican and Les Théâtres de la Ville de Luxembourg).

66 George Rodosthenous (ed.), *Contemporary Adaptations of Greek Tragedy, Auteurship and Directorial Visions* (London and New York: Bloomsbury, 2017), 13, 14.

67 Edward-Cook interview, in conversation with George Rodosthenous, 2017.

68 Edward-Cook interview.

69 Radosavljević, 'Layers'.

70 Shawn H. Katz, 'Healing the Father–Son Relationship: A Qualitative Inquiry into Adult Reconciliation', *Journal of Humanistic Psychology*, 42:3 (2002), 13–52, 18–22.

71 Anne Carson, *Sophokles: Antigone* (London: Oberon Books, 2015), 33.

72 Carson, 33.

73 Carson, 34.

74 Eric D. Miller, 'Why the Father Wound Matters: Consequences for Male Mental Health and the Father-Son Relationship', *Child Abuse Review*, 22 (2013), 194–208, 200.

75 Carson, 35.

76 Carson, 36.

77 Mark T. Morman and Kory Floyd, 'A "Changing Culture of Fatherhood": Effects on Affectionate Communication, Closeness, and Satisfaction in Men's Relationships with their Fathers and their Sons', *Western Journal of Communication*, 66:4 (2002), 395–411, 396.

78 Carson, 36.

79 Carson, 46.

80 Carson, 48.

81 Carson, 49.

82 Radosavljević, 'Layers'.

83 Sue Hamstead, 'Re-imaging *Antigone*: Contemporary Resonances in the Contemporary Revisioning of Characters, Chorus, and Staging', in Rodosthenous (ed.), *Contemporary Adaptations of Greek Tragedy*, 227–50, 244.

84 George Steiner, *Antigones: How the Antigone Legend has Endured in Western Literature, Art, and Thought* (New Haven and London: Yale University Press, 1996 [1984]), 300.

85 Carson, 24.

86 Carson, 38.

87 Carson, 39.

88 Carson, 44.

89 Carson, 47.

90 Carson, 41.

Section Two: The Festival Performances of Ivo van Hove and Toneelgroep Amsterdam

1 See 'Directing the Classics' for extended discussion of *Roman Tragedies* and *Kings of War*, especially Massai's overview to the section (19–28), Bassett (43–6) and the extract from van Hove's director's notes for *Roman Tragedies* (56–9) – eds.

2 My thanks to Carla Stewart and Shalon Webber-Heffernan for their assistance with interview transcription.

3 See the essay by P. A. Skantze in 'Creation, Adaptation, Direction' (178–87) for discussion of van Hove's *Scenes from a Marriage* – eds.

4 Emile Schra's essay in 'American Theatre' (115–21) discusses van Hove's production of *Angels in America* – eds.

5 While *Roman Tragedies* was not the first visit of Toneelgroep Amsterdam to BAM, it was the first production of its kind to bring durational Shakespeare in Dutch to New York audiences.

6 See Massai's overview essay (19–28) and Kate Bassett's contribution (42–6) in 'Directing the Classics' for more on *Othello* and Denis Flannery's essay on *The Fountainhead* (187–94) in 'Creation, Adaptation, Direction' – eds.

Section Three: American Theatre

1   Henry Hitchings, '*A View from the Bridge*, Young Vic, Theatre Review', *London Evening Standard*, 14 April 2014. Available online: https://www.standard.co.uk/goingout/theatre/a-view-from-the-bridge-young-vic-theatre-review–9258350.html (accessed 10 August 2017).

2   Paul Taylor, '*A View from the Bridge*, Young Vic, Theatre Review: "Unforgettable"', *Independent*, 14 April 2014. Available online: http://www.independent.co.uk/arts-entertainment/theatre-dance/reviews/a-view-from-the-bridge-young-vic-theatre-review-unforgettable–9258660.html (accessed 10 August 2017).

3   Lyn Gardner, 'Ivo van Hove Reinvents Arthur Miller', *Guardian*, 17 February 2015. Available online: https://www.theguardian.com/stage/2015/feb/17/view-from-the-bridge-review-ivo-van-hove-arthur-miller (accessed 10 August 2017).

4   Melia Bensussen, personal communication, 23 May 2017.

5   Marvin Carlson, *10,000 Nights: Highlights from 50 Years of Theatre-Going* (Ann Arbor, MI: University of Michigan Press, 2017), 232.

6   Ben Whishaw, personal communication, 2 May 2017.

7   Patrick Healy, '*TimesTalks*: Mark Strong and Ivo van Hove', *The New York Times*, 23 November 2015. Available online: http://ntlive.nationaltheatre.org.uk/productions/ntlout16-a-view-from-the-bridge (accessed 10 August 2017).

8   Gary Younge and Joseph Harker, 'Samuel L Jackson Hit Out at Black British Actors in Hollywood. Was He right?', *Guardian*, 9 March 2017. Available online: https://www.theguardian.com/commentisfree/2017/mar/09/samuel-l-jackson-black-british-actors-hollywood-valid (accessed 10 August 2017).

9   Bensussen, personal communication.

10 David Lan, personal communication, 18 May 2017.

11 Ben Brantley, 'A Universal Heart, Pounding with Hope: Ivo van Hove's Version of *Angels in America* at BAM', *The New York Times*, 24 October 2014. Available online: https://www.nytimes.com/2014/10/25/theater/ivo-van-hove-brings-angels-in-america-to-bam.html (accessed 10 August 2017).

12 Michelle Memram, 'Tony Kushner Gives Rave Review of Stripped-Down, David Bowie-ized Production of *Angels in America*', *Vanity Fair*, October 2014. Available online: https://www.vanityfair.com/culture/2014/10/angels-in-america-bam-ivo-van-hove (accessed 10 August 2017).

13 Marilyn Stasio, '*The Little Foxes*, Theatre Review', *Variety*, 21 September 2010. Available online: http://www.variety.com/2010/legit/news/the-little-foxes–1117943661 (accessed 2 June 2017).

14 Ivo van Hove, 'Director's Notes for *The Little Foxes*', n.d. Director's private copy.

15 Van Hove, 'Director's Notes'.

16 Van Hove, 'Director's Notes'.

17 Van Hove, 'Director's Notes'.

18 Van Hove, 'Director's Notes'.

19 Van Hove, 'Director's Notes'.

20 Van Hove, 'Director's Notes'.

21 Tennessee Williams, *Tennessee Williams: Plays 1937–1955* (New York: Library of America, 2000), 395.

22 Van Hove, 'Director's Notes'.

23 Van Hove, 'Director's Notes'.

24 Van Hove, 'Director's Notes'.

25 Lillian Hellman, *Six Plays by Lillian Hellman* (New York: Vintage, 1960), 205.

26 Hellman, 177.

27 Randy Newman, 'God's Song' (1972). Available online: http://www.lyricsdepot.com/randy-newman/gods-song.html (accessed 2 June 2017).

28 David Cote, '*The Little Foxes*: Ivo van Hove and Elizabeth Marvel Reinvent an American Classic', *Time Out*, 27 September 2010. Available online: http://www.timeout.com/newyork/theater/the-little-foxes-off-broadway (accessed 2 June 2017).

29 Michael Feingold, 'Ivo van Hove Renovates *The Little Foxes*, Lucy Thurber's *Bottom of the World* Drifts Downward', *Village Voice*, 22 September 2010. Available online: http://www.villagevoice.com/arts/ivo-van-hove-renovates-the-little-foxes-lucy-thurbers-bottom-of-the-world-drifts-downward–7134729 (accessed 2 June 2017).

30 Van Hove, 'Director's Notes.'

31 Hellman, 194, 220.

32 Van Hove, 'Director's Notes'.

33 Van Hove, 'Director's Notes'.

34 Ben Brantley, 'A Dysfunctional Family, Greedy with "the Gimmes"', *The New York Times*, 22 September 2010. Available online: http://www.nytimes.com/2010/09/22/theater/reviews/22foxes.html?pagewanted=all (accessed 10 August 2017).

35 Hellman, 201.

36 Van Hove, 'Director's Notes'.

37 Don Shewey, '*The Little Foxes*, Theatre Review', *CultureVulture.net*, 3 October 2010. Available online: http://www.donshewey.com/theater_reviews/the_little_foxes.html (accessed 2 June 2017).

38 Tony Kushner, 'Ik schrok wel van mijn "Angels" zonder decor', *NRC Handelsblad*, 23 February 2009.

39 Susan Sontag, *Aids and its Metaphors* (London: Allen Lane, 1989); Susan Sontag, *Illness as Metaphor* (New York: Farrar, Straus and Giroux, 1978).

40 Peter van Kraaij, personal communication, 5 June 2017.

41 Van Kraaij, personal communication.

42 Tony Kushner, *Angels in America: A Gay Fantasia on National Themes. Part One: Millenium Approaches* (New York: Theatre Communications Group, 2013), 125.

43 Kushner, 160 (stage direction).

44 Kushner, 172. All caps in the original.

45 Kushner, 173. Italics, capital letters and ellipses in the original.

46 Van Kraaij, personal communication.

47 Interview with Jan Versweyveld, Amsterdam, 7 June 2017.

48 Interview with Jan Versweyveld, Amsterdam, 7 June 2017.

49 Interview with Jan Versweyveld, Amsterdam, 7 June 2017.

50 Ben Brantley, 'A Universal Heart, Pounding With Hope', *The New York Times*, 25 October 2014.

51 Hans Kesting, personal communication, 20 June 2017.

52 Kushner, 'Ik schrok wel van mijn "Angels" zonder decor'.

53 Neda Ulaby, 'Artist Talk: Ivo van Hove and Tony Kushner', BAM, New York, 23 October 2014. Available online: https://www.bam.org/video/2014/kushner-van-hove (accessed 10 August 2017).

54 Ulaby, 'Artist Talk: Ivo van Hove and Tony Kushner'.

55 In Salem, nearly 200 people were accused of practicing 'the Devil's Magic'. Nineteen people were hanged at Proctor's Ledge near Gallows Hill, and 71-year-old Giles Corey was pressed to death with heavy stones. In addition to the twenty people officially executed, four others died in prison while awaiting trial.

56 Nathaniel Hawthorne, *The Scarlet Letter* (Boston: J. R. Osgood and Company, 1850), 16.

57 Arthur Miller, *Timebends* (New York: Grove Press, 1987), 348.

58 Charles McNulty, 'Meet Ivo van Hove, the Most Provocatively Illuminating Theater Director Right Now', *Los Angeles Times*, 18 March 2016. Available online: http://www.latimes.com/entertainment/arts/la-ca-cm-ivo-van-hove-20160320-column.html (accessed 10 August 2017).

59 Ben Brantley, 'Witches of Salem Are Back; You May Be One', *The New York Times*, 1 April 2016, C1.

60 Pamela Newton, 'Ivo van Hove Is Having a Moment', *American Theatre*, 11 November 2015. Available online: http://www.americantheatre.org/2015/11/11/ivo-van-hove-is-having-a-moment/ (accessed 10 August 2017).

61 Chris Jones, '*Crucible* Burns with Seductive, Predatory Deceit', *Chicago Tribune*, 1 April 2016.

62 H. S., 'What Drew Philip Glass into *The Crucible*', *The Economist*, 10 May 2016.

63 Jerry Portwood, 'Ben Whishaw on Brexit, Beards and Life After *The Crucible*', *Rolling Stone*, 8 July 2016.

64 Brantley, 'Witches'.

65 Jesse Green, 'Ivo van Hove's *The Crucible* Heightens the Vitality of a Familiar Story', *New York Magazine*, 31 March 2016. Available online: http://www.vulture.com/2016/03/theater-review-the-crucible.html (accessed 10 August 2017).

66 Arthur Miller, *The Crucible* (New York: Bantam Books, 1959), 25.

67 Miller, *The Crucible*, 67.

68 Miller, *The Crucible*, 90.

69 Ben Whishaw, personal communication.

70 Newton, 'Moment'.

71 H. S., 'Glass'.

72 Newton, 'Moment'.

73 Green, '*Crucible*'.

74 Arthur Miller, *Echoes Down the Corridor*, ed. by Steven R. Centola (New York: Viking, 2000), 286.

75 For some disbelieving critics during the première production of *The Crucible*, the parallel between Miller's play and the 1950s hysteria broke down at this point. In *The New York Times*, for example, Brooks Atkinson wrote, 'There never were any witches. But there have been spies and traitors in recent days. All the Salem witches were victims of public fear. Beginning with [US government official and Soviet spy Alger] Hiss, some of the people accused of treason and disloyalty today have been guilty'. Miller refuted the criticism. In Brooks Atkinson, '*The Crucible*: Arthur Miller's Dramatization of the Salem Witch Trial in 1692', *The New York Times*, 1 February 1953, X1.

76 Miller, *The Crucible*, 32–3.

77 Brantley, 'Witches'.

Section Four: Opera across Europe

1 M. Debrocq, 'La "Lulu" de Bernhard Kontarsky et Ivo Van Hove à Anvers L'érotisme froid des barreaux de fer', *Le Soir*, 29 January 1999. Available online: http://www.lesoir.be/archive/recup%3A%252Fopera-la-lulu-de-bernhard-kontarsky-et-ivo-van-hove-a-a_t-19990129-Z0GAAY.html (accessed 16 August 2017). Reviews in French, as here, have been translated by the author.

2 Nicolas Blanmont, 'Makropoulos, une quête contre le temps', *La Libre Belgique*, 12 September 2002. Available online: http://www.lalibre.be/culture/musique/makropoulos-une-quete-contre-le-temps-51b87a6ee4b0de6db9a79906 (accessed 16 August 2017). The production was revived in Amsterdam in May and June 2009.

3 Rudi van den Bulck, 'Iolanta', *Opéra International* 288 (March 2004), 56.

4 John McCann, 'Ghent', *Opera*, November 2006, 1323–4.

5 Nicolas Blanmont, 'Wagner, prisonnier d'un concept', *La Libre Belgique*, 16 June 2006. Available online: http://www.lalibre.be/culture/scenes/wagner-prisonnier-d-un-concept-51b88f0be4b0de6db9ae21f8 (accessed 16 August 2017).

6 J. M. Proust, 'Die Walküre', *Opéra Magazine*, 17 (April 2007), 49.

7 Nicolas Blanmont, 'Siegfried entre GTA et Sim's', *La Libre Belgique*, 6 November 2007. Available online: http://www.lalibre.be/culture/musique/siegfried-entre-gta-et-sim-s-51b89669e4b0de6db9b0d843 (accessed 16 August 2017).

8 John McCann, 'Ghent', *Opera*, March 2008, 287–8.

9 Nicolas Blanmont, 'Le Ring flamand, voie sans issue?', *La Libre Belgique*, 16 June 2008. Available online: http://www.lalibre.be/culture/musique/le-ring-flamand-voie-sans-issue-51b89c0de4b0de 6db9b2ae51 (accessed 16 August 2017).

10 John McCann, 'Brussels', *Opera*, July 2010, 826–7. At the end of the opera, the voice of Neptune is heard from off-stage, announcing that Idomeneo doesn't have to kill someone, but has to leave his throne to his son Idamante.

11 Erna Metdepenninghen, 'Amsterdam', *Opera*, January 2013, 64–5.

12 Erna Metdepenninghen, 'Lyon', *Opera*, February 2013, 196–7. This production was reprised at l'Opéra de Lyon in March 2018.

13 David Smythe, 'Mazeppa: A Thrilling Night at the Komische Oper Berlin', *Bachtrack*, 6 July 2013. Available online: https://bachtrack.com/fr_FR/review-komische-oper-berlin-mazeppa-van-hove ?destination=%2F22%2F270%2Flist-published%2F994 (accessed 16 August 2017).

14 Erna Metdepenninghen, 'Brussels', *Opera*, January 2014, 38–9. The production was reprised in January 2016 at Teater Wielki in Warsaw.

15 E. Dahan, '"Brokeback Mountain" chic et toc', *Libération*, 30 January 2014. Available online: http://next.liberation.fr/culture/2014/01/30/brokeback-mountain-chic-et-toc_976660 (accessed 16 August 2017).

16 The Nederlandse Opera, which has become a national opera, does not have a permanent orchestra and the great orchestras of the country take turns in its pit.

17 Shirley Apthorp, 'A Salome to Die For at Dutch National Opera', *Financial Times*, 14 June 2017. Available online: https://www.ft.com/content/5b5e9f92-5021-11e7-a1f2-db19572361bb?mhq5j= e2 (accessed 16 August 2017).

18 See P. A. Skantze's essay on van Hove's screen-to-stage adaptation of *Scenes from a Marriage* in this volume (178–87) – eds.

19 My discussion of *La Clemenza di Tito* is based on my review published in *Didaskalia*: 'Łaskawość Tytusa i kryzys demokracji', *Didaskalia*, 132 (2016), 119–22.

20 Agnieszka Holland, interviewed by J. Wróblewski, 'Dlaczego nie byliśmy Charlie', *Polityka*, 8 (2015), http://www.polityka.pl/tygodnikpolityka/paszporty/1609855,2,agnieszka-holland-o-tym-dlaczego-kultura-jest-tak-wazna.read (accessed 20 June 2017). Author's translation.

21 R. B. Moberly, 'The Influence of French Classical Drama on Mozart's *La clemenza di Tito*', *Music and Letters*, 55:3 (1974), 286–98.

22 John A. Rice, '*La clemenza di Tito*', in *The Cambridge Mozart Encyclopedia*, ed. Cliff Eisen and Simon P. Keefe (Cambridge: Cambridge University Press, 2006), 89–98.

23 Ivo van Hove, interviewed by M. Ulewicz, 'Mozart, Tytus, Mandela', *Łaskawość Tytusa*, Warsaw, Teatr Wielki – Polish National Opera, 2016, 34–7.

24 P. Urbański, 'Clemenza Austriaca. Nowy Sarastro i brat Mozart', in 'Mozart, Tytus, Mandela', 17–23.

25 D. Heartz, 'Mozart's Overture to *Titus* as Dramatic Argument', *The Musical Quarterly*, 64:1 (1978), 29–49.

26 Agnieszka Holland, interviewed by J. Wróblewski, in 'Dlaczego nie byliśmy Charlie', *Polityka*, 8 (2015). Author's translation.

27 Kadja Groenke, 'Frauenschicksale in Čajkowskijs Puškin-Opern', *Čajkowskij Studien*, 5 (2002), 15.

28 Ivo van Hove, 'Die Unmöglichkeit der Liebe. Ivo van Hove und Henrik Nánási sprechen über sachliche Gefühle, das Scheitern des Einzelnen und ein Stück Brot', *Mazeppa*. Programme accompanying the production at Komische Oper Berlin (2013), 8.

29 Van Hove, 'Die Unmöglichkeit der Liebe', 7.

30 Jan Brachmann, 'Kriegsgemetzel sind kein Bühnenkolorit: Die Komische Oper Berlin wächst bei Peter Tschaikowskys neuerdings vielgespieltem "Mazeppa" über sich hinaus', *Frankfurter Allgemeine Zeitung*, 26 February 2013.

31 Klaus Geitel, 'Ein Kriegsdrama im Pelzmantel: Bei der "Mazeppa" Premiere an der Komischen Oper gewinnen alle Beteiligten – nur Tschaikowsky als Kommponist verliert', *Berliner Morgenpost*, 26 February 2013.

32 Van Hove is quoted in Kester Freriks, 'Een sensuele, ingetogen "Salome"', *NRC Handelsblad*, 1 June 2017, C23. Available online: https://tga.nl/media/117642/170601_ivo_van_hove_nrc_next.pdf (accessed 6 September 2017).

33 I use Richard Strauss's spelling of the characters' names, but for ease of understanding for English-language readers, I have cited Oscar Wilde's play in Lord Alfred Douglas's 1892 translation from Wilde's French, rather than the German libretto itself.

34 Avishai Margalit and Ian Buruma, *Occidentalism: The West in the Eyes of Its Enemies* (New York: Penguin, 2004).

35 Van Hove quoted in Freriks, C23.

36 Here the singer was replaced by an actress, Laura Aris. She did not go so far as to take all her clothes off, either in the video or on stage, as Karila Mattila had done in Lev Dodin's production (2003), or as actresses often do in van Hove's theatre productions.

Section Five: Creation, Adaptation, Direction

1 A brief history of the companies and a sense of their place in Flemish theatre history can be found in the entry by Toon Brouwers, Alfons van Impe and Jaak van Schoor in *The World Encyclopedia of Contemporary Theatre Volume I: Europe*, ed. Peter Nagy, Philippe Rouyer and Don Rubin (New York: Routledge, 1994), 117–21.

2 See Keren Zaiontz's interview with van Hove in Section Two of this book (86–9) – eds.

3 Rebecca Mead, 'Theatre Laid Bare: Ivo van Hove's Raw Productions Bring Out the Elemental Drama of Classic Works', *The New Yorker*, 26 October 2015. Available online: http://www.newyorker.com/magazine/2015/10/26/theatre-laid-bare (accessed 31 August 2017).

4 Quoted in Pamela Newton, 'Ivo van Hove Is Having a Moment', *American Theatre*, 11 November 2015. Available online: http://www.americantheatre.org/2015/11/11/ivo-van-hove-is-having-a-moment/ (accessed 31 August 2017).

5   Quoted in Matt Trueman, 'Obsession: An Interview With Ivo van Hove', *National Theatre Blog* 2016. Available online: https://www.nationaltheatre.org.uk/blog/obsession-interview-ivo-van-hove (accessed 31 August 2017).

6   Trueman, 'Obsession'.

7   Trueman, 'Obsession'.

8   IMDb listing. Available online: http://www.imdb.com/title/tt1087830/?ref_=ttfc_fc_tt (accessed 31 August 2017).

9   'Ivo van Hove, in conversation with Susan Bennett and Sonia Massai', January 2017. See also Isabel Lloyd's 'Death, Dutch Novels and David Bowie', where she describes the process as 'X-raying the text', *Newsweek*, 5 September 2016. Available online: http://www.newsweek.com/2016/09/09/ivo-van-hove-director-theater-david-bowie-lazarus-barbican-london-miller-495831.html (accessed 31 August 2017).

10 Quoted in Alexis Soloski, 'A Visit to the Strange, Secretive World of David Bowie's "Lazarus"', *The New York Times*, 10 November 2015. Available online: https://www.nytimes.com/2015/11/15/theater/a-visit-to-the-strange-secretive-world-of-david-bowies-lazarus.html?mcubz=3 (accessed 31 August 2017).

11 The term is Ben Brantley's, taken from his review of the New York production, 'David Bowie Songs and A Familiar Alien in "Lazarus"', *The New York Times*, 7 December 2015. Available online: https://www.nytimes.com/2015/12/08/theater/review-david-bowie-songs-and-a-familiar-alien-in-lazarus.html (accessed 3 September 2017).

12 Interview with Ivo van Hove and Jude Law, BBC Radio 4 'Front Row', 3 May 2017.

13 Van Hove describes the excitement of putting films onstage as akin to performing *Hamlet* for the very first time ('Front Row', 3 May 2017). His loyalty to those screenplays though is also extensive and less disruptive than his deliberately confrontational adaptational methods sometimes imply: Simon Stephens' dialogue for *Obsession* treads remarkably closely to the original script and therefore retains elements of its sense of lives trapped in certain social spaces and by expectations, and, ultimately, by poverty.

14 The seminal book on the idea of the empty stage is Peter Brook's, *The Empty Space* (Harmondsworth: Penguin, 2008). On issues of familiarity and enrichment in the experience and reception of adaptations, see my own *Adaptation and Appropriation*, 2nd edition (London: Routledge, 2015 [2006]), 27.

15 See Geoffrey Nowell-Smith, programme notes to the Barbican production (6–8), and also his *Luchino Visconti*, 3rd edition (London: BFI, 2003) and Henry Bacon, *Visconti: Exploration of Beauty and Decay* (Cambridge: Cambridge University Press, 2012), 16.

16 For a varied discussion of adaptation and versioning in intermedial contexts, see Jorgen Bruhn, Anne Gjelsvik, and Eirik Frisvold Hanssen (eds), *Adaptation Studies* (London: Bloomsbury Academic, 2013).

17 The point was not lost on reviewers, see, for example, Andrew Todd in the *Guardian*, 10 July 2016: '*The Damned*: Van Hove's Chillingly Prescient Masterstroke'. The Avignon festival is an annual arts festival held every summer in the courtyard of the Palais and was founded in 1947 by Jean Vilar so can be viewed as direct product of the post-war unification effort in Europe. These links undoubtedly contributed to the nuanced political interpretations of Van Hove's production of *The Damned*.

18 On the use of live filming in contemporary theatre and specifically theatrical adaptation, see Kara Reilly (ed.) *Contemporary Approaches to Adaptation in Theatre* (London: Palgrave, 2018), esp. Adam J. Ledger, '"The Thrill of Doing it Live": Devising and Performing Katie Mitchell's International "Live Cinema" Productions,' 69–94. Van Hove's pioneering of this technique in his Shakespeare productions, *Roman Tragedies* and *Kings of War*, both staged at the Barbican as part of the 2016–17 Toneelgroep Amsterdam residency, is certainly influencing other Shakespearean productions at this time, most notably Robert Icke's acclaimed 2017 production of *Hamlet* at the Almeida with Andrew Scott in the title role. Tal Yarden's use of video work there to suggest a surveillance culture as well as the use of Bob Dylan songs throughout carry clear traces of van Hove's influence (Icke has been a significant contributor to the Toneelgroep programme in recent years as has Australian theatre/film director Simon Stone).

19 Philip Auslander, *Liveness: Performance in a Mediatized Culture* 2nd edition (London: Routledge, 2008), *passim*.

20 There are direct kinships here with the use of epic landscape back projections in van Hove's production of Charles Wuorinen's operatic version of Annie Proulx's short story (itself famously expanded into a feature-length film by Ang Lee in 2005), *Brokeback Mountain* (a 2014 co-production with Teatro Real de Madrid). The staging there deployed van Hove's by-now familiar largely bare stage invested with a few meaningful props but was enlarged by full stage screen projections of the Wyoming mountains in which the male protagonists' illicit relationship first takes place and to which Ennis del Mar returns in spirit but devastatingly alone to sing his heartbroken aria at the close. Van Hove was again determined that this opera should not be seen as an adaptation of the film ('Brokeback Mountain: The Opera to Open in Madrid', *Guardian*, 20 January 2014). Elsewhere the production made brilliant use of the sudden introduction of household objects and office furniture along with a sudden influx of other characters onto the stage as threatening and suffocating entities that merely stressed the entrapment and enclosure of the two men in a life to which they could not fully subscribe. Here, as in *Obsession*, film ironically provided the sense of the emotional reality beneath the social pretense, and a vision of the world of freedom and mobility for which Ennis and Jack like Gino and Hanna yearned.

21 Peter Conrad, *A Song of Love and Death: The Meaning of Opera* (London: Hogarth Press, 1987), 49.

22 Conrad, 356.

23 Bacon, 24.

24 Visconti directed Verdi's *La Traviata* in 1955 at La Scala in Milan with Maria Callas so it was also an artwork to which he returned. The presence of Verdi in his film-work was also sustained. His 1954 film *Senso* opens in Venice's La Fenice opera-house, midway through a performance of *Il Trovatore*. Ironically, Bacon suggests that Bregana's association with *La Traviata* and opera more generally in *Ossessione* is meant to mark him out as of an older, passing generation (27); Giovanna in the film by contrast sings recognizable snatches of popular 1930s song. Van Hove also retained this association with song in the production in moments that Barbican audiences found hard to calibrate when Hanna sang to Gino while heatedly covering the stage in all the detritus and rubbish from the night's service at the trattoria.

25 Programme notes, Barbican April–May 2017 (12)

26 In another theatrical engagement with European film, van Hove's 2011 *Antonioni Project* was comprised of re-enactments of three of the Italian director's films using both live camerawork and blue screen technology on stage. Elsewhere he has adapted work by Bergman and Pasolini, suggesting a sustained engagement with a particular moment of European filmmaking throughout his career. There is also a challenge to cultural venue programming here; is there a logic in a more sustained engagement being made available for audiences with the different versions of a work that inform a single production? The Barbican Centre London did provide a single screening of Visconti's *Ossessione* (currently unavailable to purchase or stream in the UK) but it was not strongly publicized as a linked part of the offer/season. Since several reviewers and interviewers raised the vexed question of familiarity it would repay arts administrators to at least consider what an adaptation-sensitive programme might look like in this era of convergence culture and multiple points of entry to creative artworks.

27 Jay Bolter and David Grusin note in their *Remediation: Understanding New Media* (Cambridge, MA: MIT Press, 2000) that the term can suggest improvement or repair, as in environmental engineering contexts (59) but for van Hove the remediation at work is one that is engaged with the immediate possibilities of the form in which he is working – live theatre.

28 This response came in the BBC Radio 4 'Front Row' interview on 3 May 2017 when his interlocutor suggested that audience members unfamiliar with the Visconti film might not even realize that they are witnessing car crashes.

29 All of these examples manifest the 'maximal minimalism' ascribed to van Hove by *New York Times* critic Ben Brantley: see, for example, 'A *View from the Bridge* Bears Witness to the Pain of Fate', *The New York Times,* 12 November 2015.

30 Joyce Carol Oates, *Blonde* (New York and London: Fourth Estate, 2001); and cf. Sanders, 186.

31 Auslander, 25.

32 Michel Foucault, *The Archaeology of Knowledge* (New York: Pantheon Books, 1972), 3.

33 P. A. Skantze, 'Take Me to the Bridge', in *Choreo-graphic Figures: Deviations from the Line*, ed. Nikolaus Gansterer, Emma Cocker and Mariella Greil (Berlin/Boston: Walter de Gruyter GmbH, 2017), 176.

34 Foucault, 128.

35 Odd how a polished wooden floor can begin to look like sand, give off the feel of dusty aimlessness. Something about van Hove's work seems to suggest the language of earth, reviewers refer to landscape or in Ian Shuttleworth's review of *Obsession* for the *Financial Times* the experience of watching suggests the production maps 'the character's inner geography' (*Financial Times*, 27 April 2017).

36 In a conversation with Halina Reijn published in this volume, Ruth Wilson discusses van Hove's method. Imagine someone dependent on the Meisner school of acting being told to 'staple the flowers to the wall', and when the actor probes the director, he says 'I don't psychologize'. What makes the enigmatic power a theatrical one is that the 'psychologizing' is practical, physical, a form of action.

37 Foucault, 128.

38 Duška Radosavljević, 'Changing Scenes', *Exeunt Magazine*, 20 November 2013.

39 Radosavljević, 'Changing Scenes'.

40 Henry James, *The Scenic Art: Notes on Acting and the Drama 1872–1901*, edited with an Introduction and Notes by Allan Wade (London: Rupert Hart-Davis, 1949), 3.

41 James, *The Scenic Art*, 273.

42 http://www.imdb.com/title/tt0041386/

43 Rand, *The Fountainhead* (London: Penguin, 2007 [1943]), ix.

44 Rand, *The Fountainhead*, viii.

45 Rand, *The Fountainhead*, 727.

46 https://www.youtube.com/watch?v=rAfeQjoWQKM

47 English-language publicity for *The Fountainhead*, 2014.

48 Ivo van Hove, 2012 publicity for *Husbands*, for the 2017 Tampere Theatre Festival. Available online: http://2012.teatterikesa.fi/media/taustamateriaalit-kansainvalisis/toneelgroep-amsterdam-husbands/ (accessed 3 September 2017).

49 Jean-François Perrier, 'The World of Politics: Ivo van Hove in Conversation', *Roman Tragedies* Programme, Barbican Theatre, London (2009).

50 English-language publicity for *The Fountainhead*, 2014.

51 Rand, *The Fountainhead*, 518.

52 Fabienne Darge, 'Au Milieu des Gratte-Ciel, la Liberté de l'Artiste Contre la Société de Masse', *Le Monde*, 14 July 2014. Author's translation.

53 Rand, *The Fountainhead*, 3.

54 Darge, 'Au Milieu'. Author's translation.

55 Rand, *The Fountainhead,* 121.

56 Rand, *The Fountainhead*, 207.

57 Barbara Johnson, 'Writing', in *Critical Terms for Literary Study,* ed. Frank Lentricchia and Thomas McLaughlin (Chicago: University of Chicago Press, 1991), 46.

58 Jonathan Freedland, 'Goddess of the New Right', *Guardian*, 11 April 2017, 8.

59 Rand, *The Fountainhead*, 345.

60 Rand, *The Fountainhead*, 530.

61 Billie Holliday, 'Don't Explain' (1945). Lyrics available online: https://play.google.com/music/preview/Tny6pwuslm7uvughizum47rvrri?lyrics=1&utm_source=google&utm_medium=search&utm_campaign=lyrics&pcampaignid=kp-lyrics (accessed 31 August 2017).

62 Email message, 5 September 2017.

63 Email message, 5 September 2017.

64 A copy of the Learning Resource was provided by Lauren Monaghan-Pisano, 1.

65 Learning Resource, 4.

66 Learning Resource, 1.

67 Learning Resource, 2.

68 Learning Resource, 2.

69 Learning Resource, 6.

70 Learning Resource, 6.

71 Dalya Alberge, 'David Hare: Classic British Drama "Being Infected" by Radical European Staging', *Guardian*, 29 January 2017. Available at: https://www.theguardian.com/stage/2017/jan/29/david-hare-classic-british-drama-infected-radical-european-staging (accessed 21 July 2017).

72 Alberge, 'David Hare', 15.

73 Alberge, 'David Hare', 16.

74 Alberge, 'David Hare', 24.

75 Alberge, 'David Hare', 22.

76 For example, the AQA GCSE Drama Specification 2016, 'Component 2: Devising' states that 'stimuli may be, but are not limited to: visual (such as a photograph, painting or sculpture), printed or spoken word (such as a poem, news article, story or novel), musical (such as a song, melody or instrumental piece), fact-based (such as a current, political or historical event), theme or issue-based (such as conflict, relationships, justice or freedom), myths (such as folklore or urban myth), cultural (such as traditions or festivals)'. Available at: http://www.aqa.org.uk/subjects/drama/gcse/drama-8261/scheme-of-assessment#id (accessed 21 July 2017). Although this particular specification does not explicitly forbid the use of a play text as a stimulus, the list of suggestions strongly steers teachers away from it.

77 AQA GCSE Drama Specification, 4.

78 Video interview, TEA films, YouTube, 25 Nov 2016; unlisted (accessed 21 July 2017). Lauren Monaghan-Pisano, Creative Learning Producer at Barbican/Guildhall School of Music & Drama, provided the link to this video for research purposes.

79 'NYTW announces the world premiere of LAZARUS', 2 April 2015. Available at: www.davidbowie.com/news/nytw-announces-world-premiere-lazarus-54311

80 'NYTW announces the world premiere of LAZARUS'.

81 Robert Simonson, 'The Secret Behind New York Theatre Workshop's Fastest-Selling Production Ever, Bowie's *Lazarus*', *Playbill*, 20 November 2015. Available at: http://www.playbill.com/article/the-secret-behind-new-york-theatre-workshops-fastest-selling-production-ever-david-bowies-lazarus-com-372490

82 'This Way or No Way, You Know I'll Be Free', Introduction to *Lazarus*, by David Bowie and Enda Walsh (London: Nick Hern, 2016), vii.

83 Simonson, 'The Secret'.

84 Simonson, 'The Secret'.

85 Isabel Lloyd, 'Theatre Director Ivo van Hove Talks Death, Dutch Novels and David Bowie', *Newsweek*, 5 September 2016. Available at: http://www.newsweek.com/2016/09/09/ivo-van-hove-director-theater-david-bowie-lazarus-barbican-london-miller-495831.html

86 Bowie and Walsh, *Lazarus*, 4.

87 Bowie and Walsh, *Lazarus*, 45.

88 Bowie and Walsh, *Lazarus*, 47.

89 Lloyd, 'Theatre Director Ivo van Hove'.

90 Lloyd, 'Theatre Director Ivo van Hove', 63.

91 Jill S. Dolan, *Utopia in Performance: Finding Hope at the Theater* (Ann Arbor: University of Michigan Press, 2006), 168.

92 Rishi Iyengar, 'Here's How the Internet Reacted to David Bowie's Death,' *time.com*, 11 January 2016. Available at: http://time.com/4174828/david-bowie-dead-cancer-69-blackstar/

93 See Keren Zaiontz's interview with Wouter van Ransbeek in this volume for discussion of how productions are designed with an eye to touring.

94 Paul Taylor, 'Lazarus, King's Cross Theatre, London Review: David Bowie's Parting Gift to the World', *Independent*, 8 November 2016. Available at: http://www.independent.co.uk/arts-entertainment/theatre-dance/reviews/lazarus-david-bowie-enda-walsh-review-michael-c-hall-blackstar-a7404331.html

95 Dominic Cavendish, 'Lazarus Review – Bowie Musical Lands in London, but Does it Really Make the Grade?', *Telegraph*, 8 November 2016. Available at: http://www.telegraph.co.uk/theatre/what-to-see/lazarus-review--bowie-musical-lands-in-london-but-does-it-really/

96 Michael Billington, 'Lazarus Review – Michael C. Hall is a Loving Alien in Spectacular Bowie Fantasy', *Guardian*, 8 November 2016. Available at: https://www.theguardian.com/stage/2016/nov/08/lazarus-review-david-bowie-kings-cross-theatre-michael-c-hall

97 Ian Shuttleworth, 'Lazarus, King's Cross Theatre, London – "Head-spinning"', *Financial Times*, 8 November 2016. Available at: https://www.ft.com/content/a03e1178-a5a0-11e6-8898-79a99e2a4de6

98 Cavendish, 'Lazarus Review'.

99 Billington, 'Lazarus Review'.

100 Taylor, 'Lazarus'.

Selected Further Reading

Als, Hilton. 'It's a Man's World: Forceful Women in *The Little Foxes* and *Orlando*'. *The New Yorker*, 4 October 2010.

Ball III, James R. 'Staging the Twitter War: Toneelgroep Amsterdam's *Roman Tragedies*'. *TDR* 57.4 (Winter 2013), 163–70.

Billing, Christian M. 'The *Roman Tragedies*'. *Shakespeare Quarterly*, 61 (2010), 415–39.

Bobkova, Hana. 'De Tragedies en paradijzen van Ivo van Hove'. *Ons Erfdeel: Algemeen-Nederlands Tweemaandelijks Cultureel Tijdschrift*, 38 (1995), 27–35.

Boenisch, Peter M. 'Creating X-Rays of the Text to Dissect the Present: Ivo van Hove of Toneelgroep Amsterdam in Conversation'. *Theatre and Adaptation: Return, Rewrite, Repeat*, ed. by Margherita Laera (London: Bloomsbury Methuen Drama, 2014), 49–62.

Boenisch, Peter M. *Directing Scenes and Senses: The Thinking of Regie* (Manchester: Manchester University Press, 2015).

Brustein, Robert. 'More Masterpieces'. *PAJ: A Journal of Performance and Art* 30.3 (September 2008), 1–7.

Callens, Johan. 'Tennessee Williams and Ivo van Hove at Home Abroad'. *Tennessee Williams and Europe: Intercultural Encounters, Transatlantic Exchanges*, ed. by John S. Bak (Amsterdam: Rodopi: 2014), 301–19.

Carlson, Marvin. *10,000 Nights: Highlights from 50 Years of Theatre-Going.* (Ann Arbor: University of Michigan Press, 2017).

Cartelli, Thomas. 'High-Tech Shakespeare in a Mediatized Globe: Ive van Hove's *Roman Tragedies* and the Problem of Spectatorship'. *The Oxford Hanbook of Shakespeare and Performance*, ed. by James C. Bulman (Oxford: Oxford University Press, 2018), 267–83.

Conkie, Rob. 'Graphic Shakespeare'. *Writing Performative Shakespeares: New Forms for Performance Criticism* (Cambridge: Cambridge University Press, 2016), 91–110.

Crombez, Thomas. 'Canonisation in Contemporary Theatre Criticism: A Frequency Analysis of "Flemish Wave" Directors in the Pages of *Etcetera*'. *Contemporary Theatre Review*, 24.2 (2014), 252–61.

Desrochers, Dick. 'Looking Behind the Mirror of Life: The Subtext is the Surface in Ivo van Hove's production of Molière's *The Misanthrope*'. *Theatre Forum*, 33 (2008), 86–98.

Dieleman, Cock (ed.). *Het Zuidelijk Toneel 1990–2000* (Amsterdam: International Theatre and Film Books, 2000). [The first book on Ivo van Hove. It includes testimonies, photographs and an account of the director's work in Eindhoven.]

Flannery, Denis. '"Floating in a Most Peculiar Way": *Angels in America*, David Bowie, Toneelgroep Amsterdam'. *Contemporary Theatre Review*, 24.2 (2014), 156–76.

Gener, Randy. 'A Passion for Extremes: Words and Images Clash in the Notorious Dramatic Installations of Ivo van Hove and Jan Versweyveld'. *American Theatre*, 26.9 (November 2009), 24–7, 77–8.

Maurin, Frédéric. 'Globalement, Shakespeare'. *Théâtre/Public*, 221 (2016), 81–93.

Maurin, Frédéric. *Ivo van Hove* (Arles: Actes-Sud Papiers, 2014).

Maurin, Frédéric. 'Ivo van Hove, du scénario à la scène'. *Les Damnés, L'Avant-scène théâtre*, 1404 (June 2016), 70–5.

Maurin, Frédéric (ed.). *Ivo van Hove, la fureur de créer* (Besançon: Les solitaires intempestifs, 2016). [The first collection of critical essays on the director and his work.]

Maurin, Frédéric. 'Ivo van Hove: l'opéra aux deux bouts du théâtre'. *Alternatives théâtrales*, 113–14 (2012), 28–31.

Maurin, Frédéric. 'Le prisme et le miroir: *Après la répétition / Persona* d'Ivo van Hove d'après Bergman'. *Théâtre/Public*, 211 (2014), 96–104. [Co-written with Anaïs Bonnier and Chloé Lavalette.]

McNulty, Charles. 'Commuting Beyond the Stereotypes: The Dangerous Trek of Ivo van Hove's *A Streetcar Named Desire*'. *Theatre*, 30.2 (2000), 155–9.

McNulty, Charles. 'Meet Ivo van Hove, the Most Provocatively Illuminating Theatre Director Right Now'. *LA Times*, 18 March 2016.

Mead, Rebecca. 'Theatre Laid Bare: Ivo van Hove's Raw Productions Bring Out the Elemental Drama of Classic Works'. *The New Yorker*, 26 October 2015. Available online: http://www.newyorker.com/magazine/2015/10/26/theatre-laid-bare (accessed 5 September 2017).

Muhleisen, Laurent and Frédéric Maurin. 'La puissance et le pouvoir: entretien avec Ivo van Hove, Jan Versweyveld, Tal Yarden et Eric Sleichim'. *Les Damnés, L'Avant-scène théâtre*, 1404 (June 2016), 61–70.

Newton, Pamela. 'Ivo van Hove's Sound and Vision'. *American Theatre*, 16 (January 2016), 25.

Nijhof, Jos. 'Kunstenaar voor stad en wereld: Theatreregisseur Ivo van Hove'. *Ons Erfdeel: Vlaams-Nederlands Cultureel Tijdschrift*, 60 (2017), 38–49.

Perrier, Jean-Louis. 'Au bout du texte'. *Mouvement*, 62 (January 2012), 76–9.

Reyniers, Johan. 'Ivo van Hove: "Toneel is de kunstvorm van de eenentwintigste eeuw"'. *Etcetera*, September 2013, 5–29.

Scott, Sarah K. '*Roman Tragedies*'. *Shakespeare Bulletin*, 28.3 (2010), 347–56.

Smith, Mark. 'Ivo'. *Fantastic Man*, 24 (2016), 166–75.

Thielemans, Johan. 'Ivo van Hove's Passionate Quest for a Necessary Theatre'. *Contemporary Theatre Review*, 20.4 (2010), 455–60.

Van Hove, Ivo. *Rumors (Geruchten)*, translated by D. Willinger and K. DeSloovere. *An Anthology of Contemporary Belgian Plays, 1970–1982*, ed. by David Willinger (Troy, NY: Whitston, 1984).

Van Hove, Ivo. *Disease Germs (Ziektekiemen)*, translated by D. Willinger and K. DeSloovere. *An Anthology of Contemporary Belgian Plays, 1970–1982*, ed. by David Willinger (Troy, NY: Whitston, 1984).

Willinger, David. 'Van Hove's *Geruchten*'. *TDR*, 25.2 (1981), 116–18.

Willinger, David. 'Van Hove's *Disease Germs* (Belgium)'. *TDR*, 27.1 (1983), 93–7.

Film/documentary

Cohen, Paul and Martijn Van Haalen. *Bloot: een film over acteren* [*Exposed: A Film About Acting*], prod. IDTV DOCS and NTR, 2013. Colour, 68 minutes.

Audiovisual archives (in Dutch)

Arias, Pol (mod.). *Traject Ivo van Hove: Symposium meeting Van Hove / Versweyveld*, Antwerp, deSingel, 9 October 2010. See in particular 'Ivo van Hove interviewt Jan Versweyveld over hun dertigjarige samenwerking' ['Ivo van Hove interviews Jan Versweyveld on their thirty-year long collaboration'].

http://www.youtube.com/watch?v=p3yn84lpWwY&list=PL679F712182D58809
http://www.youtube.com/watch?v=mT3HdJOnA5U&list=PL679F712182D58809
http://www.youtube.com/watch?v=5ALKNSpvcZM&list=PL679F712182D58809
http://www.youtube.com/watch?v=z2lH1Sfnem8&list=PL679F712182D58809
http://www.youtube.com/watch?v=9gks_OYt0qs&list=PL679F712182D58809

Toneelgroep Amsterdam (TGA) website

The company's website offers rich resources: https://tga.nl/en (English version), https://tga.nl/ (Dutch version). As well as information about the company and its ensemble, the site offers detailed materials on each of their productions (including synopses, cast and creative lists, links to reviews, performance calendars, photos and videos). There is also a biography of van Hove (https://tga.nl/en/employees/ivo-van-hove) that outlines a chronology of his directorial work at TGA and elsewhere. A YouTube channel offers trailers for all the productions van Hove has directed at TGA (https://www.youtube.com/playlist?list=PL27F26E48F47B7469).

Index